The Future of Hope

The Future of Hope

CHRISTIAN TRADITION AMID MODERNITY
AND POSTMODERNITY

Edited by

Miroslav Volf *&* William Katerberg

William B. Eerdmans Publishing Company
Grand Rapids, Michigan / Cambridge, U.K.

© 2004 Wm. B. Eerdmans Publishing Co.

Wm. B. Eerdmans Publishing Co.
2140 Oak Industrial Drive N.E., Grand Rapids, Michigan 49505 /
P.O. Box 163, Cambridge CB3 9PU U.K.

Printed in the United States of America

09 08 07 06 05 04   7 6 5 4 3 2 1

ISBN 978-0-8028-2752-4

www.eerdmans.com

Contents

Acknowledgments

This book had its origin in a seminar and conference, "Modernity, Postmodernity, and the Future of Hope," sponsored by the Seminars in Christian Scholarship program at Calvin College, with financial support from the Pew Charitable Trusts, in June 2000 and May 2001. We would like to thank these organizations for their support, in particular Susan Felch and Anna Mae Bush, the Director and Coordinator of the seminars program at the time, and their assistants. The seminars program also helped to pay for the process of editing the conference papers and producing the book. Thanks also go to Jamie Smith and the current seminars program staff for help with some of the final details associated with the book.

Several people helped with the process of evaluating and editing the essays in the volume. Thanks to Ivica Novakovic, Maurice Lee, and Ron Wells for input and advice. Thanks to the contributors of essays to the book for turning in drafts and responding to questions about revisions in good time and with good humor. Finally, thanks to Jon Pott, the editor in chief, and the editorial, graphic design, and promotions staff at William B. Eerdmans Publishing Company.

On the cover of the book is Paul Klee's painting *Novus Angelus*. It inspired Walter Benjamin, who described it as "the angel of history" in his famous "Theses on the Philosophy of History." Influenced by the tradition of Jewish messianism and by Marxism, Benjamin tried to find hope in a perilous time shaped by the Nazi rise to power in Germany,

Stalinism in Russia, and the Great Depression. Whether our time is so dangerous and epochal remains an open question; but like Benjamin, people today continue to look in ominous times to diverse religious and secular traditions to find and define the future of hope. The essays in this book are written in that spirit and to that end.

Introduction: Retrieving Hope

MIROSLAV VOLF AND WILLIAM KATERBERG

Over the last three decades a major cultural shift has taken place in the attitudes of Western societies toward the future. Optimism has given way to a sense of ambiguity, messianic and utopian modes of thought have capitulated before the drawing of apocalyptic scenarios.[1] This shift is not just a fleeting mood. Instead, it rides on two major cultural developments. One is the wider cultural shift from modernity, with its orientation toward the bright future, to what has been rather vaguely called postmodernity, with its stress on the extension of an ambiguous present.[2] The other and related development is an increasing awareness of the fragility of our natural and social environments, a sense of living in a "risk society" marked by "manufactured certainty," in a world where nobody knows what the risks facing humanity are.[3] Both of these developments, and their interaction, have contributed to the disappearance of the resolute optimism that characterized modernity. If

1. See John Leslie, *The End of the World: The Science and Ethics of Human Extinction* (New York: Routledge, 1996). Indicative of the predominance of apocalyptic modes of thought in religious circles is the immense popularity of the *Left Behind* series. For example, see Tim LaHaye and Jerry B. Jenkins, *Left Behind: A Novel of the Earth's Last Days* (Wheaton: Tyndale House, 1995).

2. Zygmunt Bauman, *Life in Fragments: Essays in Postmodern Morality* (Oxford: Blackwell, 1995).

3. Ulrich Beck, *Risk Society: Towards a New Modernity*, trans. Mark Ritter (London: Sage, 1992).

we trace the historical development of Western culture, following slightly modified categories proposed by Richard Rorty (in his correspondence on cultural otherness),[4] we can say that modernity's "culture of optimism," which emerged from pre-modernity's "culture of endurance," is giving way to a postmodern "culture of ambiguity."

This culture of ambiguity threatens to stifle hope at a personal as well as a social level. All of the scientific and technological innovations that promise to extend life and lighten its burden notwithstanding, we dare not hope for a future substantially better than the present. Since "hope" is both a central theological category and a component of the "cultural capital" indispensable to human flourishing, it is essential not to squander the language of hope. A major theological and cultural project must be to re-learn the forgotten language of hope or to infuse the jaded language of hope with new vitality.

There is a major obstacle to such retrieval, however. The participants in the recent consultation of theologians and scientists on eschatology at the Center for Theological Inquiry (in Princeton, New Jersey) have drawn attention to the fact that the spread of electronic media (the global expansion of satellite television and the Internet) is accompanied by "an enormous inflation of the flow of data that constantly demands fresh attention."[5] As people's attention focuses on shifting images, the so-called "hot cultural memory" — that is, memory which has the power to shape a culture — is markedly depreciated. It gives way to "cool cultural memories," which are transitory and fragmented, consumable and disposable like biodegradable plastic.[6]

From the perspective of the Christian faith, these developments are deeply disturbing. The biblical tradition, precisely that resource from the past to which Christians must take recourse in order to address the present culture of ambiguity, makes less and less claim on our contemporaries because it is ignored, forgotten, or rejected, or manipulated and marketed by its proponents. In the context of an increasing

4. Anindita Niyogi Balslev, *Cultural Otherness: Correspondence with Richard Rorty* (Shimla: Indian Institute of Advanced Study, 1991), p. 21.

5. John Polkinghorne and Michael Welker, "Science and Theology on the End of the World and the Ends of God," in their *The End of the World and the Ends of God* (Harrisburg: Trinity Press International, 2000), p. 8.

6. Jan Assmann, *Das kulturelle Gedächtnis. Schrift, Erinnerung und politische Identität in frühen Hochkulturen* (Munich: Beck, 1992).

"cooling of memories," a trend in which Christians all too often uncritically participate, a major challenge to Christian thought is to find in its own rich heritage the resources to rejuvenate a living hope rooted in the "hot memory" of God's engagement with the world in Christ's life, death, and resurrection. If Christians do not meet this challenge, they will not only fail to explicate adequately their own sources of hope for today but also fail to adequately prepare communities of Christian conviction in their proper mission to the wider culture. This mission is a matter of engagement with that culture — participating in it, drawing on it, critiquing it, and witnessing to it.

It is with roughly this kind of a challenge that a group of young Christian scholars from various disciplines met over a period of six weeks on the campus of Calvin College (in Grand Rapids, Michigan) during the summer of 2000 to reflect together on the future of hope. In a seminar, we read classical Christian sources as well as modern and postmodern thinkers; and we worked at the same time on our own projects related to the question of hope. A year later, in May 2001, we presented our work at a conference, along with three senior scholars who were invited to speak on the theme of Christian traditions and hope in a postmodern world. The seminar and the conference were sponsored by Calvin College's Seminars in Christian Scholarship program and the Pew Charitable Trusts. This book offers some of the results of our individual and collective work. It is organized into three sections, each one including an essay by one of the senior scholars and two essays by junior scholars.

The first section, "Hope amid History and Late Modern Culture," sets the context with cultural criticism of modernity. In "Progress and Abyss: Remembrances of the Future of the Modern World," Jürgen Moltmann presents an overarching historical interpretation of the modern world and humanity's destructive technological quest for progress. He argues that if "the goal of progress and the globalization of human power is to make the earth habitable, not to dominate and possess it, we must leave behind the modern Western world's God-complex of being 'the masters and possessors of nature'" and view the creation as "the shared house of all earthly created beings" and a "dwelling place of God." Moltmann's meta-historical analysis thus incorporates a social and ecological critique of the technology of progress and a sacramental Christian vision of creation renewed.

The next two essays are focused more specifically in their cultural criticism. In "Contrary Hopes: Evangelical Christianity and the Decline Narrative," Daniel Johnson analyzes contemporary evangelical fears of American cultural decline. He argues that evangelical hopes for the future are profoundly influenced by late-modern fears of the "risk society." Rather than express positive hopes about the future, evangelicals "more often find themselves guarding against discretely determined negative outcomes." "Given how steeped American evangelicals are in modern culture, we can hardly expect them to have remained immune to such a development," he explains. If they are to articulate distinctive Christian hopes, American evangelicals will have "to contend with contrary habits of hoping that have been burned in by the cultural conditions of late modernity."

William Katerberg's essay, "History, Hope, and the Redemption of Time," concludes this section. Not only did the modern quest for objective historical knowledge fail, according to Katerberg, it led modern historians and their readers to neglect questions about the meaning of time. Instead of the progressive redemption of history promised by the Enlightenment and modernity, modern history writing has become sterile and often hopeless. Engaging the writings of modern and contemporary philosophers of history, Katerberg attempts to clear spaces for Christians (and others) to express hope by emphasizing the connections between the past and traditions, on the one hand, and hope and the redemption of time, on the other.

In the second section of the book, "Early Christianity in Conversation with Contemporary Thought," the three essays explore affinities between pre-modern Christian visions of hope and twentieth-century thought. In "Seeking Justice in Hope," Nicholas Wolterstorff analyzes the relationship between justice and hope, ranging from the writings of the medieval theologian-philosopher Aquinas to postmodern thinkers and to the prayers of Allan Boesack in the struggle against apartheid in South Africa. He argues that all "conflations of Christian hope with secular optimism" are heretical, shortsighted, and arrogant. Instead, Wolterstorff contends that "Christian hope for liberating justice is confident as to its ground in Christ, while at the same time it is humble as to our ability to discern the ways in which our endeavors contribute to the coming of Christ's rule of justice."

In the next essay, "The Crossing of Hope, or Apophatic Eschatology," Kevin Hughes responds to contemporary concerns about the dangers of Christian eschatology and progressive-utopian political movements by exploring the mystical tradition of "apophatic" or "negative" theology. Negative theology "struggles to remain aware of what we do not and cannot know or say about God and the mysteries of faith. It is the disciplined speech of 'unknowing' and 'learned ignorance' before the mysterious presence of God." Hughes finds in this tradition ways to restate Christian hopes for the future that "navigate between the presumption of claiming to know too much and the emptiness of knowing nothing at all."

David Billings concludes the section with "Natality or Advent: Hannah Arendt and Jürgen Moltmann on Hope and Politics." His essay explores conceptions of "newness," specifically Arendt's discussion of "natality," which is rooted in her study of Augustine, and the idea of "advent" in the writings of Moltmann. The traumas of the twentieth century deeply shaped the work of both Arendt and Moltmann, and their very different approaches to engaging Christian tradition provide ways to address the existential and political question, "[How] can a hope based upon God be reconciled with a hope grounded in the human condition?"

The last section of the book, "Christian Hope and Postmodernity," addresses the relationship between postmodern thought, Christian tradition, and biblical hope. In "The Gospel of Affinity," John Milbank asks how the church is to manifest itself and how Christians are to articulate their faith in a postmodern world. In answer to this question he finds significant affinities between postmodernism and Christianity, but also insists that only Christianity provides a truly radical alternative to the powers of our day. "In the face of globalization and the new American empire, we must counterpose Augustine's counter-empire, the city of God," Milbank argues. "We may do this alongside many secular brothers and sisters (for example, socialists, communists, and anarchists). We should not refuse their cooperation, but yet we should insist that they have little real grasp of the counter-empire, since, for them, it is still a matter of simply unleashing more undifferentiated liberty, going yet further beyond the law." Only in Christianity can the barriers between the creation, humanity, and God be reconciled and their deep affinity recognized and regained.

In the second essay in this section, "Wounded Vision and the Optics of Hope," Robert Paul Doede and Paul Edward Hughes analyze the postmodern critique of contemporary visual culture. They critique and draw on twentieth-century philosophy and cultural theory, analyze the biblical portrait of divine vision, and explore the potential of photography to humanize and heal. In a postmodern culture so dominated by images, and so often images that exploit and dehumanize, Doede and Hughes search for "a new ethics of vision, a moral vision informed by transcendence, imagination, indeterminacy, and community — essential elements for an ecology of hope."

Finally, in "Determined Hope: A Phenomenology of Christian Expectation," James K. A. Smith critiques postmodern expressions of hope in the work of Richard Rorty and Jacques Derrida, and counters their critique of Christian hope. Postmodern hopes are without ground, he argues, and fail to offer compelling reasons to hope. They also lack "determination," a clear expression of that which is hoped for. Instead, Smith argues for Christian hope that is grounded in the revelation of God's faithfulness and has clear expectations of a redeemed creation. He concludes that "because of the Christian's commitments to God's revelation in Christ and God's faithfulness to creation, a Christian eschatology must argue that, ultimately, God is our only hope. In that regard, the question of the viability of Christian hope in late modernity differs little from the context of Augustine's *De civitate Dei:* it represents both a scandal and good news. My hope is that the demise of modern eschatologies, and the critique of postmodern hopes above, indicate an open space for Christians to unapologetically proclaim a hope that does not disappoint."

As these summary descriptions indicate, the essays in this collection are diverse in their content, methodologies, and temperament. On some matters the authors disagree. Nevertheless, the authors are united by something more than their common participation — conversing and debating — in a seminar-conference on Christianity and the future of hope amid modernity and postmodernity. They are all deeply engaged with both Christian traditions and the larger cultural and intellectual climate in which they live and work. For this reason, their essays might be read not only as attempts at retrieval of hope for today but as themselves small acts of hope, in an age when people too seldom take time to think critically and hopefully, and in an academic culture in which such daunting issues too often get buried under the minutiae of technical scholarship.

Section I

Hope amid History
and Late Modern Culture

Progress and Abyss: Remembrances of the Future of the Modern World

JÜRGEN MOLTMANN

What, then, actually happened on 1 January 2000? Was it "the turn of an age," with all the weighty solemnity of destiny this implies? Or was it a new millennium in the felicitous progress of the modern world? Was it the beginning of the world's end? Or was it merely a tremendous postmodern New Year's party in Berlin, London, Paris, and New York?

Common sense tells us that it was just a night like all other nights before and after it, without any special significance at all. And yet the year 2000, with its three zeros, does have something magical about it. So what sort of magic? It has to do with the decimal system with which we have measured time ever since the beginning of the modern world. From the beginning of modern times, linear chronology has asserted itself, a way of calculating time that takes no account of what happens in it, but simply moves on and on, from one year to the next. It fits our idea of inexorable human "progress" from the past into a better and better future. That is why at turning points in time, like 1 January 2000, we like to draw up a balance sheet, totting up the profits and the losses of the progress we have made. But about the progress itself there is no question, for it hastens on year after year, with our calendar, into an endless future. Or so we think.

But why the year 2000 in particular? According to the decimal system, there is evidently something marvelous about everything that ends with zeros, because we think that zero is "a round number," although in fact it is not a number at all. Every ten years a jubilee, every

3

hundred years a centenary, and so on, whether there is anything to celebrate or not. Why is the zero more attractive than the seven or the twelve? Like the symbol for infinity, the zero entered our numerical system at a late date, coming to us from India by way of Arabia.[1] The suspended breath or the mystic moment that belongs to what we call zero hour is apparently a difficult and mysterious affair. Can we begin again from the beginning, from zero, so to speak, without a past, and free of memories? With the three zeros of the year 2000 a new year begins, and a new decade, and a new century — perhaps even a whole new thousand years. Fascinating — four new beginnings! We get the impression that the immediate future and the wider future further ahead are both open. What a delightful illusion!

Things look very different if we take our bearings from what happens in time, for real events do not usually take any account of our time scale. What is our situation today, now that the twentieth century is at an end, and the nineteenth before it? The future in the twenty-first century will be determined by these two eras, for they are by no means past and gone, and they confront us with tremendous contradictions. On the one hand we have the nineteenth century (with its twentieth-century extensions), an age of fantastic progress in all of life's different sectors: from the steam engine to the airplane, from the telephone to the Internet, from classical physics to the theory of relativity. It was an age of discoveries and conquests. And on the other hand we have the twentieth century (as distinct from the nineteenth), an age of incomparable catastrophes: Verdun and Stalingrad, Auschwitz and the Gulag Archipelago, Hiroshima and Chernobyl. These names stand for the unimaginable crimes against humanity committed by the progressive West and the modern world. Both of these eras are still present today — their progress and their abysses. What once became possible will never again disappear from reality, but will always remain part of it. Today we are globalizing the nineteenth century's world of progress, and at the same time all the weapons of mass destruction developed and employed in the twentieth century are still kept in readiness for mass extermination, which would provide the "final solution" of the question about the human race.[2]

1. Robert Kaplan, *The Nothing That Is: A Natural History of Zero* (London: Oxford University Press, 1999).

2. For a similar analysis see Richard Bauckham and Trevor Hart, *Hope against*

In the first part of this essay I shall talk about the birth of modernity out of the spirit of messianic hope, so that we can understand the age of beginnings without end. In the second part I shall describe the age of the end without beginnings, which began with the seminal European catastrophe of the First World War. In the third part I shall ask about the future of Christian hope and hopes for humanity.

The Birth of Modernity Out of the Spirit of Messianic Hope

The modern world had at least two significant starting points before the advent of the age of Enlightenment. The first was the *conquista,* the discovery and conquest of America from 1492 onward. The second was the scientific and technological seizure of power over nature by human beings.

The year 1492 saw the beginning of the European domination over continents and peoples. According to Hegel, this was the hour when the modern world was born.[3] Before that the European powers had been unimportant, globally speaking, compared with the Ottoman empire, the Indian empire of the Moguls, and the Chinese empire. The Spanish and the Portuguese, and then the English, the Dutch, and the French, "discovered" America, each for themselves. But what does "discovered" mean here? America was neither discovered nor perceived as such. It was appropriated and molded according to the will of its conquerors.[4] "America," says the Mexican historian Edmundo O'Gorman, "is an invention of European thinking." The individual life and individual cultures of the Aztecs, Mayas, and Incas have never been perceived

---

Hope: Christian Eschatology in Contemporary Context (Grand Rapids: Eerdmans, 1999), chap. 1.

3. "America is thus the country of the future in which in the times ahead of us . . . the whole significance of world history will be revealed" (G. W. F. Hegel, *Lectures on the Philosophy of World History: Introduction, Reason in History,* trans. H. N. Nisbet [Cambridge: Cambridge University Press, 1975]). Just how unimportant the European Powers were in 1492 in the context of the world as a whole is impressively described in Paul Kennedy, *The Rise and Fall of the Great Powers* (New York: Vintage, 1989).

4. B. Dietschy, "Die Tücken des Entdeckens: Ernst Bloch, Kolumbus und die Neue Welt," *Jahrbuch der Ernst Bloch–Gesellschaft* (1992-1993): 234-51.

for what they were, right down to the present day. They were repressed as something alien, and sacrificed to the conquerors' own notions and purposes.[5] Islands, mountains, and rivers were given Spanish names, generally Christian ones. The languages of the indigenous peoples were forbidden. The legal fictions of "unclaimed property," "no-man's land," and "the wilderness" legalized the pillaging and the colonization. With the conquest of America, Christianity came forward as a European religion to rule the world.

The scientific and technological seizure of power over nature is the other foundation stone of the new world order. In the century between Copernicus and Isaac Newton, the new empirical sciences stripped nature of her magic, as Max Weber put it, and took from her the divine mystery which up to then had been reverenced as *anima mundi,* the soul of the world.[6] This also ended the taboos evoked by reverence for "Mother Earth" and for the greatness of life.[7] The sciences bring "Mother Nature and her daughters" to the human being (who is of course a man) in order to make him "the master and possessor of nature," as Francis Bacon and René Descartes interpreted this process at the time. Science and technology now restored the human being's status as the image of God, which had been lost in superstition and idolatry, and in so doing they established human lordship over the earth *(dominium terrae),* which corresponds to the lordship of God over heaven and earth. Here too new discoveries were made (and are being made still), which were adorned, down to the present day, with the name of the discoverer. Recently they have even been patented for the purposes of economic exploitation: the genome researcher Craig Venter wants to acquire the human genome for himself by way of thousands of patents, although he never "invented" it. For scientific discov-

---

5. See Enrique Dussel, *The Invention of the Americas,* trans. Michael Barber (New York: Continuum, 1995). Among older studies see the still important Tzvetan Todorov, *The Conquest of America: The Question of the Other,* trans. Richard Howard (New York: Harper and Row, 1984).

6. On the idea of the "world soul" *(anima mundi),* see Heinz Robert Schlette, *Weltseele: Geschichte und Hermeneutik* (Frankfurt: Knecht, 1993).

7. Carolyn Merchant, *The Death of Nature: Women, Ecology, and the Scientific Revolution* (San Francisco: Harper and Row, 1980); Maria Suutala, *Zur Geschichte der Naturzerstörung: Frau und Tier in der wissenschaftlichen Revolution* (New York: Peter Lang, 1999).

ery does not merely do away with our ignorance; it also makes us the determining subjects of what we have "discovered." Since the beginning of modern times, scientific reason has become what Max Horkheimer calls "instrumental reason," that is, reason whose knowledge-determining interest is power and utility. Antiquity's idea of reason as *phronesis* linked science with wisdom; but this idea was brushed aside. According to Kant's rationalization of scientific reason, reason "has insight only into what it itself produces according to its own design" by "compel[ling] nature to answer its questions."[8] "Knowledge is power," and scientific knowledge is power first over nature, then over life, and finally over the future. Through science and technology Europe acquired the instrumentalizing knowledge that enabled it to build up its world-spanning civilization out of the resources of the worlds it had colonized. With increasing globalization, the Christian world became the Western world, and the Western world the modern world, whose unique historical origins are no longer evident because Tokyo, Singapore, and Chicago now appear very similar to London, Frankfurt, and Berlin.

What hope motivated the European "discovery" of the rest of the world? It was the vision of the new world order.

Columbus was apparently looking both for God's Garden of Eden and for Eldorado, the city of gold.[9] God and gold also provided the most powerful driving force behind the *conquista*.[10] The gold was intended not just for personal enrichment but also (as we know from Columbus's journal) for the reconquest of Jerusalem. For according to Joachim of Fiore's prophecy, "From Spain will come the one who will bring back the Ark to Zion." Why Jerusalem especially? Because the Holy City was to be the capital of Christ's Thousand Years' Empire,

---

8. Immanuel Kant, *Critique of Pure Reason,* trans. Paul Guyer and Allen Wood (Cambridge: Cambridge University Press, 1998), p. 109.

9. Ernest Bloch, *The Principle of Hope,* vol. 2, trans. Neville Plaice, Stephen Plaice, and Paul Knight (Cambridge: MIT Press, 1986), pp. 772-77; Gustavo Gutiérrez, *Dios o el oro en las Indias* (San Salvador: UCA Editores, 1991).

10. Mariano Delgado, "Die Metamorphosen des Messianismus in den iberischen Kulturen: Eine religionsgeschichtliche Studie," *Neue Zeitschrift für Missionswissenschaften* 34 (1994): 39-50. When Charles V said that in his empire "the sun never sets," he was not registering a fact but asserting the claim of the universal Christian monarchy: one God in heaven — one emperor on earth — one worldwide empire which rules the whole earth.

which would be the consummation of world history. And why the Spanish? According to the political theology of the so-called Quintomonarchists, the Spanish state theologians, the worldwide Christian monarchy would be nothing less than the "Fifth Monarchy," which Daniel 7 prophesies will replace the four bestial world empires, Rome last of all. This would be the kingdom of the Son of man, in which the saints of the Most High will rule the world and judge the nations. With the stone of Daniel (Daniel 2) or with "fire from above" (Daniel 7) all the other empires will be destroyed, until at long last humanity is "one flock under one shepherd" (cf. John 10:16). According to the messianism in Iberian culture, this Christian universal monarchy would last until the end of history. It would be "the new world order," as the Spanish said, long before the United States came into being. This is "the New World" in its messianic sense.

The founders of the United States had a similar vision. *Novus ordo saeculorum* is impressed on the seal of the United States and printed on every one-dollar note. This is the messianic "faith of our fathers," the "new world order" that is so often invoked in presidential inaugural addresses.[11] The United States decided the outcome of the two world wars, and ever since the collapse of the Soviet Union it has been the only remaining superpower. It was therefore not without some justification that Henry Luce called the twentieth century "the American century." And at the moment the twenty-first century looks no different.

What hope motivated modern civilization in the "Old World"?

It was, and still is, the vision of the "new time" of modernity. The interpretive framework for Europe's rise to worldwide power, its mobilizing and orientating impulse, can be perceived in two symbols of hope for the future: first, the expectation that history will find its consummation in the "Thousand Years' Empire," in which Christ will reign together with those who are his, and will judge the nations; second, the expectation that history will find its consummation in the "Third Empire" of the Spirit, which according to Joachim of Fiore's prophecy will replace the empire of the Father and the empire of the Son, and will complete them. We call both these historical expectations chiliastic or millenarian, and their motivation of the present "messi-

---

11. Cf. Ernest Lee Tuveson, *Redeemer Nation: The Idea of America's Millennial Role* (Chicago: University of Chicago Press, 1968).

anic."[12] What they have in common is that, wherever their influence is paramount, the past no longer dominates the present, as it does in traditional societies; now the future takes precedence in the experience of time. And thus "modern society" is born. What is also common to the two expectations is that they see the consummation of history in a historical future, not in a catastrophe outside of or apart from history. And then the past really does become "the prologue to the future," and successive ages can be divided into stages or steps forward in the direction of time's completion. Like a compass that gives us bearings in space and enables us to master it, "the eschatological compass gives us orientation in time, by pointing to the Kingdom of God as the ultimate end and purpose."[13]

From the seventeenth century onwards, waves of chiliastic, messianic, and apocalyptic hopes swept through Europe.[14] We come across them in the Jewish messianism of Sabbatai Tzevi, in Puritan apocalypticism at the time of Oliver Cromwell, in Dutch "prophetic theology,"

---

12. For more detail see Jürgen Moltmann, *The Coming of God: Christian Eschatology,* trans. Margaret Kohl (Minneapolis: Fortress, 1996), chap. 3.

13. Karl Löwith, *Meaning in History* (Chicago: University of Chicago Press, 1949), p. 18. Löwith wanted to show that the modern faith in progress represents a secularization of Christian eschatology. But he did not perceive that it was the secularization only of Christian chiliasm, not of Christian eschatology as a whole. It is only if one hopes for a "completion" of world history that one can talk about its "progress." Löwith took no account of Christian apocalyptic, which must be seen as the reverse side of Christian chiliasm. That is why he called the later (1952) German version of his book *World History and Saving Event* (*Weltgeschichte und Heilsgeschehen*), and not *World History and the Events of Disaster,* although the latter title would have been considerably more plausible after 1945.

14. See Jacob Taubes, *Abendländische Eschatologie* (Bern: A. Francke, 1947). Since Taubes used only German sources, I may point to Richard Bauckham, *Tudor Apocalypse: Sixteenth-Century Apocalypticism, Millennarianism and the English Reformation: From John Bale to John Foxe and Thomas Brightman* (Oxford: Sutton Courtenay Press, 1978). Marjorie Reeves's *Joachim of Fiore and the Prophetic Future* (London: SPCK, 1976) shows how greatly English Protestantism and the English Enlightenment were colored by Joachim's messianic spirit. Not least influential, finally, was the book *Spes Israelis* (1650), written by Manasseh ben Israel, the Chief Rabbi of Amsterdam, which was dedicated to Oliver Cromwell, and brought about the readmission of the Jews to the British Isles. See here Avihu Zakai, *Exile and Kingdom: History and the Apocalypse in the Puritan Migration to America* (Cambridge: Cambridge University Press, 1992), and Zakai's "From Judgment to Salvation: The Image of the Jews in the English Renaissance," *Westminster Theological Journal* 59 (1997): 213-30.

and in the expectations of "better times in the future" that appear at the beginning of German pietism, with Amos Comenius, Philipp Jakob Spener, and the Württemberg theologians Johann Albrecht Bengel and Friedrich Ötinger. They all fused the hope for the millennium of Christ soon to dawn with the ancient world's expectation of the Golden Age, which they had learned from Virgil would replace the Age of Iron. There had always been similar expectations about the end in Christianity. But in the seventeenth century, with the beginning of modernity, a new time was proclaimed. Now the time of fulfillment has arrived, it was said; this hope can be realized in the present. Antiquity and the Middle Ages are past; the "new time" is beginning, and that is the time of consummation. Now world history will be completed. Now humanity will be perfected. Now unhindered progress in all spheres of life is beginning. There will be no more qualitative changes.

Gotthold Ephraim Lessing's famous essay "On the Education of the Human Race" (1777) became the foundational document of the German Enlightenment. Lessing felt that he was the prophet of "the Third Age of the Spirit" announced by Joachim of Fiore. The time is coming, Lessing wrote, when everyone will know the truth for himself without the mediation of the church, and will recognize and do the good *because* it is good, not out of fear of punishment. This new time is beginning now, with the transition of men and women from historical faith in the church to general belief in reason. God's revelation in history will become the promise of that which human beings can now perceive for themselves. God's hidden providence will become the manifest pedagogical plan of education for rising and forward-striving humanity.[15]

In Kant too we find the same chiliastic solemnity that heralds the transition of humanity into the new era of pure faith in reason.[16] For devout Christians, the French Revolution was a sign of the apocalypse

---

15. Karl Aner, *Die Theologie der Lessingzeit* (Hildesheim: G. Olms, 1964); Wolfgang Philipp, *Das Werden der Aufklärung in theologiegeschichtlicher Sicht* (Göttingen: Vandenhoeck und Ruprecht, 1957).

16. Immanuel Kant, *Das Ende der Dinge* (1794); *Ob das menschliche Geschlecht im beständigen Fortschreiten zum Besseren sei?* (1798; reprint: Berlin-Leipzig, W. de Gruyter, 1912). In his *Ideen zu einer allgemeinen Geschichte in weltbürgerlicher Absicht* (1784; reprint: Berlin-Leipzig: W. de Gruyter, 1912) he wrote: "We see: philosophy too can have its chiliasm" (Eighth Proposition).

of the Antichrist. For Kant it was a historical sign that the human race was developing for the better. What had formerly been called the kingdom of God became for Kant the symbol of the ethical goal humanity had endlessly to approach. Part of this chiliasm was also his vision of the perfect civil union of the human race in a league of nations that would guarantee eternal peace; for peace is the promise of what were at that time called "the rights of man" — human rights.

In view of this messianism of the "new time" in Europe, it is not surprising that for Kant the primary religious question was not, "What links us with our origins in the past?" or, "What gives us support in eternity?" The real religious question was, "What can I hope for?" Only a future for which we can hope can give meaning to life in historical time, to historical acts, and to suffering in history. "All's well that ends well." In this solemn, religiously charged sense, the "future" became for the modern world the new paradigm of transcendence.

The nineteenth century, which began, as it were, in 1789, after the marked caesura in Europe, and ended in 1914, was indeed an age of beginnings, utopias, and revolutions. What earlier had been no more than something to be hoped for was now to be realized. For the first time people saw the alternatives to the faulty condition of the world as it exists, not in the world to come but in the future of this world now, not in an intangible other world but in real alterations to this one.

The French Revolution was the matrix of the democratic vision of popular sovereignty on the basis of human and civil rights, and was the source of the great promise: liberty, equality, fraternity (sisterhood had to be added later). From England came the industrial revolution, sister of the democratic revolution, with its promise of general prosperity and the greatest happiness for the greatest number.[17] The socialist revolution was intended to complete the democratic revolution by producing the classless society in the "realm of freedom" built upon the industrial "realm of necessity."

The sense of progress, fired by ever more new scientific discoveries and technological inventions, trusted in a beginning without an end. Great philosophies of history, like those of Auguste Comte, Hegel, and Marx, set historical progress in the context of the perfecting of the

17. Joachim Ritter already maintained this theory in connection with Hegel; see his *Hegel und die französische Revolution* (Frankfurt: Suhrkamp, 1965).

world. At the same time, the great European powers divided up the globe into their colonial empires, undoubtedly with the pernicious intention of ruling the world, but also with the benevolent aim of contributing to the education and development of backward, underdeveloped humanity.

Throughout the nineteenth century, the educated classes in Europe cherished the dream of the moral betterment of humanity. This moral optimism also had an ancient apocalyptic premise. According to Revelation 20:2-4, in Christ's Thousand Years' Empire "Satan will be bound for a thousand years," so that the good can spread unhindered. Around 1900, the fulfillment of this dream seemed to be within the grasp of the European powers. After the Boxer rising, they set about dividing up the last major country that was still independent, China. All the Christian missions fell upon the allegedly backward Chinese with the end-time hope formulated in the slogan: "The evangelization of the world in this generation."

The hallmarks of the sixteenth through the nineteenth centuries in Europe were progress and evolution, growth and expansion, utopias and the revolutions of hope.

The Age of Catastrophes

Walter Benjamin gave us one of the most moving symbols of the swing from hopeful progress to the appalling catastrophes of the modern world in his image of the angel of history:

> A [Paul] Klee painting named *Angelus Novus* shows an angel which looks as if he is about to move away from something at which he is staring. He is wide-eyed, his mouth is open, and his wings are spread. This is what the angel looks like. His face is turned to the past. Where we see a chain of events, he sees a single catastrophe which unceasingly heaps up ruins upon ruins, and throws them down at his feet. The angel would perhaps like to tarry, to awaken the dead, and to piece together what has been broken. But a tempest is blowing from Paradise, it is caught up in his wings, and is so strong that the angel can no longer fold them. This tempest is sweeping him inexorably into the future to which he has turned his

back, while the heap of rubble in front of him rises up to heaven. What we call progress is this tempest.[18]

Where do we find these "ruins upon ruins" which our progress has left behind in history? Let us try to find the sources of tormenting memories so that by becoming aware of them we can seek to heal them.

The glossy messianic surface of European history has its ugly apocalyptic downside: the victorious progress of the European peoples in the nineteenth century led to the regress of many peoples, with heavy losses. Only a third of the modern world is the modern First World; two-thirds of it is the modern Third World. The "new time" has produced them both, both modernity and submodernity, as I should like to call them. For the oppressed, long-enslaved, and always exploited peoples of the Third World, the messianism of modern European times has never been anything but the apocalypse of their destruction. Only the mass enslavement of the Africans from 1496 to 1888 made the colonial latifundia economy in America possible; sugar, cotton, coffee, and tobacco were "slave" crops. It was gold and silver from Latin America that first created the capital used to build up European industrial society.[19] The wealth of the European countries grew out of the triangular transatlantic trade of slaves from Africa to America, raw materials and precious metals from America to Europe, and merchandise and weapons from Europe to Africa. But through the slave trade this wealth destroyed Africa's kingdoms and cultures, and through export economy America's subsistence economy; and the indigenous peoples in the Americas were offered up on the altar of European development.

Nature did not fare much better. The beginning of modern indus-

18. Walter Benjamin, *Illuminationen: Ausgewählte Schriften* (Frankfurt: Suhrkamp Verlag, 1961), pp. 268ff., my translation. *Illuminations* is available in English, trans. Harry Zohn (New York: Schocken, 1977), although the text is not identical in content to the German edition. See Gershom Scholem, *Walter Benjamin und sein Engel* (Frankfurt: Suhrkamp, 1983); Stéphane Mosès, *L'Ange de l'histoire: Rosenzweig, Benjamin, Scholem* (Paris: Seuil, 1992). The painting *Angelus Novus* is on the cover of the present volume.

19. Still of fundamental importance here is Eduardo Galeano, *Open Veins of Latin America,* trans. Cedric Belfrage (New York: Monthly Review Press, 1973). For the history of slavery, see Daniel Pratt Mannix and Malcolm Cowley, *Black Cargoes: A History of the Atlantic Slave Trade* (New York: Viking, 1962).

trial society was also the beginning of "the end of nature."[20] The spread of scientific and technological civilization as we have known it up to now has led to the extermination of more and more plant and animal species. Industrial emissions are producing the greenhouse effect, which is going to change the earth's climate radically in the coming years, with severe consequences. Rain forests are being felled, pastureland overgrazed, deserts are growing. In the last sixty years — my own lifetime — the world's population has quadrupled, and it will go on increasing. Foodstuff requirements will grow proportionately, and so will the amount of refuse produced. The ecosystem of our planet is losing its equilibrium. This is not just a crisis of the natural environment. It is also a crisis of the industrial world itself. The destruction of nature that we can see every day with our own eyes is based on the disturbed relationship of modern men and women to nature. It is impossible to make oneself "the master and possessor of nature" if one is still part of nature and dependent on it. The modern culture of mastery has produced its own downside, which reveals its catastrophic effects in the disappearance of natural living spaces. Here Benjamin's "ruins upon ruins" are very evident. If we look at the development of the newest industrial products on display at shows such as EXPO 2000 we get a sense of progress. But if we see the growing refuse dumps on earth, in the sea, and in space, fears of catastrophe creep in on us. Does our progress really justify these consequences?

In the First World War of 1914-18, the great Christian powers in Europe destroyed each other. It was a war of extermination without any detectable war aims on either side. Its symbol was the Battle of Verdun in 1916.[21] According to the German idea, this was to be "a battle of attrition." It was the idea of annihilation that dominated military thinking, not the hope of victory. The first six months of the war brought over 600,000 dead and almost no territorial gains or losses. Then Germany began the gas war, and gained nothing. The enthusiasm for war in 1914 turned into the naked bestiality of pure nihilism. "The lamps are going

---

20. William Leiss, *The Domination of Nature* (New York: G. Braziller, 1972); Bill McKibben, *The End of Nature* (New York: Random House, 1989).

21. German Werth, *Verdun: Die Schlacht und der Mythos* (Bergisch-Gladbach, 1982), p. 53, writing on German strategy and military planning, says, "Military thinking at the turn of the century was dominated by the idea of 'annihilation.' At Verdun the intention was not to win, as in Sedan in 1870, but to 'annihilate.'"

out all over Europe," said Edward Grey, the British Foreign Secretary, "and we shall not see them lit again in our lifetime." And it was not just the lamps in Europe that went out; the lights of the Enlightenment and of resplendent progress toward a better world went out too. It was as if progress had turned on itself and had devoured its own children. What we suffered in the twentieth century, and are still suffering, is an apocalypse without hope, extermination without justification, pure pleasure in torture, rape, and murder. The "Decline of the West" (the title of Oswald Spengler's well-known work) was fueled in Europe by the drive for self-destruction. The age that began in 1914 and whose end we do not know — perhaps it ended with the end of the East-West conflict in 1989 — became what W. H. Auden called "the age of anxiety."

The Second World War of 1939-45 continued the modern world's nihilistic work of annihilation. Disguised under those misused symbols of hope "the Third Reich" or "the Thousand Years' Reich," in Germany "the final solution of the Jewish question" was pursued at Auschwitz, while the peoples of eastern Europe were exterminated through forced labor and hunger. In 1945 Germany's self-destruction was met by cynical comments from its Führer. The expulsion of whole populations began, with millions of victims. Japan was punished in August 1945 by two atomic bombs, which killed hundreds of thousands of people on the spot. In fascist dictator cults, naked, naked power — power requiring no legitimation — was idolized, and industrial output was ruthlessly pursued. In the Soviet Union, Stalin exterminated whole classes and populations, first through hunger, then through labor and disease in his Gulag Archipelago. Mao Tse-tung adopted the same party system and state terrorism imposed from above. Numerous petty tyrants, such as Pol Pot in Cambodia, learned from them how to murder their own people. Ethnic cleansing became the word — or rather the non-word — of this era. The relapse into forms of personal cruelty against the weak — forms that people thought had long been overcome — in the Balkans, in Africa, and now in Germany, too, is horrifying. It would be cynical to go on talking today about the moral progress of humanity through civilization. Hitler and Stalin and all their willing henchmen have convinced us that the power of radical evil is unbroken. That is why end-of-the-world scenarios, catastrophe fantasies, and *Apocalypse Now* films seem to us more realistic than the fine, hopeful images of the nineteenth century about the golden age and eternal peace.

The twentieth century brought no new ideas, visions, or utopias into the world that could lend history a meaning. We have seen the killing fields of history forbid every attempt to find a meaning for them, and every theodicy, every ideology of progress, and every satisfaction in globalization fails to suffice. In that century progress left in its wake ruins and victims, and no historical future can make this suffering good. No better future can assure us that their suffering was not for nothing. In the twentieth century, a total inability to find meaning in the face of history as it has hitherto been replaced the nineteenth century's credulous faith in the future. If the achievements of science and technology can be employed for the annihilation of humanity — and if they can, they will be, some day or another — it becomes difficult to enthuse over the Internet or genetic engineering. Every accumulation of power also accumulates the danger of its misuse. But one thing at least the twentieth century should have taught us, as we look back at the nineteenth: it is impossible for history to be consummated in history. No historical future can do that. And it is impossible to complete history if we ourselves are merely historical beings.

Bridges to the Future

I am calling the hopes pointing toward the next thousand years "bridges to the future" because they have to be built over the abysses of annihilation that we have experienced in the twentieth century. They are practically the same hopes which called the modern world to life in the nineteenth century — in the democratic and the industrial revolutions — but today they are hopes that have become wise through bitter experience. We will no longer be so credulously confident about progress as we once were, when these hopes first saw the light of day, or so blind to the risks. Today our hopes will have to be cautious hopes, and hopes that count the costs. We have to hope and work for the future without arrogance and without despair. The nineteenth century's hopes for humanity have left us living on the mass graves of the twentieth. Whether we look upon the next millennium in exuberant hope or with skepticism, we need to be reconciled with the past of the twentieth century, so that for us that century can become the past, and its catastrophes do not close in on us again.

The Future of Christian Hope:
The Raising of the Dead, Hope for Those Who Have Gone

Before I explore further the links between the secular hopes of the nineteenth century and the experience of the twentieth, I should like to return to Walter Benjamin's "angel of history." Wide-eyed, the angel sees before him in the past "ruins upon ruins"; the wreckage of history rises up to heaven before him. He is petrified, for "the tempest blowing from Paradise" is caught up in his wings, so that he cannot fold them again. But what did this angel really want to do? For what purpose was he sent? "He would like to tarry, to awaken the dead and piece together what has been broken." But he is unable to do so as long as the tempest is caught up in his wings. "What we call progress is this tempest," says Benjamin. So we might conclude, conversely, that if we could interrupt this tempest, and could get away from the wind of progress, the angel would be able to waken the dead and piece together what is broken, and our memories would be healed.

We find the biblical image behind this description in Ezekiel 37, which tells of Israel's resurrection and reunification. In the Spirit of the Lord, the prophet is led out to "the wide field full of dead bones." That is a reference back to Israel's history of suffering. And the bones "were very dry." Then the prophet hears the voice: "Behold, I will cause breath [*ruach,* vital energy] to enter you, and you shall live. . . . [And you shall] say to the breath . . . Come from the four winds, O breath, and breathe upon these slain, that they may live" (vv. 5, 9 RSV). After he has experienced this vision of the raising of the dead, the prophet goes to his people and proclaims: "Behold they say, 'Our bones are dried up, and our hope is lost; we are clean cut off.' . . . [But I the Lord GOD] will put my Spirit within you, and you shall live, and I will place you in your own land" (vv. 11, 14 RSV).

"Waken the dead and piece together what has been broken." That is a future hope for the past. There is no historical future in which it could happen. It must be a future for the whole of history, and therefore it must have a transcendent foundation. For mortal beings will not awaken the dead, and those who have done the breaking will not be able to put together what is broken. No human future can make good the crimes of the past. But in order to be able to live with this past, with its ruins and victims, without repressing it and without having to repeat it, we need this transcendent hope for the raising of the dead and the healing of what has been broken. Because of the raising of the broken Christ, the Christian hope for the future is at its heart a hope for resurrection. Without hope for the past there is no hope for the future, for what will be, will pass away; what is born, dies; and what is not yet, will one day be no longer.[22] The resurrection hope is not directed toward a future *in* history; it points toward the future *of* history, in which the tragic dimensions of history and nature will be dissolved.

But if the future of history is defined by the raising of the dead, then in that raising we encounter our own past too. Among the dead there come to meet us the fallen, the gassed, the murdered, and the "disappeared." The dead of Verdun, Auschwitz, Stalingrad, and Hiroshima await us.

Only the person who remembers can look this future in the face, the future called "the raising of the dead." And only the person who looks into this future is able really to remember those who have gone, and to live in their presence. Today, many people are asking for a "culture of remembrance," but such a culture must be sustained by a "culture of hope," for without hope for a future of the past and those who are past, remembrance sinks into nostalgia and ultimately into a powerless forgetting; or it clings to the remembered so closely that it can no longer free itself, because it cannot let go what it remembers. "Remembrance hastens the redemption" is written over Yad Vashem in Jerusalem. "The dead are dead, but we awaken them," said the historian Leopold von Ranke. "We walk with them and look them in the eye. They demand the truth from us."[23]

If we compare Benjamin with Ezekiel, we see that the tempest we call progress blows in the opposite direction. It blows "from Paradise," says Benjamin. That is to say, it drives people further and further from their original home. The tempest of the resurrection does not blow from the past into the future; it blows from the future into the past, and brings back what cannot be brought back — the dead — and heals what is unhealably broken — the ruins. We already feel it in the Pente-

---

22. No enduring hope can be based on an "ontology of not-yet-being" (Ernst Bloch, *Philosophische Grundfragen I: Zur Ontologie des Noch-Nicht-Seins* [Frankfurt: Suhrkamp Verlag, 1961]).

23. In Reinhard Wittram, *Das Interesse an der Geschichte* (Göttingen: Vandenhoeck und Ruprecht, 1968), p. 32.

costal Spirit that makes us live "through the powers of the age to come" (Heb. 6:5).

How are these two tempests, "progress" and "resurrection," related to each other? How can the transcendent hope for God be joined with the immanent hopes of men and women? I believe in their opposition.[24] Because (and in so far as) the resurrection hope sees a future for those who are gone, those who are living in the present gain courage for the future. Because of a great hope for the overcoming of death and transience, our little hopes for future better times gain strength, and do not fall victim to resignation and cynicism. In the midst of the age of anxiety we hope "against hope" and still do not give ourselves up to despair. We gain the courage to be, in spite of non-being, as Paul Tillich aptly put it.[25] Our limited human hopes for those to come then become a reaction to the divine future for those who have gone.

The Future of the Democratic Revolution

We owe the democratization of political life to the American and French revolutions. With them the nineteenth century began. After tremendous struggles and sacrifices, since 1989 liberal democracy has come to prevail in the Western and modern world, in the face of fascist tyranny and the communist "dictatorship of the proletariat." But today we have democratic politics under different conditions from those of the nineteenth century.

One such condition might be described as *absentee democracy*. Modern democracies today are threatened not so much by totalitarian right- or left-wing parties as by the apathy of the people from whom, when all is said and done, "all state power" issues.[26] The diminishing

---

24. Benjamin suggests how "progress" and "resurrection" are *not* related: "Consequently nothing in history can attempt of itself to relate to the messianic. Thus the kingdom of God is not the *telos* of historical dynamic. . . . Seen historically, it is not a goal but an end. . . . The secular is therefore not a category of the kingdom, but it is a category, and the most appropriate category, of its stealthiest approach" (Benjamin, *Illuminationen*, p. 280; the passage is not included in the English translation; see note 18 above).

25. Paul Tillich, *The Courage to Be* (New Haven: Yale University Press, 2000).

26. *Basic Law for the Federal Republic of Germany* (Bonn: Foreign Office of the Federal Republic of Germany, 1969), Article 20.2.

turnout at elections is only a symptom of this apathy. What is the deeper cause? I believe the reason is that we view democracy as a condition we possess, not as a process we are involved in. But democracy is an open, expanding process which can never be completed in history, and which requires the active participation, participatory interest, and personal commitment of the people. If this democratizing process flags, then the political interest of the people flags too. The participatory democracy that is necessary is replaced by a strange absentee democracy. People withdraw into private life or into their business concerns and don't want to be bothered with politics any longer. They lose interest and no longer take part. A political class then becomes estranged from the people, and the people lose trust in the politicians. The result, as Richard von Weizshäcker complained, is party rule. The parties by no means fulfill their function of helping to form the will of the people, as the Basic Law requires.[27] Instead they impose their own will on the people.

A second condition is that democracy as a process open to the future remains alive only as long as it is motivated and mobilized by *hope for the realization of human rights*. The civil rights guaranteed in various national constitutions are just, provided they correspond to universal human rights, which are well summarized and defined in the Universal Declarations of Human Rights of 1948 and 1966.[28] As we can see from the struggles for the rights of women, children, the disabled, asylum seekers, and other underprivileged groups, the democratic implementation of human rights in the civil rights of our political community has by no means been completed. Many free and spontaneous citizens' action groups on local and regional levels must be mobilized if human rights are to be realized. Participatory democracy is worth it, I believe, for the sake of the implementation of human rights.

Human rights are universally valid; they apply to all human beings. They are indivisible. It follows that every person is not only the member of a people, the citizen of a nation, the adherent of a religious community, and so forth, but also has "inalienable human rights." Today human rights are not just a United Nations "ideal," as the Preamble

---

27. *Basic Law for the Federal Republic of Germany* Article 21.1.

28. Jan Milič Lochman and Jürgen Moltmann, *Gottes Recht und Menschenrechte* (Neukirchen-Vluyn: Neukirchener, 1977).

says; they can be claimed through international courts of law, where these exist. What happened in the Balkans was frightful, but the fact that people responsible for crimes against humanity and infringements of human rights are brought before the international court of justice in the Hague and are condemned by it is a small step forward. Crimes against humanity and one day — as I hope — crimes against the environment too must be punished, so that human rights and the rights of nature may become the fundamental rights of a global human society.

A third reality of our world today, the *nuclear threat*, means that the peaceful regulation of conflicts between countries is a duty. Nuclear armaments and other means of mass extermination are not military weapons; they are political ones.

The avoidance of the nuclear annihilation of the world (which is possible at any time, even if not very probable at the moment) means that an age-old apocalyptic task is again being imposed on the modern state and the community of states as a whole. The power that was to hold back the end-time annihilation was called the Kat'echon. This "power of restraint" derives from the prophecy about the Antichrist in 2 Thessalonians 2:7ff.: "the mystery of lawlessness is already at work; only he who now restrains it will do so until he is out of the way" (RSV). For Christians in the Roman Empire, the one that now "restrains" it meant the Roman state; for Carl Schmitt, it was the anti-revolutionary Holy Alliance in the nineteenth century and, in the twentieth, the "anti-bolshevist" Hitler dictatorship.[29] We can forget these two ideological anxieties. Today, the annihilation of the human race and the inhabitable earth is the real threat. So every country has the urgent task of restraining humanity's nuclear self-annihilation.

"We are living in the 'End-time'," said Günter Anders, and rightly so, for he did not mean any form of apocalyptic prophecy; he meant the time in which the end is possible at any moment.[30] Consequently, the state not only has the power of restraining the nuclear catastrophe; it also has the positive task of gaining time, and extending the time-limit.[31] With every year in which the annihilation is put off, we gain time for life

29. Heinrich Meier, *Die Lehre Carl Schmitts: Vier Kapitel zur Unterscheidung Politischer Theologie und Politischer Philosophie* (Stuttgart: J. B. Metzler, 1994), pp. 243-49.

30. Günter Anders, *Die atomare Drohung* (Munich: Beck, 1983).

31. Johann Baptist Metz, *Faith in History and Society*, trans. David Smith (New York: Seabury, 1980), pp. 169-79.

and for peace. We do not have endless time. That was an illusion of the nineteenth century, with its credulous belief in progress. We exist in limited time, and must gain time. This is a truly global historical task for the modern state in the shadow of nuclear extermination.

Is there a *Christian hope for the political world* which motivates Christians for responsible cooperation and, if circumstances require it, justifies their resolute resistance?

It is the task of the Christian community to remind the civil community unceasingly, through word, act, and presence, of the righteousness and justice of God and of his coming kingdom. The church is not like a sect, separate, and there only for itself. It is there for all human beings, and for nature in this earthly creation. The future for which Christians hope is not the consummation of the church in the downfall of this world, nor the salvation of the redeemed at the world's end; it is the kingdom of God, which will redeem everything and put all things to rights, the kingdom which will come "on earth as it is in heaven." Consequently the church cannot intervene politically simply on behalf of its own interests. It must above all intervene on behalf of the justice which, in the spirit of Jesus, is there for the poor and the powerless first of all. The church has no "public claim" for itself, but only for the cause of the kingdom of God it propounds. Its task is not to "churchify" the world but to prepare the way for the coming kingdom. There is no such thing as nonpolitical Christianity. Indeed, the modern axiom that "religion is a private matter" was a political decision, directed against the old form of state church and political religion (*cuius regio, eius religio:* a person's religion is the religion of his ruler).

In the history of this still unredeemed world, Christians will not aim to bring about the kingdom of God. God will do that himself. But they will press for parables and correspondences to God's righteousness and justice and his kingdom, and insist that circumstances that are in contradiction to them are diminished. Christianity's motivating vision is the descent to earth from heaven of the *polis* Jerusalem (Rev. 21:2), in whose light the nations are to live in peace (21:24).

Because Christians know that they have the rights of citizenship in the coming kingdom (*politeuma,* Phil. 3:20), they will do what is best in the kingdom of the world in which they live, and will contribute their ideas about justice and freedom to their political community. Because of their hope, they cannot escape into the absentee democracy but will be present wherever political ways out of the perils have to be sought. In these perils of the world they can show where deliverance is to be found.

The Future of the Industrial Revolution

The industrial revolution awakened the mobilizing faith in progress that was the mark of the nineteenth century. Today we no longer have any need to justify such a belief. Nor do we need to criticize it any more, for the competitive principle makes progress compulsive for all production. Indeed, industries and markets are condemned to a continually accelerating progress. Whatever fails to modernize and rationalize has already lost. Progress has got itself into the acceleration trap. "The person who rides the tiger can never get off again."[32]

This means that there is not much point in criticizing progress as such. What does have a point is to question its goals, so as to correct its course if that is desirable. Progress itself is only a means to an end; it does not itself prescribe humane ends. We generally measure progress by the increase of economic, financial, military, and cultural power. But power itself is not a humane goal; it is only an accumulation of the means whereby humane goals can be attained. Every year we are better equipped to achieve what we want — but what do we really want?

Most major technological projects were started not because this was the democratically established will of the people, but because the will of the people was bypassed. In Germany there was no democratic decision about the building of nuclear power stations. And there are no democratic discussions today about genetically modified foodstuffs.

Since the end of the East-West conflict, progress has come to be called "globalization." This process already got under way in the nineteenth century and at the beginning of the twentieth. Since 1989, the end of the East-West conflict, we have reverted to the views held before 1914. But like progress, globalization is, to be precise, merely a quantifying term: what once applied to particular cases is now deemed univer-

---

32. Klaus Backhaus and Holger Bonus, *Die Beschleunigungsfalle oder der Triumph der Schildkröte* (Stuttgart: Schaffer-Poeschel, 1994).

sal. What used to be local is now considered global. Like progress, globalization is therefore only the means to an end, not a humane end in itself. As long as it is merely a matter of acquiring power, the process of globalization does not exist, qualitatively speaking. Initially it is manifestly only a matter of dominating, exploiting, and marketing nature. Commerce starts to be shared out between fewer and fewer global players, but these players get bigger and bigger. But if short-term profiteering is not to lead in the long term to the bankruptcy of humanity and the collapse of the ecosystem, we must begin a public discussion about humane goals and the purposes of globalization.

In order to avoid the destruction of the earth through ruthless exploitation, it is good to concentrate on the holism of creation, and to protect life through bioethical conventions. It is also important to support sustainable development. But this focus inevitably ends up as an ethos of conservativism, and conservative ethics are always too late. It is better to develop a counter-model to the globalization of power which concentrates on finding humane goals and purposes for it.

We have a model of this kind for defining humane goals of globalized power, and hence for correcting the course of the modern world's development. We can find it in the inconspicuous term *ecumenism,* which has up to now been used only for relations between the churches.[33] In Greek, *oikoumenē* is a term of quality and means "the whole, inhabited globe," a meaning that reflects its root in the word *oikos* (house). From a world inhabited by human beings we can derive the goal of a habitable world for a humanity that is at home on this earth. The "housekeeping" of this earth requires the keeping of a dwelling place fit for human beings; while, for their part, human beings should be prepared to live in the ecosystem, and no longer stand against and apart from nature as hostile aliens.[34]

---

33. Geiko Müller-Fahrenholz, "Ökumene — Glücksfall und Ernstfall des Glaubens," *Evangelisches Pressedienst-Dokumentation* 28 (1998): 3-16.

34. If this is correct, then a new ecological anthropology is required. The modern anthropology of Max Scheler, Arnold Gehlen, Helmuth Plessner, Wolfhart Pannenberg, and others starts from the "openness to the world" and the "self-transcendence" of human beings, as a way of distinguishing them from animals. But this distinction goes back to Johann Gottfried Herder, *Abhandlung über den Ursprung der Sprache* [*Essay on the Origin of Language*] (München: Hanser, 1978). Herder writes: "Nature was his most severe stepmother, just as she was the most tender of mothers towards every insect" (my trans-

If the goal of progress and the globalization of human power is to make the earth habitable, not to dominate and possess it, we must leave behind the modern Western world's God-complex of being "the masters and possessors of nature," which is what Descartes promised in his scientific theory at the beginning of modern times.[35] The earth can live without the human race, and did so for millions of years; but the human race cannot exist without the earth, for it is from the earth that we were taken. So human beings are dependent on the earth, but the earth is not dependent on human beings. It follows from this simple recognition that human civilization must be integrated into the ecosystem and not the converse — that nature has to be subjected to human domination.[36]

Only interlopers exploit nature, cut down the forests, fish the seas empty, and then pass on like nomads. People who live in these places, and want to live there, are concerned to preserve the foundations on which their life depends, and will preserve their natural environment so that it is capable of sustaining life. They will try to compensate for every intervention in nature, and to establish an equilibrium. Today's economic-ecological conflicts are largely conflicts between foreign corporations and indigenous peoples — that is to say, they are conflicts between interests in exploitation on the one hand, and the habitability of nature on the other.

Having globalized power, we logically need to globalize responsibility. We cannot stand still at a point where the economy is globalized but politics are still nationally limited. The economy needs its political correlate, and politics need humane goals about which human beings can unite.

Humanity's scientific and technological potential will have to be developed further, but it must not be employed in a destructive struggle for power. Rather, it should be used to make the earth sustainably habitable by human beings. Then earthly creation will not be simply

---

lation). There is an English translation of the book by Alexander Gode (Chicago: University of Chicago Press, 1986). In the new ecological anthropology, the insights of modern feminist anthropology must also be taken into account.

35. See René Descartes, *Discourse on Method* (1637), trans. John Veitch (New York: Dutton, 1969).

36. Jürgen Moltmann, *God for a Secular Society: The Public Relevance of Theology,* trans. Margaret Kohl (Minneapolis: Fortress, 1999), pp. 92-116.

"preserved" (to use the conservative vocabulary hitherto employed); it will develop further toward its goal. For it is destined to be the shared house of all earthly created beings, and to be the home and dwelling place for the community of all the living. The earth is even to become the dwelling place of God "on earth as it is in heaven."

When the Eternal One comes to "dwell" on the earth, the earth will become God's cosmic temple, and the restless God of hope and history will come to his rest. That is the great biblical — Jewish and Christian — vision for this earth. It is the final promise: "Behold, the dwelling of God is with [human beings]. He will dwell with them, and they shall be his people" (Rev. 21:3 RSV, following Ezek. 37:27). The ultimate *Shekinah,* this cosmic incarnation of God, is the divine future of the earth. In this expectation we shall already treat the earth as "God's temple" here and now, and cherish its creatures as sacred. We men and women are not "the masters and possessors" of the earth, but perhaps we shall one day become its priests and priestesses, representing God to the earth, and bringing the earth before God, so that we see and taste God in all things, and perceive all things in the radiance of his love. That would be a sacramental view of the world which would be able to take up and absorb into itself the worldview held at present in science and technology.

Contrary Hopes: Evangelical Christianity and the Decline Narrative

DANIEL JOHNSON

In February 2000, a curious title appeared among the offerings of the Christian Book Distributors, a catalogue marketer of Christian books, videos, gifts, and software. The singularity of the new title was surely not lost on CBD's cataloguers, to whom fell the task of placing it into one of the company's extant subject headings. They eventually settled on "Inspirational." So it was there, among the several helpings of *Chicken Soup for the Soul* and various doses of Norman Vincent Peale's thoughts on the power of positive thinking, amid the prayer guides, devotional guides, and countless tales of miracles big and small, that CBD browsers would also find an uplifting little volume entitled *Slouching Towards Gomorrah: Modern Liberalism and American Decline,* by Robert H. Bork.

That CBD should wind up selling such a book is in many ways unremarkable. The company does carry a wide range of other secular titles, and these do include the occasional work of social commentary or criticism. It was perhaps inevitable that Judge Bork's book would one day be counted among them, given the near iconic status that Bork had attained within much of the evangelical Christian community. After the United States Senate rejected his appointment to the nation's highest court, Bork had become a martyr of sorts — not for the Christian faith, to be sure, but for the sociopolitical convictions that had done so much to define the Religious Right.

Slouching Towards Gomorrah is, in the main, a repackaging of those very convictions. Most of what is wrong in America today, Bork maintains, stems from a liberalism that has run amok. Two principal developments stand out in this respect. First, the egalitarianism associated with traditional liberal thought has been taken to an extreme, overriding the natural differences between people in a quixotic quest for equalized outcomes. Second, the liberal emphasis on individualism has been similarly radicalized, with efforts now given to clearing away all that might curb the personal pursuit of pleasure. These developments are to blame for the rootless hedonism and the void of personal responsibility that supposedly plague the country, and Bork's one hope is that the American people will somehow find the will to reverse the tide.[1]

It seems fitting at this point to ask *why* this sort of message resonates so strongly within evangelical Christian circles. As it happens, social scientists in recent years have offered several explanations. Perhaps the resurgence of the ideological Right, both within Christianity and without, stems from a deep-seated "fear of falling" down the status hierarchy that plagues the established middle class.[2] Or perhaps it is symptomatic of the deep restructuring of American political culture, in which the most salient fault lines are increasingly defined by the fundamentally opposed moral visions that coalesced in the aftermath of the Enlightenment.[3] Maybe it reflects the ongoing need for American evangelicals to define themselves as an embattled community, whose moral convictions are routinely under assault.[4] Or maybe it is yet another instance of a community finding in the rhetoric of the jeremiad a tool for galvanizing support, especially in prosperous times, when the threat of moral turpitude looms larger and a sense of security blunts the impact of milder forms of cultural criticism.[5] Clearly, there is much that might

---

1. Robert H. Bork, *Slouching Towards Gomorrah: Modern Liberalism and American Decline* (New York: Regan, 1996).

2. Barbara Ehrenreich, *Fear of Falling: The Inner Life of the Middle Class* (New York: Pantheon, 1989). Ruth Levitas makes a similar argument in connection with the middle class embrace of decline narratives in "Dystopian Times? The Impact of the Death of Progress on Utopian Thinking," *Theory, Culture and Society* 1 (1982): 53-64.

3. James Davison Hunter, *Culture Wars: The Struggle to Define America* (New York: Basic, 1991).

4. Christian Smith, *American Evangelicalism: Embattled and Thriving* (Chicago: University of Chicago Press, 1998).

5. Sacvan Bercovitch, *The American Jeremiad* (Madison: University of Wisconsin

help us to account for why CBD thought its patrons would be so attracted to works such as *Slouching Towards Gomorrah*.

Even so, we ought not let the ease with which we can explain it keep us from recognizing the significance of the fact that this particular book appeared in this particular place. And it *was* a significant occurrence, though in a much humbler way than we are used to considering. It does not signal a moment of epochal transformation, nor does it mark a new point of advancement for some inexorable historical trend. Rather, it is a trace left by the diffuse and mercurial history of a social element called "hope." Accordingly, it prompts reflection on the character of the social hopes that evangelical Christians entertain today.

I will begin these reflections with a cursory analysis of the nature of hope, with special emphasis on the critical role that narrative plays in the experience and expression of hope. I will then examine some of the countervailing tendencies that have marked evangelical expressions of social hope, finding among them certain elements that may dovetail nicely with Bork's story. Finally, I will suggest two ways of thinking about why evangelicals concerned with "this-worldly" action have gravitated toward tales of decline to express their social hopes. The first suggests that "the postmodern condition" results in nothing less than the loss of genuine social hope; the second proposes that developments in "late modern" societies typically foster experiences of hope in a "negative" mode. Ultimately, I believe that the latter is the more promising way of understanding the evangelical embrace of decline narratives, but I run ahead of myself.

Hope and Its Narrative Instantiation

While sociologists of religion have not traditionally given much thought to the matter of hope, two recent exceptions bear some consideration here. In very different ways, Andrew Greeley[6] and Charles Lemert[7] each advance an argument that the experience and expression

---

Press, 1978). See also Frank L. Borchardt, *Doomsday Speculation as a Strategy of Persuasion: A Study of Apocalypticism as Rhetoric* (Newliston, N.Y.: Edwin Mellen, 1990).

6. Andrew M. Greeley, *Religion as Poetry* (New Brunswick, N.J.: Transaction, 1995).

7. Charles Lemert, "The Might Have Been and Could Be of Religion in Social Theory," *Sociological Theory* 17 (1999): 240-263.

of hope is essential to all religion. Given how self-evident the theme of hope is in the specific Christian traditions that concern us here, there is little need to take up such expansive theoretical claims. What Greeley and Lemert provide instead are two important observations regarding the experience and expression of hope.

First, Greeley and Lemert refresh a phenomenology of hope that will be instrumental for our purposes. In both accounts, the experience of hope is that which brings human limitedness into view while at the same time hinting at the possibility of moving beyond those limits.[8]

In a passing comment, Greeley suggests the term "horizon experience" to describe this phenomenon. While the horizon metaphor carries a lot of excess baggage, having been widely used for very different purposes, it is helpful here insofar as it emphasizes that the limits encountered in these sorts of experiences are not absolute; for the significance of a horizon is not just that it demarcates all that is visible to us at a given moment. It does do this, of course, but because it does so ambiguously, and because we have acquired a sense of what it means to move about in space, a horizon is always suggestive of things that are not visible to us. Put another way, a horizon may signify an end, but not an end beyond which there is nothing. Rather, it is an end beyond which there is *necessarily* something, something that we could very well see for ourselves if only we were somewhere other than where we are.

So it is with the metaphorical horizon that swings into view anytime we find ourselves hoping. The limits of the human are limits only on account of our humanness — our finite nature, our fixity in time and space, and the contingencies that lead us to occupy particular places in time and space. Any time we encounter such limits and see this, glimpsing there a hint of something beyond what we can realize at that moment, we hope.[9]

_____

8. Greeley does so explicitly, equating his "experiences that renew hope" with certain of the "limit-experiences" that David Tracy made the centerpiece of his early work (see David Tracy, *Blessed Rage for Order: The New Pluralism in Theology* [New York: Seabury, 1975]). Lemert, meanwhile, says very little to characterize hope directly, but he assumes much the same idea.

9. Paul Pruyser nicely captures the view in his reprise of Gabriel Marcel's analysis of hoping: "From a structural point of view one might say that at the moment hoping sets in, the hoper begins to perceive reality as of larger scope than the one he has hitherto dealt with. He can faithfully take all that he himself and mankind has ever known

Second, Greeley's thoughts in particular help to draw special attention to narrative forms when thinking about hope. It has become quite fashionable to extol the study of narrative as key to understanding the social world,[10] and sociologists of religion have gamely worked to stay in fashion.[11] The rationale is generally methodological: much of what social actors do to make sense of the world is tell stories, and so those who take the interpretivist's task seriously must deal seriously with the stories that people tell. This is all well and good, but Greeley actually encourages us to make a more basic observation regarding how hope is instantiated. As he sees it, it is only by means of narrative that hope is experienced in the first place.

The assertion is well founded, for the experience of hope has a narrative structure built right into it. When people hope, they lay a story arc over a certain span of history, one that identifies the limitations of the present, offers a vision of how those limitations may be overcome in the future, and furnishes grounds for expecting that that future will be realized. The story may not be fully articulated in the experience itself, of course, but the narrative structure is there just the same. And it becomes even more pronounced as soon as people try to express hope, packaging their experiences in such a way that they might share them with others and revisit them themselves.

This is not to say that the hopeful stories that people tell offer

---

about reality, acknowledge it without abrogation, and yet envisage it as only a part of a larger reality which contains, because of its wider scope, also certain unknowns. This need not be a view of two worlds — it is more likely to be two views of one world. When one sees the world with oneself in it as an open-ended process, finiteness refers only to the crystallized things of the past, and all knowledge becomes only a knowledge of parts. But the summation of knowledges of parts does not yield the knowledge of the whole, which still thrusts toward novelty" (Paul W. Pruyser, "Phenomenology and the Dynamics of Hoping," *Journal for the Scientific Study of Religion* 3 [1963]: 93).

10. See Norman K. Denzin, "The Sociological Imagination Revisited," *Sociological Quarterly* 31 (1990): 1-22; David R. Maines, "Narrative's Moment and Sociology's Phenomena: Toward a Narrative Sociology," *Sociological Quarterly* 34 (1993): 17-38; Patricia Ewick and Susan S. Silbey, "Subversive Stories and Hegemonic Tales: Toward a Sociology of Narrative," *Law and Society Review* 29 (1995): 197-226; and the collection of essays compiled in Ruthellen Josselson and Amia Lieblich, eds., *The Narrative Study of Lives* (Thousand Oaks, Calif.: Sage, 1993).

11. David Yamane, "Narrative and Religious Experience," *Sociology of Religion* 61 (2000): 171-89.

unalloyed access to the experiences that lead to their telling. Hopeful narratives are reflexive, mediated accounts of hopes and their fulfillment, and as such they are invariably shaped by factors external to the experience of hope.[12] Still more, the tense of the story often shifts from the experience to the retelling. While many narratives of hope are expressly about an as-yet-unrealized future, many others involve recounting the completed events of the past. Yet even the stories told in past tense remain fundamentally future-oriented. They may be given more to maintaining plausible grounds for future hopes than to detailing what is hoped for, but they nonetheless orient their hearers to a certain understanding of what the future may hold.

We thus find narrative to be the principal vehicle through which hope is experienced, expressed, and cultivated.[13] This raises interesting questions concerning the kinds of stories through which evangelicalism has traditionally sustained its social hopes, and how tales of decline like Judge Bork's might conceivably fit in. It is to such matters that we now turn.

The Contrarieties of Evangelical Social Hope

So how does a community that has so much to do with hope pay so much attention to such seemingly unhopeful stories as *Slouching Towards Gomorrah?*

There is likely more than one answer to this question, and that is so for a couple of reasons. For one thing, the evangelical subculture is far from monolithic. While there are a few common understandings that hold it together, what we call "the evangelical community" is actually made up of distinct subgroups with quite different theological and cultural commitments. As such, an answer that seems to work in one pocket of that community may not suffice when we turn our attention to others. More important still, evangelical theology (especially on a popular level) contains certain countervailing tendencies where the

---

12. This theme echoes throughout the interpretivist literature, but it is perhaps best associated with Alfred Schutz, *The Phenomenology of the Social World,* trans. George Walsh and Frederick Lehnert (Evanston, Ill.: Northwestern University Press, 1932).

13. This understanding informs many of the essays in the present volume. See especially William Katerberg's contribution.

fulfillment of Christian social hope is concerned. Where various strands of that tradition pull in opposing directions on such matters, spaces appear for diverse, even conflicting, tales of decline to be woven into the theological fabric.

A thorough accounting of the myriad social groupings that comprise the evangelical subculture is beyond the scope of this essay, as is any effort to retrace all that evangelicals through the years have said regarding their hopes for this world. We can, however, identify the most conspicuous ways in which the narratives of hope that evangelicals have entertained have occasionally pulled against each other.

We begin by noting that for a certain segment of the evangelical population, the question of social hope simply does not register. For many within the evangelical community, salvation and deliverance from sin are purely personal propositions, rooted exclusively in the hope that each individual who has received such things will live on after death. Within such interpretive circles, the central stories of the Christian tradition — the incarnation of God in the person of Jesus, the events of his life, and the Easter tale of his crucifixion and resurrection — become tokens of this purely personal hope. The ancient Jewish messianic narrative is completely transformed in view of its fulfillment in the Christ event, and any elements of social, political, or global hope that marked the Jewish tradition are thereby excised from it. Even the lingering messianism expressed in the hope of Christ's return comes to be understood in this way. Christ is to come back for one purpose only, and that is to receive his own into the new life promised for them. All of the individual heirs to that promise will thus enjoy a continuity of life, having been ushered beyond the personal horizon of death, but nothing else of the world they have known need be transported.

Here, then, is an open space for stories like Bork's to fill. The natural and social worlds alike may well be slated for long-term decline, or even annihilation, as there is a total break between this creation and the heavenly realm that awaits the faithful.

Yet, if we consider the whole of the Christian tradition, this is clearly a minority view. The bearers of that tradition have routinely projected their hopes onto more levels than just the personal, and the evangelical community is no exception. Throughout their history, evangelicals have held out hope for the redemption of all things human, both individual and social.[14] They also have anticipated the healing of the natural world and the reestablishment of healthy relations between humanity and nature. Finally, they have spoken hopefully about the future of the entire cosmos and have even suggested that God's own future history may be part of the story of hope as well.[15]

To entertain hopes in connection with all of these things is to presuppose some continuity between that which is and that which is to come. While there may be some kind of break in the future history of the creation — some sense in which present realities will be made like new — the coming of that new world cannot be predicated on the complete cessation of the present one. In other words, the "new creation" cannot be a creation *ex nihilo,* since the hopes being entertained are hopes for *this* creation. It is *this* social and natural world that awaits transport across the horizons of the present; it is the *present* cosmos and the *present* God that will somehow see the fulfillment of all hopes in the future that is yet to come.

This understanding generally lends a proximate quality to the objects of such hopes. If present realities somehow persist into the world to come, then the promise of realizing at least some of what is hoped for extends back into the present.[16] This is readily acknowledged where it concerns the purely personal dimension of Christian hope. No matter how firm the conviction that personal perfection will come only with a

14. Analyses of the development of evangelical social thought can be found in David O. Moberg, *The Great Reversal: Evangelicalism and Social Concern* (Philadelphia: Lippincott, 1972); Donald W. Dayton, *Discovering an Evangelical Heritage* (New York: Harper and Row, 1976); and Timothy L. Smith, *Revivalism and Social Reform: American Protestantism on the Eve of the Civil War* (Gloucester, Mass.: Peter Smith, 1976). For an assessment of more recent evidences of evangelical social concern, see James Davison Hunter, *Evangelicalism: The Coming Generation* (Chicago: University of Chicago Press, 1987), pp. 40-46.

15. Jürgen Moltmann, *The Coming of God: Christian Eschatology,* trans. Margaret Kohl (Minneapolis: Fortress, 1996).

16. Even if such a move is not deemed theologically necessary, certain practical exigencies may force the theological hand. It is not easy for even the most self-assured religious community to sustain a vital sense of hope for an as yet unrealized future. As John Lofland found in his seminal study of the nascent Unification Church, one of the principal strategies by which they do so involves defining "the present as preparatory to a later time, when, helped by things done now, other things would *really* happen" (*Doomsday Cult: A Study of Conversion, Proselytization, and Maintenance of Faith* [Englewood Cliffs, N.J.: Prentice-Hall, 1966], p. 251).

final act of divine intervention, Christians have long insisted that the journey toward that state of perfection begins in the present. The same is true where things social are concerned. While the specifics of their accounts certainly have varied, most Christians through the years have allowed that the divine social order is somehow breaking in even on this side of the eschaton. For them to think otherwise threatens to make the whole of human history and culture a meaningless exercise.[17]

This is the greatest point of tension for evangelical deliberations on social hope. For a tradition that invests so much in the idea of human depravity (and the resultant expectation that God alone will bring redemption), it is difficult to say much about what might be realized short of the divine reconstitution of the social order. To do so is to raise the suspicion that one is placing faith in what humans can achieve on their own. Accordingly, the evangelical community has been less sanguine than most about the prospects of actually fulfilling social hopes in the present age.[18]

The narrative structure of apocalypse helps to relieve the tension that thus builds here. Fittingly, apocalyptic accounts reproduce within themselves the basic phenomenal structure of hope that we observed above. The image of apocalypse evokes the requisite sense of human finitude, in that it unmistakably signals an end — and not just any end, but the ultimate sort of end that renders a judgment regarding what humans can and cannot do. This is even the case with the apocalyptic visions that have done so much to shape popular consciousness in the nuclear age. Yet the historic Christian understanding of apocalypse goes beyond such unqualified doomsday scenarios, for apocalypse is the revelation of God to the world. This involves judgment and the de-

---

17. I say "threatens" because even if it is not taken as a time when godly governance of human social relations is already breaking in, that history may yet be construed as meaningful. If it heightens social awareness of the limits to human enterprise, drawing attention to the futility of human efforts to establish a heaven on earth, it may be valued insofar as it engenders a sense of humility and dependence on God that may be thought necessary for the kingdom of God to break in.

18. Indeed, conventional accounts of the rise of Christian fundamentalism and evangelicalism have them first emerging as self-conscious movements largely in reaction to modernist progressivism. See George Marsden, *Fundamentalism and American Culture* (New York: Oxford University Press, 1980), and Martin Marty, *Protestantism in the United States: Righteous Empire,* second ed. (New York: Scribner's, 1986).

lineation of limits, to be sure, but it also entails the coming-to-be of the "like new" world that is the ultimate object of social hope. Apocalypse thus marks the point at which humanity finally reaches the heretofore receding horizon and crosses over to the always possible world beyond.

By all indications, popular forms of apocalyptic narrative are alive and well within Christianity today, especially within evangelical circles.[19] The packaging of the story may have changed through the years — from C. I. Scofield's reference Bible to Hal Lindsey's *Late Great Planet Earth* to the *Left Behind* series of Jerry B. Jenkins and Timothy LaHaye — but its appeal certainly has not. Lindsey's book was the best-selling book of any kind in the United States through the decade of the 1970s, while the *Left Behind* series continues to rack up similarly impressive sales today.

This appetite for apocalyptic narrative (and particularly for this kind of apocalyptic narrative) furnishes another space where secular tales of decline, like Bork's, may slide into the mindset of many evangelicals. The dispensationalist premillennialism espoused by the likes of Scofield, Lindsey, Jenkins, and LaHaye did much to define the evangelical movement at the turn of the twentieth century,[20] and it continues to hold sway over many within that tradition. This is significant since dispensational thought forecasts that things in the present age will get steadily worse as the apocalypse of Christ and the establishment of his millennial kingdom draw near. And while works like *Slouching Towards Gomorrah* offer no visions of apocalyptic purges or triumphant messianic returns, perhaps many evangelicals are so attuned to this story that they have taken to filling in those religious bits that are left out of the secular stories.

I do not doubt that this is at least partly true. Many evangelicals appear not just resigned to visions of their world in decline, but positively affirming of them.[21] Their eagerness in this respect might signal

---

19. Peter Boyer, *When Time Shall Be No More: Prophecy Belief in Modern American Culture* (Cambridge, Mass.: Belknap, 1992).

20. This is completely consonant with the reaction against modernist progressivism noted previously. See again Marsden, *Fundamentalism and American Culture*.

21. In a recent national survey of over two thousand respondents (James Davison Hunter and Carl Bowman, eds., *The 1996 Survey of American Political Culture* [Ivy, Va.: In Medias Res Educational Foundation, 1996]), nearly two-thirds (64.4 percent) of all evangelicals indicated that they believe the United States as a nation is in decline. Roughly

just how ready they are to incorporate such secular visions into an overarching dispensationalist account. This is probably not all that is going on, though. For one thing, we cannot completely ignore the fact that Judge Bork offers his readers a very different take on history than the one that so many of his would-be "translators" apparently entertain. On their own terms, works like Bork's are straightforward tales of civilizational decline, following a narrative formula that is far more aligned with the ideological discourse of modernity than with Christian tradition. This formula is actually a companion to the modernist ideal of perpetual progress, and the positive prospects that it suggests are either (1) that we will stay the course of progress into the future, deftly avoiding the potential nastiness that gives rise to such misgivings in the present, or (2) that we will recapture the squandered advances of the past and return to the trajectory that supposedly prevailed before things got so far off track.[22] Bork's ultimate hope turns out to be the latter, and there is nothing to say that his fans in the evangelical community have not embraced the whole of his story. If so, then evangelicals may actually be harboring the very this-worldly hopes that they ostensibly reject.

Indeed, many within the evangelical community seem at least as taken by the modernist faith in this-worldly progress as by the eschatological visions of Christianity, dispensationalist or otherwise. This goes even for those who are eager to embrace the image of a civilization heading downhill. For example, of those evangelicals who in a recent survey[23] declared that America as a whole is in decline, nearly half went on to affirm the seemingly contradictory idea that the nation's "best years are in the future." All told, three out of every ten evangeli-

---

half of those (31.4 percent) characterized that decline as "strong." All told, this group was at least 50 percent more likely to say these things than was any other religiously defined group, and its members were three times more likely to do so than were self-identified secularists. When we look just at devotees of the Religious Right, the differences become even more extreme. Better than four out of every five (81.0 percent) members of the Religious Right claimed that the United States is in decline, and nearly half (45.2 percent) described that decline as strong. This pattern remains when the focus shifts to specific areas of life in the United States.

22. This idea is forcefully explicated in Arthur Herman, *The Idea of Decline in Western History* (New York: Free Press, 1997).

23. Hunter and Bowman, eds., *The 1996 Survey of American Political Culture*.

cals simultaneously professed that America is declining *and* that it is destined for better years ahead. So while they see little cause for hope in the concrete developments of the present, such people still hold on to the vague hope that things will ultimately get better, and this without anything so messy as an apocalyptic overhaul of the entire social order.

Perhaps more telling is the level of activism found within that portion of the evangelical community that identifies with the political stance that Bork and others have taken. One can presume that such people act in the hope that valued social and political change *can* be realized in this world. This is the enigma that is the Religious Right: a community that is largely committed to premillennialist eschatology is at the same time fully mobilized in the pursuit of this-worldly hopes. In this sense, the evangelical consumption and production of decline narratives seem to support Sacvan Bercovitch's observation that American jeremiads generally have motivated rather than discouraged positive social action.[24]

What should we make of this paradox, that the tales of decline embraced by so many evangelicals may actually express a kind of social hope? If evangelicals do harbor hopes for the future of the social order, why do their expressions of these hopes seem limited to expositions of how the present world is falling apart (and the attendant calls to prevent this from happening)? Works that portray in positive terms the new world that may be dawning rarely gain a wide following in the evangelical community. But why should this be, if that community is so willing to fudge on its premillennialist convictions and imagine good things for the future of this world?

Hope Lost or Reconfigured?

In what follows I offer two possible interpretations of the evangelical reliance on decline narratives to express this-worldly social hopes. While we do not have time here to defend or try to prove them empirically, they may help us to think about some of the unique challenges that confront evangelicals today.

24. Bercovitch, *The American Jeremiad.*

One ready-made answer to the questions posed above is that evangelical Christianity is not unlike the rest of the contemporary culture, which has generally lost its ability to sustain a substantively significant social hope. Consider, for example, Andrew Delbanco's recent "meditation on hope."[25] Delbanco's account is itself a narrative of decline, one that purports to account for the difficulty that modern Americans have in shaking the nagging suspicion that their world is falling apart.[26] Delbanco terms this suspicion *melancholy,* the "dark twin" of hope. And what is it that keeps this melancholy sense at bay? Delbanco's answer should hardly come as a surprise: "The premise of this book is that human beings need to organize the inchoate sensations amid which we pass our days — pain, desire, pleasure, fear — into a story. When that story leads somewhere and thereby helps us navigate through life to its inevitable terminus in death, it gives us hope."[27]

This understanding leads Delbanco to construct a history of social hope in America in terms of three great narrative phases through which it has passed. Most important here is the third phase, when the kinds of stories that animated the first two phases have lost the ability to unite the national community under a common conception of where it has been, where it is now, and where it is going from here. While vestiges of such stories linger here and there, the withering ef-

---

25. Andrew Delbanco, *The Real American Dream: A Meditation on Hope* (Cambridge: Harvard University Press, 1999).

26. Delbanco operates within a Geertzian framework, so he describes this suspicion in terms more aligned with Geertz's concern with the prospect of meaninglessness than with the narrative construction of history as decline. Yet Delbanco also force-fits some new terminology atop Geertz's basic framework. While Geertz's symbol systems provide *meaning* for those who inhabit them, Delbanco has them furnishing the rather different good called *hope.* And while Geertz is content to describe the menace that symbol systems ward off as the "threat of meaninglessness," Delbanco interjects his notion of melancholy. He does so mainly to highlight the subjective experience that attends the failure of narrative structures, a subjective experience best described as a sense of decline: "This idea is contained not only in certain theological and psychological doctrines, but in the colloquial terms with which we speak about the EXPERIENCE of melancholy: we sink, droop, break down. Even the etymology of our modern word, depression — from the Latin, DE PREMERE, to press down — contains this idea of a fall" (Delbanco, *Real American Dream,* p. 4).

27. Delbanco, *Real American Dream,* p. 1.

fects of consumer culture generally have sapped our ability to establish a common narrative structure. The consequences of such deprivation in the realm of narrative are clear. Lost is "any conception of a common destiny worth tears, sacrifice, and maybe even death."[28] Also lost is our capacity "to deliver the indispensable feeling that the world does not end at the borders of the self."[29] Hope may well exist in a world devoid of shared narratives, but not as social hope. "Today," it seems, "hope has narrowed to the vanishing point of the self alone."[30]

Delbanco's account is clearly a lamentation, told with a certain erudite wistfulness. He is hardly alone in offering such an account, although not all who do so are inclined to offer laments. At least since Jean-François Lyotard's seminal work on how the postmodern "incredulity toward metanarrative" has undermined modern science's legitimating grand narratives,[31] social commentators of various ideological stripes have been keen to document the effects of our apparent inability to tell certain stories with any degree of conviction. This effort has unquestionably made its mark on contemporary deliberations on social hope. It can be found in Jean Baudrillard's kaleidoscopic reflections on the vanishing of history and its shift into reverse as it nears the "end."[32] It is present in Zygmunt Bauman's diagnosis that, as postmodernity has nestled in alongside modernity, the life lived with ambivalence has gradually replaced the life lived in hope.[33] It is Richard Rorty's taken-for-granted starting point for his own efforts to revive the discourse of "criterionless hope" that he finds in the works of Emerson and Dewey.[34] And it is the assumption that both liberates and chastises Jacques Derrida as he opens himself to the coming of the *tout*

28. Delbanco, *Real American Dream,* p. 97.

29. Delbanco, *Real American Dream,* p. 5.

30. Delbanco, *Real American Dream,* p. 103.

31. Jean François Lyotard, *The Postmodern Condition: A Report on Knowledge,* trans. Geoff Bennington and Brian Massumi (Minneapolis: University of Minnesota Press, 1984).

32. Jean Baudrillard, *The Illusion of the End,* trans. Chris Turner (Stanford, Calif.: Stanford University Press, 1994).

33. Zygmunt Bauman, *Modernity and Ambivalence* (Ithaca, N.Y.: Cornell University Press, 1991).

34. Richard Rorty, *Achieving Our Country: Leftist Thoughts in Twentieth-Century America* (Cambridge: Harvard University Press, 1998), and *Philosophy and Social Hope* (New York: Penguin, 1999).

autre, that indeterminate messianic figure that is always coming but never comes.[35] So whether it is judged as a lamentable or laudable development, there is little question in such circles that the collapse of compelling shared narratives has made conventional forms of social hoping unsustainable.

Yet this bit of received wisdom does not get us very far in the present discussion. For one thing, the evangelical Christian subculture in America has *not* found it impossible (or even particularly difficult) to rally around shared narratives. In fact, the very thing that we might take as evidence that they have lost the ability to sustain social hope *is* itself a narrative. Images of civilizational decline structure an understanding of past, present, and future history just as surely as did those other putatively hope-inducing stories. For this reason, we can at least call into question the claim that the kinds of shared narratives that have historically sustained social hopes are no longer tenable, at least within this particular religious community.

Ultimately, however, I would not say that Delbanco and those with similar views have gotten it wrong so much as that their perspective is simply less helpful here. Rather than concluding that people have lost the capacity to sustain social hopes, I think we do better to suggest that developments in advanced modern societies are actually transforming the very experience of hope, and in ways that shape the forms of social hoping that we observe. In short, I would argue that hope has come to be experienced more in a negative form — as a desire that certain bad things *not* occur — than in the more conventional form of aspiring toward a positively defined future.

The basic distinction between positive and negative modes of hoping is nicely prefigured in the opening stanzas of Robert L. Heilbroner's *Inquiry into the Human Prospect:*

> There is a question in the air, more sensed than seen, like the invisible approach of a distant storm, a question that I would hesitate to

35. Jacques Derrida, "Psyche: Inventions of the Other," trans. Catherine Porter, in *Reading de Man Reading,* ed. Lindsay Waters and Wlad Godzich (Minneapolis: University of Minnesota Press, 1989), pp. 25-56; Jacques Derrida, *Specters of Marx: The State of the Debt, the Work of Mourning, and the New International,* trans. Peggy Kamuf (New York: Routledge, 1994). See also John D. Caputo, *The Prayers and Tears of Jacques Derrida: Religion without Religion* (Bloomington, Ind.: Indiana University Press, 1997).

ask aloud did I not believe it existed unvoiced in the minds of many: "Is there hope for man?"

In another era such a question might have raised thoughts of man's ultimate salvation or damnation. But today the brooding doubts that it arouses have to do with life on earth, now, and in the relatively few generations that constitute the limit of our ability to imagine the future. For the question asks whether we can imagine that future other than as a continuation of the darkness, cruelty, and disorder of the past; worse, whether we do not foresee in the human prospect a deterioration of things, even an impending catastrophe of fearful dimensions.[36]

Heilbroner's first gloss on his opening question reflects more of the conventional understanding of what hope looks like. To have hope is to anticipate a future that is somehow better than what has been and is now.[37] But he goes on to say something altogether different. For it seems that hoping could also mean imagining a future history of civilization's decline, or even of its catastrophic closure, and holding onto the prospect that such things will *not* come to pass. Put another way, having hope could simply mean that we do *not*, finally, "foresee in the human prospect a deterioration of things," or even "an impending catastrophe of fearful dimensions."

The rest of Heilbroner's book is a transparent example of the latter sensibility in action. Stepping deliberately through each major arena of modern life, Heilbroner finds everywhere either the threat of calamity or indications that the fabric of the world is unraveling. Yet Heilbroner also scrupulously identifies the resources that might be used in staving off the dystopia that he divines for the future. In this respect, he is clearly articulating a hope, if not for a brighter tomorrow, then at least for the perpetuation of today.[38]

36. Robert L. Heilbroner, *An Inquiry into the Human Prospect* (New York: W. W. Norton, 1974), p. 3.

37. The sheer negativity of Heilbroner's take on the historical record — his testament to "the darkness, cruelty, and disorder of the past" — is purely incidental. It is consistent with his own insistent pessimism, but we need not denigrate past and present in order to hope in the conventional sense.

38. Accordingly, some have characterized this sort of account as "a form of disguised optimism" (Joe Bailey, *Pessimism* [New York: Routledge, 1988], p. 53).

This negative mode of hoping is not exactly new to the world. Yet as commentators like Ulrich Beck and Anthony Giddens point out, two related and rather conspicuous developments have dramatically transformed how (and how often) we hope in this way.

The first involves a dramatic change in the complexion of what we hope against most. Modern society has achieved a level of control over nature that drastically reduces our sense of helplessness in the face of it. This control comes via several means, of which raw technological mastery over nature is the most salient. Yet technological mastery is double-edged: the very technology that reduces our exposure to some of nature's more capricious forces, and even enables us to harness those forces, also carries the capacity for catastrophes of wider scope and more devastating consequence than ever before imagined. So while contemporary society is still beset by what Beck calls "threats" (apparent hazards that still loom beyond our ability to control, technologically or otherwise), the greatest of these are now principally human in origin.[39] It is not so much against drought, earthquakes, or epidemics that we must hope, but against those threats that emerge as a direct consequence of the very mastery we have acquired over physical and, to a lesser degree, social nature.[40] We can imagine our managing the prospect and/or effects of even the most potentially devastating natural disaster, but we cannot fathom what it would take for a society to deal with a full-scale nuclear conflict or the accidental release of a lethal and transmissible bioagent.[41] The only thing we can do is trust the experts (their often contradictory claims notwithstanding) and hope

39. The distinction is between "threat" and "risk." It figures prominently in most of Beck's "risk society" work, but he does the most with it in his *Ecological Enlightenment: Essays on the Politics of the Risk Society*, trans. Mark Ritter (Atlantic Highlands, N.J.: Humanities Press International, 1995).

40. This characterization is a little too neat, as it is often the volatile interaction of the natural world with human technologies that stimulates the discourse of threat — hence the concern with global warming, or with the prospect of a mutant, airborne strain of *ebola* spreading as fast as our jets can carry it.

41. Indeed, in terms of both probabilities and their effects, such threats are literally incalculable. This does not, however, prevent expert organizations from treating them as though they were manageable, generating elaborate contingency plans that serve to reassure both the experts and the public that things are under control. See Lee Clarke, *Mission Improbable: Using Fantasy Documents to Tame Disaster* (Chicago: University of Chicago Press, 1999).

that such things will not come to pass. As Giddens puts it, "'Human beings only set for themselves such problems as they can resolve': for us Marx's principle has become no more than a principle of hope."[42]

The emergence of this new class of threats has other significant cultural consequences.[43] For one thing, it has largely stripped the apocalyptic narrative of its capacity to generate hope. The apocalyptic scenarios that we can most readily entertain still speak of an end, but it is no longer the sort of end that marks the inbreaking of a new and hope-fulfilling order of things. It is hard to picture the Kingdom of God on the other side of a nuclear winter. Accordingly, our apocalypses are only to be avoided.[44] Moreover, the apparent link between technological advance and increasing threat has contributed to the difficulties many people have buying into either utopian visions or the modern fantasy of perpetual and unalloyed progress.[45] While technological advance

42. Anthony Giddens, "Living in a Post-Traditional Society," in *Reflexive Modernization: Politics, Tradition and Aesthetics in the Modern Social Order,* ed. Ulrich Beck, Anthony Giddens, and Scott Lash (Stanford, Calif.: Stanford University Press, 1994), p. 59.

43. Those who analyze risk from a more Foucauldian perspective have faulted Beck for his ontological realism in portraying risks and threats, and for his consequent disregard for the full range of risk rationalities that render the "incalculable" calculable and hence amenable to governmentalist interventions of various kinds. See especially Mitchell Dean, "Risk, Calculable and Incalculable," in *Risk and Sociocultural Theory: New Directions and Perspectives,* ed. Deborah Lupton (New York: Cambridge University Press, 1999), pp.131-59. In the main, I find this critique (and the perspective in which it is embedded) to be compelling, but it does not deny the cultural significance of the newly constructed category of threat that Beck describes.

44. Here it is worth noting a curious literary amalgam of the post-nuclear age: accounts that entertain (sometimes quite graphically) the possibility of an apocalyptic end to the world and yet hold out the millennial hope of a new world placed beyond such possibilities, and this not through rebirth in a realized apocalypse, but through technological advances that finally render all such possibilities impossible. R. Buckminster Fuller's *Utopia or Oblivion: The Prospects for Humanity* (New York: Bantam, 1969) and Bertrand Russell's *Has Man a Future?* (New York: Simon and Schuster, 1962) are prototypical examples.

45. This development has been so thoroughly analyzed from so many angles that we hardly need to document it. Even so, it is easy to get carried away. Visions of technological progress are clearly alive and well in many circles, and they are not without influence. We need only recall then U.S. House Speaker Newt Gingrich's insistence that all of Congress read Alvin and Heidi Toffler — specifically, *Creating a New Civilization: The Politics of the Third Wave* (Atlanta: Turner, 1994) — to establish this. (Those with tastes more meliorist than millenarian can turn to, say, Virginia Postrel, *The Future and Its Enemies:*

still occurs, today it is largely unaccompanied by the grand myths of progress once taken for granted. Rather, it occurs largely in the context of a growing awareness of the attendant dangers of technology and a growing inclination to devote the technical resources of modernity to the problems that modernity itself has wrought.[46]

All of this lends a certain negativity to the political contests that materialize. Beck comments that where political consciousness is dominated by threat, "distributional conflicts over 'goods' (income, jobs, social security), which constituted the basic conflict of classical industrial society and led to attempted solutions in the relevant institutions, are covered over by the distributional conflicts over 'bads'."[47] The most conspicuous "bads" to be distributed are threats themselves, as considerable political, legal, and cultural resources are tied up in the effort to determine which populations should be exposed to recognized hazards. Where do we place a nuclear power facility, or a large chemical plant, or a transfer station for industrial waste? These are potentially headline-grabbing clashes, but the more ordinary and consequential of the conflicts over "bads" are all about distributing responsibility. They involve the efforts of businesses, government agencies, advocacy groups, and others to normalize or deny the threats with which they are associated,[48] to frame and draw attention to supposedly greater threats elsewhere, and to prospectively or retrospectively assign the blame for any incident to some other party. Nothing is won in these

---

The Growing Conflict Over Creativity, Enterprise, and Progress [New York: Free Press, 1998].) Clearly, we are dealing more with general cultural tendencies here than with the total sea change that some accounts suggest.

46. Those given to dividing human history up into discrete phases have called this a period of "reflexive modernization." The term is often traced to Ulrich Beck, *Risk Society: Towards a New Modernity,* trans. Mark Ritter (London: Sage, 1992), but the three main essays in Beck, Giddens, and Lash, eds., *Reflexive Modernization,* provide a more well-rounded orientation to how it has been used in the risk society literature.

47. Ulrich Beck, "The Reinvention of Politics: Towards a Theory of Reflexive Modernization," in Beck, Giddens, and Lash, eds., *Reflexive Modernization,* p. 6. See also Beck's repeated discussions of these matters in *Ecological Enlightenment.* I leave aside Beck's extended (and more hopeful) reflections on the emergence of a complementary realm of "sub-political" activism. While important in its own respect, this development does not alter the basic dynamics emphasized here.

48. Charles Perrow, *Normal Accidents: Living with High-Risk Technologies* (New York: Basic, 1984), is the classic statement on the strategy of normalization.

contests; the only thing "winners" achieve is an avoidance of loss . . . for now.

It is easy to see how conventional expressions of social hope might wane as a political resource under such conditions. If many of the principal actors in a political environment are accustomed to engagements wherein "avoidance imperatives predominate,"[49] then they have little cause to entertain positive visions of what the world could become. Still less do they have cause to come together in pursuit of such visions. It is enough to hope and strive against their darker dreams.

That said, we have yet to see just how deeply ingrained this negative mode of hoping may be within the thought life of individuals. This leads us to the second difference that separates the context in which we hope today from that of an earlier time.

Technology has taken us only so far in our efforts to control the natural world. Where nature has resisted our efforts to master it, where we are still left vulnerable to what it might throw at us in the future, we have found a measure of control through the calculation and management of *risk*. While we may not be able to prevent certain bad things from happening, we can at least assess the chances of their happening and engage in practices that minimize those chances. Sometimes we can even insure against their happening, mapping payment and compensatory schedules onto our risk assessments in an effort to deal beforehand with whatever the future may hold.

Owing largely to the painstaking work of François Ewald in documenting the emergence and functioning of modern insurance mechanisms,[50] some observers have treated insurance as the purest form of risk management.[51] Yet Ewald and others are quick to point out that modern societies have actually constructed many different types of risk

49. Beck, *Ecological Enlightenment*, p. 9.

50. One of his most accessible accounts is his "Insurance and Risk," in *The Foucault Effect: Studies in Governmentality*, ed. Graham Burchell, Colin Gordon, and Peter Miller (Chicago: University of Chicago Press, 1991), 197-210.

51. Beck, for example, contends that insurance marks "the boundary between calculable risks and incalculable threats" (*Ecological Enlightenment*, p. 2). Giddens, meanwhile, treats it as the ideal-typical expression of our efforts to "colonise the future" (see his *The Consequences of Modernity* [Stanford, Calif.: Stanford University Press, 1991] and *Modernity and Self-identity: Self and Society in the Late Modern Age* [Stanford, Calif.: Stanford University Press, 1991]).

and devised many different strategies for managing it. The crucial feature of most of them is that they make the individual the focal point of a discourse of risk. In medical discussions about the potential for exposure to contaminated blood,[52] in the race to set up community policing programs,[53] in the preventive strategies used to manage populations of mental patients,[54] and so on, the individual in his or her natural and social environment is methodically transformed into "a combinatory of *factors,* the factors of risk."[55] With the promise that a routine genetic screening will soon yield a complete rundown of an individual's chances of contracting almost any genetically linked disorder, the process should only intensify in the coming years.

Most analysts of such developments are primarily concerned with documenting how the transformation of subjects into bundles of risk makes them responsible for monitoring their own behavior. The idea is that individuals must manage ever more scrupulously the risks that beset them, and do so through a variety of sanctioned practices. Arguably, this development has important consequences in its own right.[56]

In the present context, however, it is enough to note the mere fact that individuals find themselves the focal point of an ever-expanding array of risk discourses. This has the simple effect of increasing the number of concerns that they must harbor about the future. And while the prescribed regimes for avoiding various risks promise to allay the mounting concerns, they do so only by challenging individuals to prevent certain adverse outcomes or render them less harmful should they occur. This inevitably shapes a basic defensive posture toward the future. In short, while the inhabitants of societies less obsessed with managing the future may have found themselves hoping against a mere

52. Nick J. Fox, "Postmodern Reflections on 'Risks', 'Hazards' and Life Choices," in *Risk and Sociocultural Theory,* ed. Lupton, pp. 12-33.

53. Dean, "Risk, Calculable and Incalculable."

54. Robert Castell, "From Dangerousness to Risk," in *The Foucault Effect,* ed. Burchell, Gordon, and Miller, pp. 281-98.

55. Castell, "From Dangerousness to Risk," p. 281.

56. Most notably, the death of "society" as a salient category in deliberations about political action, and yet another take on why social hopes have seemingly passed away: where responsibility for action is increasingly shunted to individuals, the impulse to coordinate action and orient it toward a collective future disappears. See Mitchell Dean, "Sociology after Society," in *Sociology after Postmodernism,* ed. David Owen (Thousand Oaks, Calif.: Sage, 1997), pp. 205-28.

handful of the largest and most generic negative outcomes, individuals today have cause and opportunity to practice a negative form of hoping almost everywhere they turn.

If this is so, then I suspect that it has profound implications for the sorts of social hopes that many are prepared to entertain. It stands to reason that habits of hoping that have been long cultivated in consideration of one's personal future should remain when the focus shifts to the future of the social world at large. It also might stand to reason that such risk calculation would affect the apocalyptic religious hopes of evangelicals and other Christian believers, though that is a more complicated matter.

Conclusion

The evangelical embrace of decline narratives like *Slouching Towards Gomorrah* can be variously understood. As we have seen, we can explain the basic attraction in a number of different ways, and we can find a number of countervailing tendencies in evangelical expressions of social hope which make room for tales of decline (and perhaps even enable faithful premillennialists to strive to realize social hopes in this world). Yet there remains the question of why decline narratives and not something else . . . something, well, more positive.

I have suggested that we should view this focus, at least partly, as an indication of how hope is characteristically experienced at a time when risk calculations are paramount. In short, the principal orientation toward the future in evidence today encourages a negative form of hoping. Rather than reaching out toward a positively defined future, those who hope in this day and age more often find themselves guarding against discretely determined negative outcomes. Given how steeped American evangelicals are in modern culture, we can hardly expect them to have remained immune to such a development, and this may help to account for their satisfaction with purely negative expressions of social hope.

If this is indeed the case, then the practical consequences of it are considerable; for if some are committed to revitalizing a properly Christian, hopeful vision for the future of this world, they will need to contend with contrary habits of hoping that have been burned in by the cultural conditions of late modernity.

History, Hope, and the Redemption of Time

WILLIAM KATERBERG

Introduction

Is it possible to redeem the past? The millenarian promise of the great modern meta-narratives was the redemption of the future and perhaps of the present (at the "end of history").[1] But what does socialism offer to workers who died with their revolutionary dreams unfulfilled? What can liberal democracy do for the enslaved of the past? Christianity promises God's divine judgment and the resurrection of the dead at the end of time. What redemption can the utopian and progressive movements of the modern age extend to the past? Don't all emancipatory projects beg the question: What about the dead?

What about historians? In his classic study, *Meaning in History*, Karl Löwith claims that humanity's interest in the past arises out of the "quest for happiness" and "the basic experience of evil and suffering." In the final analysis, he contends, "The interpretation of history is . . . an attempt to understand the meaning of [the past] as the meaning of suf-

---

1. See Francis Fukuyama, *The End of History and the Last Man* (New York: William Morrow, 1992). *Post*modernism is an end to "endism," a rejection of teleology or notions of purpose and coherence in history. See, for example, Jean Baudrillard, *The Illusion of the End* (Oxford: Blackwell, 1992).

The writing of this essay was supported by the Pew Fellowships and the Calvin College Seminars in Christian Scholarship.

fering by historical action." In short, history is akin to theodicy.[2] If this is so, do historians "redeem" the past when they teach classes and write books? Do they "resurrect" the dead when they tell the stories of forgotten people who lived in times gone by? Can historians offer final judgment or heal the wounds of those who suffered in the past?

These questions sound theological and rightly so. Behind the competing ideologies and myths of progress that once gave meaning to modernity and the Enlightenment project lies the Christian promise of the new heaven and new earth.[3] Insofar as modern historiography has been defined by that project — in its assumptions, methods, and goals — theological questions have shaped what historians do, however implicitly and however distantly.[4] And yet, very few historians would be comfortable with the burden of "redeeming" the past (let alone saving the present and the future). But if not historians, then who?

This question is not as odd or arrogant as it may seem. Until quite recently, according to David Harlan, "history was one of our primary forms of moral reflection." In *The Degradation of American History* he argues that the eminent historians of previous generations held up "a mirror to our common past." They addressed their readers as fellow citizens and encouraged them to say, "This is what we value and want, and don't yet have. This is how we mean to live and do not yet live."[5] This way of thinking about the past fell into decline during the 1960s and 1970s. Some historians attacked it as elitist and turned to microstudies of daily life, while others became preoccupied with methodology and the reliability of historical knowledge. As a scholarly guild, historians have become skeptical of expressions of hope and suspicious of moral reflection. Most have tried to leave behind — and some have explicitly attacked — modern meta-historical narratives. Their chief con-

---

2. Karl Löwith, *Meaning in History* (Chicago: University of Chicago Press, 1949), p. 3. Perhaps it is also a matter of anthropodicy.

3. See Löwith, *Meaning in History*. In *The Legitimacy of the Modern Age* (Cambridge, Mass.: MIT Press, 1983), Hans Blumenberg argues that "progress" filled the space left by "providence."

4. See Joyce Appleby et al., *Telling the Truth about History* (New York: Norton, 1994); David Harlan, *The Degradation of American History* (Chicago: University of Chicago Press, 1997); and John Michael, *Anxious Intellects: Academic Professionals, Public Intellectuals, and Enlightenment Values* (Durham: Duke University Press, 2000).

5. Michael Walzer, quoted in Harlan, *Degradation,* p. xv.

cerns have become professional authority and the ongoing accumulation of historical knowledge about particular, local narratives.[6]

The question is whether, in the debris of modern history and historiography, there is any hope of redemption. Does the "postmodern" turn signal an end to moral reflection and hope? Or, between the cracks in the facade of modernity, might some revelatory light shine?[7] At the "end of history" what hope is there for the past? Do the dilemmas of modern history signify an "end" to meaningful notions of history? Or, might historians approach the past in new ways and recapture what was lost in modern historiography?[8] *Can history be redeemed, and be redemptive, after all?* The grandiosity of this question is doubly appropriate. First, as Walter Benjamin once observed, "Like every generation that preceded us, we have been endowed with a *weak* Messianic power, a power to which the past has a claim. That claim cannot be settled cheaply."[9] Second, the meaning of the past concerns not only historians but citizens and members of various kinds of communities more generally — in short, all those who desire to look to the past and future with hope.

The Contradictions of Modern History

The practice of historiography today, by both professional scholars in the academy and those who write for popular audiences, remains pro-

6. See Keith Jenkins, ed., *The Postmodern History Reader* (New York: Routledge, 1997). For moderate stances, see Thomas Haskell, *Objectivity Is Not Neutrality* (Baltimore: Johns Hopkins, 1998); and Richard Bernstein, *Beyond Objectivism and Relativism* (Philadelphia: University of Pennsylvania Press, 1983).

7. The term *postmodern* marks a transition. On continuities between postmodernity and modernity, see Marshall Berman, *All That Is Solid Melts into Air* (New York: Simon and Schuster, 1982); and David Harvey, *The Condition of Postmodernity* (Oxford: Blackwell, 1990).

8. For an example of what was lost, see Yosef Hayim Yerushalmi, *Zakhor: Jewish History and Jewish Memory* (Seattle: University of Washington, 1982). David Lyon traces the ties between providence, progress, and nihilism. Intellectuals exploring postmodernity rarely consider a return to anything pre-modern, suggesting their continued adherence to linear understandings of time; see his *Postmodernity* (Minneapolis: University of Minnesota, 1994).

9. Walter Benjamin, *Illuminations,* trans. Harry Zohn (New York: Schocken, 1977), p. 254.

foundly modern in its assumptions, methods, and goals. Critics contend that modern historiography has failed on two counts: as a form of stable, reliable knowledge and as a "discourse capable of generating moral decision-making and action."[10] Such "failures" stem from the competing purposes of modern historiography.

On the one hand, in the spirit of modern science and rationality historians have aspired to objective, disinterested knowledge, in which the knowing subject (the historian) remains separate from the object of study. Accordingly, historians have long asserted that temporal distance from the past is what makes objective knowledge possible, and thus have cast suspicion on those who pursue mere contemporary history.[11] Properly, knowledge is to be accumulated for its own sake. On the other hand, when asked why study history, historians usually have pointed to the need for people to have ties to the past for the sake of vigorous citizenship, coherent cultural identities, and the spiritual evolution of humanity. The first of these purposes demands separation from the past, which is a lifeless object held up for careful scrutiny. The second calls for continuity with the past and participation in living traditions. The resolution to this incongruity seems to be the hierarchy of knowledge assumed in modern thought, where verifiable facts are deemed the most trustworthy foundation for moral decision-making, truth claims, and action. The starting point is empirical knowledge and understanding; and, on this foundation, interpretation and application follow. As in the modern sciences generally, historiography thus privileges factual knowledge and relegates to secondary status questions of meaning, aesthetics, moral reflection, and political action.[12]

Tensions between the dual purposes of modern historiography

10. Robert Anchor, "On How to Kick the History Habit," *History and Theory* 40 (2001): 104. The most thorough critique of modern historiography is Robert Berkhofer Jr., *Beyond the Great Story: History as Text and Discourse* (Cambridge, Mass.: Belknap-Harvard, 1995).

11. Most historians no longer see perfect objectivity as possible, but it remains the standard of measure. Bias, perspective, theory, and utilitarian approaches to history must be overcome in the properly objective-minded search for reliable, value-free facts. The ideal of distance from the past is the one perspective deemed compatible with objectivity.

12. For a critique of this model, see Hans-Georg Gadamer, *Truth and Method*, trans. Joel Weinsheimer and Donald Marshall (New York: Continuum, 1998), part 2, section 2.

can be seen in debates over what, properly, may be considered "history." For whom does the historian speak, the living or the dead? Scholars such as John Patrick Diggins, Christopher Lasch, and Michael Walzer have lifted eminent thinkers out of their particular historical contexts to have them converse with intellectuals in distant times and places and address present-day questions not yet asked in a given thinker's own time. Diggins calls this type of historiography "exercises in theoretical confrontations."[13] For example, progressive-era pragmatists might speak not just to their own time but to postmodern theorists, or Augustine and the seventeenth-century Puritans to twentieth-century existentialists.[14] In a recent volume, Diggins uses Abraham Lincoln's free-soil liberalism to address present-day American dilemmas. Historian Gordon Wood has objected to this use of the past in a recent book review, saying, "Diggins thinks of himself as an intellectual historian, but in fact he is not a historian at all. He is a cultural critic who uses history to make his points about contemporary culture."[15] Such use of the past to "challenge Americans to come to terms with the nature of their society" is a meaningful practice, Wood concedes.[16] By definition, however, it is not history. History must always and can only be "an accumulated science, [one] gradually gathering truth through the steady and plodding efforts of countless practitioners turning out countless monographs." Historians such as Diggins "who cut loose from this faith do so at the peril of their discipline."[17]

Wood probably need not fear the peril to historiography represented by Diggins. Despite its competing goals, the historical profession typically rewards only history as knowledge, and historians cast suspicion on those who pursue the past primarily in the interests of moral decision-making, good citizenship, or other present-day concerns. Historians may claim practical or even spiritual purposes for the study of the past, and welcome the idea that present-day needs often

13. Quoted in Harlan, *Degradation*, p. 29.

14. See John Patrick Diggins, *The Promise of Pragmatism* (Chicago: University of Chicago Press, 1994); Perry Miller, *The New England Mind*, 2 vols. (Cambridge: Belknap-Harvard, 1939, 1953).

15. Gordon Wood, "Review of Diggins' *On Hallowed Ground: Abraham Lincoln and the Foundations of American History*," *The New Republic* 223, no. 18 (30 October 2000): 38-43.

16. Quoted in Harlan, *Degradation*, p. xxviii.

17. Gordon Wood, "Review of Diggins'."

will influence historical perspectives, but they seldom address matters of citizenship and public life or reflect on the human experience of temporality.[18] The long process of becoming a certified expert on the past focuses on the ability to collect and analyze facts, not on divining the meaning of time and history. Indeed, both professional and amateur historians typically consider scientific methods, facts, and objectivity to be the foundation of historical knowledge and truth. Except as an occasional aside or a concern implicit in historiographical debates, the human experience of temporality is left to philosophers, sociologists, and theologians.[19] Similarly, while historians may address political issues in occasional editorials, these projects only rarely in any fundamental and determinative way shape the hundreds of thousands of books, essays, lectures, and dissertations that they write. In short, as a form of cultural criticism written for the sake of the present, "engaged" history is done in spite of the profession and seldom is a practice for which a historian might be rewarded.[20]

That the contradictory purposes of modern history writing have brought historians to a crossroad is evident in the rhetoric of endings and crisis common among them today. The most vociferous defenders and eager critics of modern historiography contend that we have arrived at an epochal turning point and a moment of truth. History may be going to hell in a handbasket, or a new day of history writing, one free of the "totalitarian" pretensions of modern methods and dis-

18. Teaching is an exception. In their classes, historians often practice engaged history for the sake of the present. History teachers defend required history classes by referring to the cultural and civic purposes of history. Engaged history also keeps students more interested. My point is not that historians are not interested in the "mission" of history; but, in general, the institutions and practices of the profession discourage engaged history and promote "scientific" historical knowledge.

19. This may be changing, but only slowly. See Beverly Southgate, *Why Bother with History?* (Harlow, U.K.: Pearson Education, 2000).

20. Parallels can be seen in the culture of universities, where the legitimating role of education for the state and churches has declined and we hear empty slogans about "measurable outcomes" and "excellence." But outcomes for whom and for what purpose? Corporations? The meta-narratives that once gave purpose to academic life no longer do so convincingly. See Michael, *Anxious Intellects;* Bill Readings, *The University in Ruins* (Cambridge, Mass.: Harvard, 1996). On religion: Brian McKillop, *Matters of the Mind* (Toronto: University of Toronto Press, 1994); and George Marsden, *The Soul of the American University* (New York: Oxford, 1994).

course, may be dawning. In either case, we are at the end of history as we know it. Other equally insistent voices reject both naive realism and obscurantist theory-mongering to champion practical realism, "thoughtful and moderate interventions," and the "contested-but-democratic" institutions of the historical profession.[21] These "chastened modernists" may reject the idea that modernity and its ideals have reached an end, but they are addressing the same discourse about the end of history.

The "moment of truth" today has aspects that threaten historical knowledge in general and national histories in particular. Observers on the Left and the Right regularly express fears of fragmentation and link crises in turn-of-the-millennium nation-states to declining awareness of historical and cultural identities.[22] Conservatives claim that social history, in which each little group must have a voice, threatens coherent political histories. Many historians worry that criticism of scientific rationality, objectivity, and the reliability of facts will lead to moral and intellectual relativism. Others fear that the relentless historicism of cultural studies, literary criticism, and social theory undermines the ideal of a universal human nature and rationality.[23] In particular, progressive-minded historians often contend that the fashionable relativism of postmodernity is a reckless form of intellectual consumerism that threatens to subvert the emancipatory project of the Enlightenment and the great modern revolutions.[24] Those defending modernity often espouse chastened versions of Enlightenment science, reason,

21. See Ian McKay, "The Liberal Order Framework," *Canadian Historical Review* 81, no. 4 (2000): 618. Also see Appleby et al., *Telling the Truth,* chaps. 7-8.

22. See Chris Lorenz, "Comparative Historiography: Problems and Perspectives," *History and Theory* 38, no. 1 (1999): 25-39. A representative book is J. L. Granatstein, *Who Killed Canadian History?* (Toronto: HarperCollins, 1998). Also see Ian McKay, "After Canada: On Amnesia and Apocalypse in the Contemporary Crisis," *Acadiensis* 28, no. 1 (1998): 76-97.

23. Examples include Keith Windschuttle, *The Killing of History: How Literary Critics and Social Theorists Are Murdering Our Past* (New York: Free Press, 1996), and Richard Evans, *In Defense of History* (New York: Norton, 1997).

24. See Bryan Palmer, *Descent into Discourse* (Philadelphia: Temple University Press, 1990). For a defense of the Enlightenment and its emancipatory projects, see Harvey, *The Condition of Postmodernity;* Lyon discusses such "chastened modernists" in *Postmodernity,* pp. 100-105. A good example of a chastened historical defense of modernity is Haskell, *Objectivity Is Not Neutrality.*

and emancipation. Crucially, most of the groups defending civilization (as it is or as it might become) against postmodernity do so on the basis of "objective" foundations. They continue to believe that political action and moral decision-making depend first and foremost on the stability of scientific knowledge. The specific historiographical problems explored in this essay thus have wider implications, as examples of more general concerns about knowledge, hermeneutics, politics, and the search for truth and meaning in our time.[25]

Such fears — that extreme forms of social history, cultural theory, or literary criticism are killing the past, present, and future, and promoting relativism — do not look deeply enough into the basic assumptions of modern historiography. The privileging of facts and scientific methods over meaning, moral decision-making, and action (indeed, the very categorical distinction between knowledge, interpretation, and application) is at the root of whatever crises historians are confronting today. Modern historians have failed to produce stable, objective knowledge about the past. And, worse, by privileging the accumulation of disinterested knowledge about the past for its own sake, rather than writing history for the sake of the living, unwittingly they may have been killing the past.

Killing the Past

How is it that historians who are devoted to studying history for its own sake, and who bear a self-proclaimed responsibility to the past, are killing it? In *Truth and Method,* Hans-Georg Gadamer argues that the scientific pursuit of knowledge alienates us from the past. "Objective" historical consciousness may recognize the otherness of the Other, that people in the past lived and thought in fundamentally unique ways, but it refuses to let the past speak to us today. True hermeneutical experience, what he calls "historically effected consciousness," demands that we be open to the truth claims of the past. "I must allow [a]

25. Because of the wider implications of historiographical problems, I have chosen to pursue my argument via authors generally associated with hermeneutics, such as Gadamer and Heidegger, rather than those concerned more specifically with historical science, such as Wilhelm Dilthey.

tradition's claim to validity," Gadamer insists, "not simply in the sense of acknowledging the past in its otherness, but in such a way that it has something to say to me."[26] True openness requires going beyond merely understanding Chinese communists, medieval Muslims, or colonial American Puritans on their own terms, which is to control and contain them. We must let them speak to us and open ourselves to their claims to truth. Gadamer concedes the vast gulf between the past and present but argues that hermeneutical understanding means overcoming such distances in authentic conversations with the past — that is, in practices of communication and interpretation that lead to a fusion of horizons. "To reach an understanding in a dialogue," he explains, "is not a matter of putting oneself forward and successfully asserting one's own point of view, but being transformed into a communion in which we do not remain what we were."[27] Pre-modern thinkers treated their predecessors as contemporaries, not objects. Gadamer does not suggest a return to such anachronistic naiveté; nevertheless, pre-modern authors were open to their interlocutors in ways that modern historians have not been.[28]

For Gadamer, then, mere historical consciousness is useful but inadequate. It is a failure of understanding rooted in a refusal to open oneself to the past and allow a "fusion of horizons." For Friedrich Nietzsche, modern historical consciousness is deadly. He diagnoses the West as suffering from a culture of despair, a "sickness unto death." His prophet declares in *Thus Spoke Zarathrustra,*

> I saw a great sadness come over mankind. The best turned weary of their works. A doctrine appeared, a faith ran beside it: all is empty, all is alike, all hath been. . . . To be sure we have harvested; but why have all our fruits become rotten and brown?[29]

In search of truth for its own sake, historians and other modern scientists have forsaken their duty to life and have cultivated despair. Historiography has become a spectacle that displays its motto boldly: "let

26. Gadamer, *Truth and Method,* pp. 360-61.
27. Gadamer, *Truth and Method,* p. 379.
28. Gadamer, *Truth and Method,* p. 537.
29. Friedrich Nietzsche, *Thus Spoke Zarathustra,* quoted in Löwith, *Meaning in History,* pp. 216-17.

there be truth and may life perish." Nietzsche thus condemns so-called "pure thinkers who only contemplate life" or are "satisfied with mere knowledge." Life, he insists, demands action, moral decisions, and commitment.[30]

In the meditation *On the Advantage and Disadvantage of History for Life*, Nietzsche depicts the consequences of disinterested, scientific methods of history. The "natural relation of an age, a culture, [or] a people to history," he contends, is "brought on by hunger, regulated by the degree of need, held within limits by the inherent plastic power" of life. In short, "knowledge of the past is at all times desired only in the service of the future and the present, not to weaken the present, not to uproot a future strong with life." This is obvious to everyone except scientists.[31] Taken in "excess without hunger, even contrary to need," their scientific knowledge does not serve "as a transforming motive impelling action." Instead, science forces people to drag around "an immense amount of indigestible knowledge," like stones rattling around in their bellies. Modern historical consciousness thus is not a living culture, not a "real culture at all, but only a kind of knowledge about culture," one that "stops at cultured thought and cultured feelings but leads to no cultured decisions."[32] In their obsession with reliable methodologies and the accumulation of knowledge, historians have taken the wonder out of history. "Every living thing needs to be surrounded by an atmosphere, a mysterious circle of mist," declares Nietzsche. "[If] one robs it of this veil, if one condemns a religion, an art, a genius to orbit as a star without an atmosphere, then one should not wonder about its rapidly becoming withered, hard and barren."[33]

Against ideals of abstract knowledge accumulated for its own sake, Nietzsche claims that if history is to have a positive purpose it must serve life. History belongs to the living insofar as they are active and striving, preserving and admiring, or suffering and in need of liberation. "Monumental" history provides timeless models for people to emulate. "Antiquarian" history is a matter of revering, of giving thanks

---

30. Nietzsche, *On the Advantage and Disadvantage of History for Life,* trans. Peter Pruess (Indianapolis: Hackett, 1980), p. 23.

31. Nietzsche, *On the Advantage and Disadvantage,* p. 23.

32. Nietzsche, *On the Advantage and Disadvantage,* p. 24.

33. Nietzsche, *On the Advantage and Disadvantage,* p. 40.

for existence and preserving the past for those who will come later. "Critical" history serves life by dissolving the past, by dragging a tradition "to the bar of judgment," interrogating it, and finally condemning it.[34] And yet, even such useful history can choke life. Monumental history may lead people to fool themselves with "tempting similarities" and forget that in the past which is inconvenient. Antiquarian history degenerates when present-day life no longer animates it and reverencing the past encourages people to hate everything that is new. Finally, critical history destroys life when it puts a knife to the roots of a people or allows revolutionaries to fool themselves into thinking that they have not inherited the passions, errors, and aberrations of the past.[35] In short, if scientific history kills by its nature, even forms of history that are intended to serve life can undermine it. Would not people be better off without history? Is it only the "unhistorical" culture that is truly alive?[36]

Perhaps the pursuit of history is a Faustian bargain, a form of literary sorcery that defies the control of any storyteller. Whether in the service of science or life, history easily degenerates. It thus is difficult to escape Walter Benjamin's angel of history. In his theses on the philosophy of history Benjamin comments on a painting by Paul Klee (see the cover of this book), in which an angel stares, his mouth open and wings spread, as he is swept up by something he is contemplating:

> Where we perceive a chain of events, he sees one single catastrophe which keeps piling wreckage upon wreckage and hurls it in front of his feet. The angel would like to stay, awaken the dead, and make whole what has been smashed. But a storm is blowing in from Paradise; it has got caught in his wings with such violence that the angel can no longer close them. This storm irresistibly propels him into the future to which his back is turned, while the pile of debris before him grows skyward. This storm is what we call progress.[37]

---

34. Nietzsche, *On the Advantage and Disadvantage*, pp. 14-15, 19, 21.

35. Nietzsche, *On the Advantage and Disadvantage*, pp. 17, 20, 21, 22.

36. Nietzsche, *On the Advantage and Disadvantage*, p. 46.

37. Benjamin, *Illuminations*, pp. 257-58. Benjamin meant that the modern-Enlightenment projects (liberal and socialist) had been piling up debris. I am suggesting that modern historiography, which finds its roots in the larger modern project, has been doing the same.

By defining history as a science, and relegating to secondary status the demands of citizenship, cultural identities, and moral decision-making, have modern historians silenced the past? By turning the past into an object of study, one distant and separate from people living in the present, have they been piling up lifeless debris?

This is the fear of David Harlan, that history has lost the stuff of salvation.[38] Historians have not universally abandoned the calling to write in the service of life, but the "evangelizing" mission of history has been buried under scientific imperatives of accumulating disinterested knowledge. The irony is profound, he says. Historians normally assume that their first responsibility is to the people of the past — after all, "they lived through those times and we did not." But does "history" (i.e., not "the past" itself) belong primarily to the dead? "The only way we, as historians, can fulfill our responsibility to the dead," Harlan argues, "is by making sure their works do not get lost in the past." We, to-day, must raise "them up from the graveyard of dead contexts" and help "them take up new lives among the living. The best way to respect the dead is to help them speak to the living." Paradoxically, only by making history our own, only by starting in our own context and pursuing a dialogue with the dead, can we help their voices be heard again, give them due justice, and breathe life into the past.[39]

Redeeming the Past

If Nietzsche wondered whether life is lived better without history, Martin Heidegger claimed that temporality defines human existence. To be human is to be "thrown" into time and "caught" between a past which defines us and a future which we can only wait for or anticipate. We live as "always-already-having been" and "being-ahead-of" or "coming-toward" ourselves.[40] Scientific study of the past thus can only be derivative and secondary because it is rooted in the primordial temporal experience of human existence. By rooting history and philosophy in life,

38. Harlan, *Degradation,* pp. xv-xvi.
39. Harlan, *Degradation,* pp. xxxii-xxxiii.
40. Martin Heidegger, *Being and Time,* trans. John Macquarrie and Edward Robinson (London: SCM, 1962), pp. 300-301; Michael Gelven, *A Commentary on Heidegger's Being and Time,* rev. ed. (DeKalb: Northern Illinois University Press, 1989), p. 181.

Nietzsche and Heidegger subverted science and became harbingers of the postmodern critique of modernity. Postmodern critics have continued this project of deconstructing modern historiography, and in so doing have provided historians with an opportunity to return to the questions of ethics, purpose, and meaning.[41] Despite exhausting debates over methodology, however, historians have only begun to articulate new models of history that give priority to meaning and life, rather than knowledge, and do so without abandoning modern historical techniques and the obligations of the historian to the past itself.[42] In short, the postmodern turn signals a new beginning for the practice of historiography, but it also offers an opportunity to return to the best resources of the pre-modern and modern eras.

A means to begin redeeming historiography can be found in Heidegger's discussion of the kinds of knowledge that people exercise. In *Being and Time,* he contends that the "primordial" form of knowledge is "ready at hand," such as when a carpenter instinctively picks up a hammer and uses it to pound a nail, or when a young parent unthinkingly remembers how her father comforted a frightened daughter. This "ready at hand" knowledge is rooted in humanity's condition of "being-in-the-world." Our being is always specific, "being-there" and "being-with" others, being part of the world, not abstracted and set apart from it. This primordial knowledge is by definition useful, significant, and purposeful. In contrast, scientific knowledge is derivative and secondary, merely "present at hand," in Heidegger's words. To reflect on a hammer's nature and use, or to analyze the status of memories, is to mentally set ourselves above or outside the world. It is, in a sense, to perform an unnatural exercise. Scientific techniques are powerful and not necessarily pernicious, but as a starting point for "being-in-the-world" and understanding the human condition they are woefully inadequate.[43]

41. On postmodernity and ethical obligations, see Lyon, *Postmodernity,* chap. 6; and Zygmunt Bauman, *Postmodern Ethics* (Oxford: Blackwell, 1993).

42. New ways to do history usually are explored by writers outside the historical profession. For example, see Walter Davis, *Deracination: Historicity, Hiroshima, and the Tragic Imperative* (Albany: State University of New York Press, 2001).

43. Heidegger talked about viewing and relating to the world. I use "knowledge" to compare scientific knowledge and useful-relational knowledge. See Heidegger, *Being and Time,* pt. 1, chap. 3, sect. 14-20; Gelven, *A Commentary,* pp. 61ff. Note that the

If Heidegger is right, then history must begin with the human experience of temporality, not with abstract, ostensibly objective knowledge claims about the past, as if historians can look at the world with God's all-seeing eye. The most basic concern of historiography should not be causal explanations, or descriptions of particular events, but rather the unavoidable experience of being thrown into time, caught between past and future. "The future is meaningful in the sense of 'I *am* as coming toward,'" explains Michael Gelven, while "the past is meaningful in the sense of 'I *am* as having been.'"[44] Both the past and the future thus are "ever-present" aspects of being human. For Heidegger, the purpose of history thus is to reveal the "silent power of the possible."[45] Facing the future with "anticipatory resoluteness," with hope, rather than passively accepting the present as it is given, as just the way things are, requires a "retrieval" of resources from the past. Natalie Zemon Davis makes this point in an interview on her work.

> I want to show how different the past was. I want to show that even when times were hard, people found ways to cope . . . and maybe resist. I want people today to be able to connect with the past by looking at the tragedies and the sufferings of the past, the love the people had, and the beating that they had. They sought power over each other, but they helped each other, too. They did things both out of love and fear — that's my message. Especially I want to show that it could be different, that it was different and that there are alternatives.[46]

An authentic relationship to the past cannot be distant and objective, a matter of studying the past "for its own sake." History and memory

---

chief failure of Heidegger's work is inadequately dealing with the intersubjectivity of human experience; I am using his work here without accepting it uncritically in all of its aspects.

44. Gelven, *A Commentary*, p. 181.

45. Heidegger, *Being and Time*, p. 360. On him, see Rüdiger Safranski, *Martin Heidegger*, trans. Ewald Osers (Cambridge: Harvard University Press, 1998); Charles Bambach, *Heidegger, Dilthey, and the Crisis of Historicism* (Ithaca, N.Y.: Cornell University Press, 1995).

46. Interview with Davis in MARHO (The Radical Historians Organization), *Visions of History* (New York: Pantheon, 1983), pp. 114-15.

must be "ready at hand," to allow people to anticipate the future and uncover the potentialities of their existence.

Heidegger called this approach to being and time "historicity," and claimed that it is prior to the science of history. In other words, the past, present, and future can be separated from life and thus "objectified" only because they are primordial and "always-already" intertwined in our day-to-day human experience. Historical accuracy and facts are useful — *and necessary* — but they are secondary to questions about the meaning of time. If historians are to act responsibly as citizens, tell hopeful stories, serve as cultural timekeepers, and help people to understand authentic human existence and live well, they cannot let scientific impulses define their work. They must consider historicity and time, not merely history. In short, they need to reconfigure their priorities. The imperatives of meaning and purpose must become the starting point of historical study rather than distantly held motivations and goals.

Heidegger's account of human existence and historicity fits closely with the work of his student, Gadamer, on historical hermeneutics. Like his mentor, and like Nietzsche, Gadamer rejects scientific notions of historical truth. He argues that historians cannot reconstruct the past, cannot see through texts (or other evidence) to the actual experiences of people in the past. The past itself is done and gone. More important, even if attainable such a goal is inadequate. Any historical hermeneutic that regards "understanding as reconstructing the original" can do little more than hand down a dead meaning. For Gadamer the true "historical spirit consists not in the restoration of the past but in thoughtful mediation with contemporary life."[47] Mediation, or the "fusion of horizons," is the true goal. Historians cannot claim to understand Plato as he understood himself or fully re-create the context in which Plato wrote. They cannot even claim to read his writings objectively, free of the prejudices of their own age. Indeed, Gadamer attacks the Enlightenment "prejudice" against prejudice and tradition. History does not "belong to us," he explains; "we belong to it. Long before we understand ourselves through the process of self-examination, we understand ourselves in a self-evident way in the family, society, and state in which we live."[48] Traditions constitute our identities and make

47. Gadamer, *Truth and Method,* pp. 167-68.
48. Gadamer, *Truth and Method,* pp. 276-77.

reason possible. Subjectivity may be a "distorting mirror," Gadamer acknowledges. But "[the] self-awareness of the individual is only a flickering presence in the closed circuits of historical life. That is why the prejudices of the individual, far more than his judgments, constitute the historical reality of his being."[49] Such "prejudice" is a matter of pejorative "bias" but also includes the assumptions and prejudgments necessary for basic communication. We cannot exist apart from the world and cannot exercise reason except within specific historical-cultural circumstances and languages. Our "being-in-the-world," our finitude, sets formidable limits around our knowledge and truth claims but also makes meaning possible for us.

Hermeneutics and historical understanding thus must be thought of not as subjective acts, but as intersubjective, "participating in an event of tradition, a process in which past and present are constantly mediated." If so, then historical research is less a scientific method than a dialectical process of handing down our own traditions and encountering others'.[50] We cannot experience the past as it was, nor read Plato's writings and fully understand his ideas as he understood them. And yet, if we are open to letting his ideas say something to us, from within our own traditions we can "hear the past resound in a new voice." Put simply, though we can make sense of Plato's writings only from within the contexts of our own time, it is possible to be confronted by his words and ideas. Texts do have a power of their own if we let them speak. If the reader is open, neither the reader nor the text rules the other. In short, we cannot use reason to shed our prejudices or escape traditions, per se, and find a universal, objective plane, but we can fuse our horizons with Plato's writings, experience a form of alienation, and expand outward from our traditions. Such "alienation" may be painful, upsetting, or liberating. But the notion and goal of "historically effected consciousness" demands that we take part in intersubjective encounters with the past that have the potential to change who we are.

This sort of "alienation" is profoundly different from that produced by scientific history. It does not ask historians to reject their own subjectivity or deny the truth claims of people in the past. It asks them

49. Gadamer, *Truth and Method*, pp. 276-77.
50. Gadamer, *Truth and Method*, pp. 290, 284.

to listen and be open to the truths of voices from the past. Nietzsche mockingly describes the scholar as "neither man nor woman, nor even hermaphrodite."[51] Rather than being indifferent or disinterested — perpetual spectators, passive sounding boards, or voyeurs — Gadamer asks historians to participate in conversations with the past, in the process both giving and taking. Never passive, never neutral, always open, the "fusion of horizons" is not a method but a deeply humanistic, humble ideal. If we cannot and perhaps should not try to escape the human condition (our "being-in-the-world" and all traditions), we can refuse to remain what we are and enrich ourselves by entering into communion with others, past and present. If we cannot leave behind our cultures and languages to arrive at some transcendent form of reason, we can add to them. Such finitude and alienation make meaning and truth possible for us as mortal beings. Through "historically effected consciousness" and the "fusion of horizons" we can make "infinite use of [our] finite means."[52]

Though it makes no promises about certainty and claims no transcendent knowledge, this approach to historical study does provide warrant for moral engagement. It also offers an approach to truth not as an object to be grasped but a series of pilgrimages to follow. This may sound radical and relativistic; and yet, Gadamer's validation of tradition and his insistence that effective historical consciousness requires a fusion of horizons have some troubling "conservative" implications.[53] Does he undermine cultural criticism, by promoting veneration of the past at the expense of revolutionary change? Does his emphasis on tradition and the truth claims of the past impose their weight on the present and future? Does his "openness" mean "acceptance"? No, at least not inevitably so.[54] Rather than tradition per se,

51. Nietzsche, *On the Advantage and Disadvantage*, p. 31. He also compares the scholar to the eunuch (p. 29). The images of voyeurs, etc., also belong to Nietzsche; see Southgate, *Why Bother with History*, pp. 122-23.

52. Wilhelm von Humboldt, quoted in Gadamer, *Truth and Method*, p. 440. On alienation, see Gerald Bruns, *Hermeneutics Ancient and Modern* (New Haven: Yale University Press, 1992), especially chaps. 9-10.

53. Jürgen Habermas has made this critique of Gadamer; see Bernstein, *Beyond Objectivism and Relativism*.

54. Gadamer addresses this question specifically in "The Problem of Historical Consciousness," trans. Jeff L. Close, in *Interpretive Social Science: A Reader*, ed. Paul

historians must insist on the obligation to fuse their horizons with multiple, competing, and even conflicting traditions and resist the totalizing claims of any one undisputed tradition. If we cannot judge traditions with objective reason, we can listen to competing voices with minds open to change, and seek opportunities to question and expand our horizons. Such a diverse and dialectical attitude toward "effective historical consciousness" will lead to the "alienating" experience of "being transformed into a communion in which we do not remain what we were." But it does not require uncritical acceptance of truth claims from the past, simply openness to them.[55]

But is this enough? Whether hopeful or unnerving, some "alienation" perhaps is inevitable today, given the cultural diversity of postmodern societies. Theorists such as Emmanuel Levinas and Zygmunt Bauman have shown that the preeminent moral dilemmas of our time come when we encounter the Other.[56] In so doing they have echoed the ancient biblical question: Who is my neighbor? As in our postmodern city streets, historians today come upon the Other when they examine the remains of the past — whether texts, material artifacts, or people who remember. Such encounters suggest complex moral obligations. Yes, we must approach the past open to the claims of both our own traditions and those of others. But, in fusing our horizons with competing and conflicting traditions, what do we give and what do we take? When we confront others in the past, whose stories do we embrace? Whose do we judge or resist? When do we seek redemption? And, when do we offer it? Can we avoid assimilating the Other into our own horizons?[57] In concepts such as "retrieval," "anticipation," "effective historical consciousness," and "fusion of horizons," and categories of "critical," "monumental," and "antiquarian" history,

---

Rabinow and William M. Sullivan (Berkeley: University of California Press, 1979), pp. 107-8.

55. Gadamer, *Truth and Method*, p. 379. That is, openness to those claims *as claims* on us, and not merely as distant-held objects of study that had claims in the past, but no longer today.

56. In *Postmodern Ethics* and *Life in Fragments* (Oxford: Blackwell, 1995), Bauman provides a useful introduction to some of Levinas's ideas. For an introduction to Levinas, see J. Llewelyn, *Levinas: The Genealogy of Ethics* (New York: Routledge, 1995).

57. Levinas makes the point that the Other must remain Other. To incorporate the Other into "the Same" would be an act of violence.

Heidegger, Gadamer, and Nietzsche offer intriguing formal approaches to the past. Yet they provide no specific direction in matters of judgment. This is a critical dilemma, because, as Walter Benjamin insists, "Only that historian will have the gift of fanning the spark of hope in the past who is firmly convinced that *even the dead* will not be safe from the enemy if he wins." The same danger threatens the dead, the living, and their traditions: "that of becoming a tool of the ruling classes." For these reasons, "In every era, the attempt must be made anew to wrest tradition away from a conformism that is about to overpower it."[58] But how do we distinguish potential "allies" from "adversaries"?

The Messianic Moment

Recognizing that they were incomplete, Walter Benjamin did not intend his "Theses on the Philosophy of History" to be published.[59] Nevertheless, these fragments have inspired much creative reflection. In his "theses" Benjamin rejects modern notions of linear progress. Steeped in Jewish messianism as well as Marxist materialism, he speculates that redemption will break into time, suddenly, rather than be an immanent product of it. He does not view time as a sequence of events, in which the present evolves in linear fashion between the past and the future, but proposes a "conception of the present as the 'time of the now,'" an advent moment "shot through with chips of Messianic time." Despite Talmudic proscriptions against investigating the future, and Marxist critiques of utopian thought, Benjamin refuses to turn the future into a "homogenous, empty time." Every moment of time, he insists, is "the strait gate through which the Messiah might enter."[60]

Benjamin's messianism thus transcends linear notions of time. It is rooted in Jewish (and Christian) traditions in which God redeems

58. Benjamin, *Illuminations*, p. 255. Whether the face-to-face relations with the Other discussed by Bauman and Levinas can be replicated in historical study, when only textual-material evidence remains, is an open question.

59. Julian Roberts, *Walter Benjamin* (London: Macmillan, 1982), pp. 196-97.

60. Benjamin, *Illuminations*, pp. 263-64. The material on Benjamin in this paragraph comes partly from my own reading, but also Rainer Rochlitz, *The Disenchantment of Art: The Philosophy of Walter Benjamin*, trans. Jane Marie Todd (New York: Guilford, 1996), chap. 3.

time itself — not just the present and the future but the past as well. The meta-historical narratives of emancipation that defined modernity offer little to the dead. Indeed, they have often inspired destruction. The debris witnessed by the angel of history is the "storm" of "progress." Furthermore, while Benjamin emphasized the unity of time (traditions are in danger in the past as well as the present and future, and the present and future can reshape the history of the past), he also judged that the redemption of time requires that it be ruptured in the messianic moment. Such a view of time and history can be read as a product of his experiences in the 1930s — the advance of fascism in Nazi Germany, and uncertainty about the direction of communism in Stalin's Russia. Benjamin's hope was mystical and often despairing. (He committed suicide near the Spanish border, in 1940, while fleeing the Nazi occupation of France.) In an age of political crisis, when modern meta-historical narratives of linear progress no longer seemed convincing, his "retrieval" of the Jewish messianic tradition and his notion of the revolutionary "now time" expressed a hope that was cryptic, melancholic, and defiant.[61] But what use are such "messianic" horizons to historians concerned with studying the past and, in some fashion, "redeeming" time?

First, Benjamin's messianic "now" time provides us with a way to postulate transcendent viewpoints from which to evaluate our encounters with the past. His messianic moment might be viewed as a utopian horizon — a vision of the possibilities of human existence, the kingdom of God, or the good society.[62] In his *Lectures on Ideology and Utopia*, Paul Ricoeur says that utopian visions allow us to imagine a "no place," a "ghost city," that offers "an exterior glance" on our reality. He asks, "Is not utopia — this leap outside — the way in which we radically rethink what is family, what is consumption, what is authority, what is

---

61. On the revival of Jewish messianism during the 1920s and 1930s, see Jürgen Moltmann, *The Coming of God,* trans. Margaret Kohl (Minneapolis: Fortress, 1996), pp. 29-46. On the crisis of historicism, see Bambach, *Heidegger, Dilthey, and the Crisis of Historicism.*

62. I do not mean to ignore the distinction between messianic and utopian traditions. For the former, the Messiah typically comes from outside of time and redemption happens to time. For the latter, people typically build utopias in the linear course of history. Nevertheless, here I am stressing the common ground between them. On the distinction, see Moltmann's discussion of Rosenzweig in *The Coming of God,* pp. 34-35.

religion, and so on? Does not the fantasy of an alternative society and its exteriorization 'nowhere' work as one of the most formidable contestations of what is?" In other words, utopian horizons allow us to put our own culture "at a distance." They provide us with a starting point from which to judge ourselves and others whom we encounter in the present or the past. Utopian horizons are not products of objective knowledge, known with scientific certitude, but products of desire rooted in faith and dreams of what might be.[63] Nor are they "transcendent" in the sense that they allow us to escape finitude or provide us with direct access to the universal and the infinite. All utopian horizons evolve within traditions (such as the Judaism and Marxism of Benjamin), even as they aspire to reach beyond their cultural origins in critically and hopefully dreaming of the redemption of time.

Second, Benjamin returns us to the apocalyptic fears and hopes expressed about the past and the present in our own day. Like his time, ours is one filled with danger, despair, and hope. His view of history and time thus legitimizes the eschatological questions of our age, even as it upsets them with its emphasis on both ruptures and continuity and its critique of objective historical facts as a stable form of knowledge. Critics today worry about historical truth and the fate of nations and other communities of memory. Is historiography in crisis, as a science and as a discourse capable of generating moral decision-making? What is left of the redemptive promises of the Enlightenment and the modern meta-historical narratives?[64] Here, Benjamin reminds us of our obligations to the past. He insists on the "weak Messianic power" of those living in the present and on the need to redeem the past. If in nothing else, then, he follows Nietzsche and Heidegger in his assump-

---

63. Paul Ricoeur, *Lectures on Ideology and Utopia* (New York: Columbia, 1986), pp. 16-17. From this perspective, the notion of objectivity is a utopian horizon, in which the scientist imagines a "no place" beyond the subjective experience of the world. The problem is a lack of self-awareness that objectivity is a utopian projection. The literature on utopian thought is immense. For an introduction, see Ruth Levitas, *The Concept of Utopia* (Syracuse: Syracuse University Press, 1990). Note also Tom Moylan, *Scraps of the Untainted Sky* (Boulder, Colo.: Westview, 2000); and Tom Moylan and Jamie Owen Daniel, eds., *Not Yet: Reconsidering Ernst Bloch* (London: Verso, 1997).

64. In general, see Daniel Wojcik, *The End of the World as We Know It* (New York: New York University Press, 1997); and Thomas Robbins and Susan Palmer, eds., *Millennium, Messiahs, and Mayhem* (New York: Routledge, 1997).

tion that history is not static or fixed.[65] Rather than the weight of undisputed traditions, the universal-linear time of modern historical consciousness, or the weightlessness of postmodernity, we might conceptualize history as "rhythmic," as including both ruptures in time and continuities between the past, present, and future.[66] This metaphor of "rhythmic time" is frustratingly vague, as well as compellingly enigmatic. The point is to consider new ways of thinking about the past, history, and the possibilities of the present and the future. This does not mean that we should wholly abandon the methods of modern historiography or impose a newly hegemonic mode of normal history. But it does require us to open history writing, in our postmodern time, to diverse goals and methods.[67]

Third, this discussion suggests ways in which history writing has the potential to redeem the past and transform the present. In the "now" moment the Messiah will break into history and redeem time, Benjamin believes. But historians are "caught" in time and cannot literally change the past. None of us is the Messiah. Nonetheless, we do have a "weak messianic power." If we are open to the alienating truths of the past, to both ruptures and continuities, we can remember the dead and share a kinship and a solidarity with them. The danger is that they will be subdued and forgotten. In reawakening the past we rescue the dead, in a partial way, from the oblivion of forgotten histories erased by remembered oppressors. In the present and future, we can redeem a small part of the happiness that the oppressed could not achieve in their own day. The process of "reawakening" history and cutting ourselves off from oppressive traditions also can rescue us in the present and help us to anticipate the future. There is a hopeful kinship,

65. Richard Wolin critiques those who link the thought of Benjamin and Heidegger; cf. Wolin, *Walter Benjamin: An Aesthetic of Redemption* (New York: Columbia University Press, 1982), p. 102. I view Benjamin and Heidegger as responding differently to the same crisis in historicism.

66. Though my use is different from hers, on "rhythmic" history, see Elizabeth Deeds Ermarth, *Sequel to History* (Princeton, N.J.: Princeton University Press, 1992).

67. "Normal history" echoes Thomas Kuhn, in *The Structure of Scientific Revolutions* (Chicago: University of Chicago Press, 1962), on paradigm shifts. In everyday science, practitioners assume and reinforce the institutions and methods of the "normal" paradigm. So too in modern historiography. In *Beyond the Great Story,* Berkhofer applies Kuhn's model to historiography.

or at least a potential one, between the dead, the living, and those yet to come. If we are open to the past and the future, and if we question the totalizing power of linear time, then the weight of inevitability and the despair that life simply is the way it is may be broken. We must envision messianic-utopian horizons that rupture our sense of time and foster new forms of communion between the present, the past, and the future. Time is not fixed. At the "end of history" we may yet be able to rewrite the past and radical new beginnings may be possible. If we are "thrown" into time, as Heidegger claims, we are not only thrown toward death but also thrown from birth, and toward "second birth."[68]

Conclusion

Can history be redeemed, and be redemptive? This essay has been an exercise in clearing spaces for hope within the contested modern and postmodern discourses through which we think about history and time. Messianic-utopian horizons reach toward the "now" time and anticipate the redemption of history. At the same time, whatever transcendent horizons we imagine, all of our hopes have an essentially finite, relative, contested quality. Our being is in the world and the bonds of traditions and communities tie us together and oftentimes tie us down. Such bonds also make human knowledge and meaning possible. The monumental, antiquarian, and critical aspects of history, and the "alienating" experience of encountering the Other, exemplify this condition.

The open-ended and contested view of history, hope, time, and traditions articulated here compares to accounts of politics given by theorists of "radical democracy," who insist that both pluralism and conflict are inescapable and necessary aspects of hopeful politics. Democracy cannot be based on "neutral" procedural rules, because such rules do not exist apart from normative concerns, political principles, and utopian horizons (such as liberty and freedom). At the same time, the values of democracy and visions of the good life must remain "endlessly" contested because they are always defined and practiced

---

68. I am referring to the Christian notion and Hannah Arendt's concept of "natality." See David Billings's essay in this volume.

within a specific historical context. Democracies cannot function without normative principles; but they cannot avoid injustices in some form unless they remain open to fundamental changes. Likewise, political communities need to remain open to including people who have been excluded in the past. The unavoidable danger is the likelihood of excluding others in the process — hence the "agonal" quality of politics (and likewise hope). Democracy thus is not an end so much as an ongoing ordeal.[69] It cannot be "fixed," not if it is to remain open and hopeful.

Messianic-utopian horizons are, similarly, a necessary aspect of hope, the experience of time, and historical study. Though I have made a formal argument here, and avoided explicitly defining or providing apologetic warrant for my own messianic-utopian horizon, individuals and communities do need to posit, think, and live in the light of specific horizons.[70] At the same time, when we do not recognize their finite and agonal quality, our expressions of hope and history threaten to become totalizing and contribute to the debris piled up at the feet of the angel of history.[71] The refusal to resolve with finality the deepest questions that humanity can pose — whether historical, political, or

69. On agonal democracy, see Chantal Mouffe, ed., *Dimensions of Radical Democracy* (London: Verso, 1996).

70. The implicit point here is that such horizons are, at some level, exclusive. To hold to and live in the light of a messianic-utopian horizon is to believe that it is better and more true than other postulated horizons. My argument is that there is no independent stance from which to determine which postulated horizon is the truest one; and my burden is to ask how, if this is so, we can live hopefully. Our choices thus should not be thought of in consumerist terms, where all choices are equally significant and insignificant. Instead, our choices must be hopeful and agonal, because they are indeterminate in their reach for something transcendent.

71. Both the formal theoretical argument I have made here, and any posited utopian or messianic horizon, can be used in foolish and oppressive ways. I have made use of Heidegger's thought to make my argument. His career presents a sad example of such foolishness, as scholars who have examined the relationship between his philosophy and the Nazi regime of the 1930s and 1940s have shown. But this does not *necessarily* delegitimize my case or every aspect of his thought. Foolishness and destruction have been justified in the name of scientific objectivity and a host of other religious, political, and philosophical perspectives, including liberal democracy. My case is built on the "agonal" assumption that specific hopes and normative principles are both necessary and dangerous; consequently, I allude to and would advocate something like the agonal form of politics discussed by Mouffe and others in *Dimensions of Radical Democracy*.

spiritual — arguably is an indispensable aspect of any radical form of commitment and openness that is at once transforming, alienating, unnerving, and hopeful.[72] This hope demands ruptures, continuities, and utopian horizons. Things can be different. Time and history are not fixed. And we can make infinite use of our finite means and be transformed in "a communion in which we do not remain what we were."[73]

72. My thinking on this has also been shaped by Michel Foucault; see "Subject and Power," in *The Foucault Reader,* ed. Paul Rabinow (New York: Random House, 1984).

73. The phrases quoted and paraphrased are from Gadamer, *Truth and Method,* pp. 379, 440.

Section II

Early Christianity in Conversation with Contemporary Thought

Seeking Justice in Hope

NICHOLAS WOLTERSTORFF

Every human endeavor that is not coerced requires, as a minimum, the hope that its goal will be achieved. Optimism is not required — optimism being understood as the expectation that one will achieve what one endeavors. The ambulance attendant who endeavors to resuscitate the person pulled down by waves at the beach may not expect to succeed in his endeavor; he may expect that he will not succeed. He may not be at all optimistic. Yet as long as he sees some hope, he tries — as long as there's a chance. If he thinks there is no hope, he gives up and stops trying.

Maybe there are one or two sorts of exceptions. Imagine a person who has just suffered considerable paralysis as the result of an accident. The doctors are now trying to determine the extent of the paralysis. One of them says to the patient, "See if you can wiggle your right thumb." So the patient tries. In this case, the person does not know whether there's a chance of his wiggling his right thumb. He does not know one way or the other as to whether it is hopeless. He tries to wiggle his right thumb so as to find out. But apart from cases in which one tries to do something so as to find out whether it's hopeless, or alternatively, to prove that it is hopeless, endeavor presupposes hope — not optimism necessarily, but hope. Though let it be said that often we give up on an endeavor if we are not optimistic about its success; it's just not worth trying.

I

In this essay I want to reflect on the sort of hope that working for justice requires. Working for justice does not, in my judgment, require optimism; often one works for justice, and is called to do so, in situations like that of the ambulance attendant who tries to resuscitate his patient without expecting to succeed. What such work does require is hope — hope of a peculiar sort. It will shortly become clear, but perhaps I should nonetheless state it here at the beginning, that these will be *Christian* reflections on the sort of hope that the struggle for justice requires.

I will have to begin by talking about the sort of hope, and, correspondingly, the sort of justice, that I have in mind. The easiest and most lucid way to do that is to begin by highlighting the sort of hope that I do *not* have in mind. In the first Part of the second Part of his *Summa theologiae,* Question 40, Article 1 *(resp.),* Aquinas offers a characteristically lucid analysis of hope. Hope, at bottom, is a special form of desire. It is unlike fear in that its object is a *good* of some sort — or at least, something that the agent regards as good. It is unlike joy in that its object is a future rather than a present good. It is unlike the desire for small things in that, in Aquinas's words, its object is "something arduous and difficult to obtain." We do not, he says, "speak of anyone hoping for trifles which are in one's power to have at any time." And it is unlike despair in that "this difficult thing is something possible to obtain: for one does not hope for that which one cannot get at all." An admirable analysis, I say!

Later, in Question 62 of the same Part of his *Summa,* Aquinas considers whether hope, along with faith and charity, is appropriately regarded as one of the theological virtues. First he asks what makes a theological virtue different from an intellectual or moral virtue. After observing that, for habits in general, what makes two habits belong to different species is a "formal difference of their objects," he goes on to apply this principle of species-differentiation to the virtues as follows:

> The object of the theological virtues is God Himself, Who is the last end of all, as surpassing the knowledge of our reason. On the other hand, the object of the intellectual and moral virtues is something comprehensible to human reason. Wherefore the theological

virtues are specifically distinct from the moral and intellectual virtues. (Art. 2, *resp.*)

With this conceptual scaffolding in hand, Aquinas is ready to argue that there are three theological virtues: faith, hope, and charity. His argument goes like this. For human beings, there is the possibility of a "supernatural happiness," such happiness consisting in a cognitive-appetitive relation to God that goes beyond what is available to us by the employment of our ordinary creaturely capacities. The enjoyment of supernatural happiness requires a cognition of things beyond those that can be known by our ordinary creaturely intellect; and it requires a fastening of the will onto a good that goes beyond those goods that can be discerned by the ordinary creaturely intellect. It follows that, if we human beings are to achieve supernatural happiness, we need some sort of supplement to our creaturely intellectual and volitional capacities and to what can be achieved by their employment — some sort of "supernatural" addition. This is exactly what faith, hope, and charity are. Aquinas explains the relationship between them:

> First, as regards the intellect, man receives certain supernatural principles, which are held by means of a Divine light: these are the articles of faith. . . . Secondly, the will is directed to this end, both as to the movement of intention, which tends to that end as something attainable, — and this pertains to hope, — and as to a certain spiritual union, whereby the will is, so to speak, transformed into that end, — and this belongs to charity. (Art. 3, *resp.*)

What I want to take from this quick dip into the deep waters of Aquinas's *Summa theologiae* is the claim that Christian hope is hope for consummation — consummation here being understood as a supernatural mode of union with God. Christian hope is not hope for what might transpire in history but hope for a state of *eudaimonia* that transcends history. Hence it has nothing in particular to do with the struggle for justice within history. Christian hope is not hope that our struggle for justice will bear fruit; nor is it hope that our longing for justice will be satisfied. I judge that in thus understanding hope, Aquinas is representative of a long and prominent strand of Christian thought.

It has been my experience that to breathe a word critical of Aquinas is to bring down upon oneself the wrath of Aquinas scholars — St. Paul seems no match for St. Thomas when it comes to infallibility! It is not my main aim here to engage in Aquinas exegesis, but rather to have before us a *type* of view. Nevertheless, I think I had better protect my flanks against the charge of those who will claim that I have misinterpreted Aquinas. They will point to Aquinas's discussion "Of Hope, Considered in Itself," found in Question 17 of the second Part of the second Part of the *Summa theologiae*. There, in the course of once again taking up the question of whether hope is a theological virtue, Aquinas speaks of "hope that has for its object not only God but also other goods" (Art. 5, obj. 1). So presumably justice in history is a candidate for hope.

Maybe so; but maybe not. What must be noticed is that to the above remark, Aquinas immediately adds the clause, "which we hope to obtain from God." Let me repeat the entire phrase — "hope that has for its object not only God, but also other goods which we hope to obtain from God." The preceding article makes clear what Aquinas has in mind by this qualifying phrase. In any example of hope, he says, we can always pick out the object of the hope, that is, the good hoped for, and the means by which, so it is hoped, that object will be attained. Furthermore, in the former, which is the final cause of the hope, we can often distinguish between the principal cause and a secondary cause, the principal cause being the last end, and a secondary cause being that which, in Aquinas's words, "is referred to that end." Somewhat similarly, in the latter, which is the efficient cause of the hope, we can distinguish between the principal efficient cause, this being the ultimate cause of all that happens, namely God, and some secondary or instrumental agent.

One implication is that whatever it may be that the Christian hopes for, God will be there within one's hope as the ultimate agent of that whole stream of agency that one hopes will bring about the good hoped for. Hope for some incursion of justice within history will be, in this respect, an example of the theological virtue of hope if one's hope concerning means goes beyond purely historical events to hoping that God will bring about that good of justice — by whatever secondary causes God chooses to use. In Aquinas's own words, "in so far as we hope for anything as being possible to us by means of the divine assistance, our hope attains God himself, on whose help it leans" (Art. 1, *resp.*).

If this were all Aquinas says that is relevant to the matter, the objection to my interpretation would stand: though Christians will hope for a variety of different things, always the ultimate ground of their hope will be that God, by whatever means, will bring about the thing hoped for. But that is not all he says. What he also says is that in every case of authentic hope, the beatific vision is "properly and chiefly" the "principal end" of the hope — that is to say, the beatific vision is always the principal good hoped for. In the Second Article of Question 17 Aquinas raises the question, "Whether Eternal Happiness is the Proper Object of Hope?" His answer goes as follows:

> Now an effect must be proportionate to its cause. Wherefore the good which we ought to hope for from God properly and chiefly, is the infinite good, which is proportionate to the power of our divine helper, since it belongs to an infinite power to lead anything to an infinite good. Such a good is eternal life, which consists in the enjoyment of God Himself. For we should hope from Him for nothing less than Himself, since His goodness, whereby He imparts good things to His creature, is no less than His Essence. Therefore the proper and principal object of hope is eternal happiness.

Aquinas does not explain in what way anything that one hopes for other than eternal blessedness ought to be "referred to" one's eternal blessedness as its proper and principal goal or end.[1] The most natural interpretation is that whatever else one hopes for, one should hope for it as a means to one's eternal blessedness; Christian hope is to be confined to the hope for consummation and to the means for achieving consummation. If, for example, one hopes for justice in history, one does so because such justice, or perhaps the struggle for such justice, is a means to eternal blessedness.

---

1. In the reply to Objection 2 he says this: "We ought not to pray God for any other goods, except in reference to eternal happiness. Hence hope regards eternal happiness chiefly, and other things, for which we pray God, it regards secondarily and as referred to eternal happiness. . . ."

II

I hold that it is a theological mistake thus to see hope for consummation as the only legitimate form of Christian hope. Recall the numinous episode of the burning bush, as reported in Exodus 3. The curiosity of Moses, the fugitive shepherd, was piqued one day by a flaming bush that was not consumed. He went to investigate. As he approached, he heard, from the region of the bush, the sound of a voice calling him by name, telling him to keep his distance and to take off his shoes, for this is holy ground. The speaker then identifies himself — what Moses heard was indeed the speech of a speaker, not just sounds in the air or voices haunting a disturbed mind. "I am the God of your father, the God of Abraham, the God of Isaac, and the God of Jacob," says the speaker. Having thus identified himself, God goes on to say that "I have seen the affliction of my people who are in Egypt, and have heard their cry because of their taskmasters; I know their sufferings, and I have come down to deliver them out of the hand of the Egyptians, and to bring them up out of that land to a good and broad land, a land flowing with milk and honey."[2]

Now jump to the song (in Luke 1) that the elderly Zechariah was moved by the Spirit to sing upon the birth of his son, John, the one known to us as John the Baptist:

> Blessed be the Lord God of Israel,
> for he has visited and redeemed his people,
> and has raised up a horn of salvation for us
> in the house of his servant David,
> as he spoke by the mouth of his holy prophets from of old,
> that we should be saved from our enemies,
> and from the hand of all who hate us;
> to perform the mercy promised to our fathers,
> and to remember his holy covenant,
> the oath which he swore to our father Abraham, to grant us
> that we, being delivered from the hand of our enemies,
> might serve him without fear,

2. Biblical quotations in this essay are taken from the Revised Standard Version of the Bible.

in holiness and righteousness [justice] before him
all the days of our life.

The theme in both passages is not consummation but deliverance
— and correspondingly, not the hope for consummation but the hope
for deliverance. Let me explain. As the result of working through a
magnificent, but yet-unpublished, manuscript on theological anthropology by my colleague David Kelsey, I have come to see with far greater
clarity than ever before that the story Christian Scripture tells of how
the triune God relates to what is not God is a story that has three independent, though mutually involving, story lines: there is the story line
of how God relates to all that is not God as creator and sustainer, there
is the story line of how God relates to all that is not God as
consummator, and there is the story line of how God relates to all that
is not God as deliverer or redeemer. Christian theology, though it does
not itself usually take the form of a narrative, is nonetheless unique
among the theologies and philosophies of humankind in that it articulates this narrative — that is, articulates the threefold way in which the
three-person God relates to all that is not God.

I said that the three story lines, though certainly mutually involving, are nonetheless independent; none is a mere component or implication of another. To a person who has heard of God only as creator
and sustainer, the news of consummation and of redemption comes as
news — good news. Consummation and redemption are not simply the
outworking of the dynamics of creation. Likewise the story line of consummation does not imply that of redemption, nor vice versa. If God's
creatures had acted as God wanted them to act, so that there was no
need for the deliverance of which the One in the burning bush spoke
nor for that which Zechariah now expected, nonetheless God might
have promised and effected consummation. Conversely, God might
have redeemed us from the sin that so strangely haunts creation without offering us that consummation which is a *new* creation. The consummation and redemption story lines do not even presuppose the creation story line. They do, of course, presuppose that there are beings
who can be redeemed and whose existence can be consummated by a
mode of existence that goes beyond what "the flesh" is capable of. But
they do not, as such, presuppose that the totality of what is not God
has been created by God, nor, if it has been created by God, that the cre-

ating and sustaining God is also the God who consummates and redeems.

Insofar as theology blurs the distinctness of these three story lines, thus far does theology depart from one of the deepest and most distinctive characteristics of the Christian Scriptures' presentation of God's relation to all that is not God. There are, of course, other, equally fundamental, ways of departing — such as by not acknowledging that it is one and the same God who is the prime agent in each of these story lines, or by not acknowledging that the one God who creates and sustains, consummates, and redeems is a Trinity of Father, Son, and Spirit.

III

What is it that God delivers people from? From affliction and the suffering caused by affliction, says God to Moses. From our enemies, says Zechariah. Those whom God delivers are delivered from those who wrong them — or to put it in the passive voice, from those by whom they are wronged. I do not say that God's deliverance is *confined* to the deliverance of those who are wronged from those who wrong them; we must allow that God also delivers from that sort of suffering which is not the consequence of wrongdoing — "natural evils," as they are called. But the deliverance of which God spoke in the burning bush and which Zechariah now expected is deliverance from being wronged.

What is it to be wronged? It is to fail to receive or enjoy what is *due* one. It is not to fail to receive or enjoy what one would *like,* nor to fail to receive or enjoy what would be good for one. Each of us finds ourself in the situation of lacking all sorts of things that we would like to have, and lacking things that it would be good to have. By itself, however, that is not a sign that we are being wronged. We are wronged just in case we are deprived of some good that is due us.

I could just as well have described being wronged in terms of rights: one is wronged only when one is deprived of some good to which one has a right. The concept of some good *being due one* is the same concept as that of *having a right to* that good.

Most readers will know that this concept of *some good being due one* was already used by some of the philosophers and jurists of antiquity to articulate the concept of justice — and correctly so, in my judgment. Injustice occurs when someone is deprived of some good that is due him or her — that is, when a person is wronged, when that person is deprived of something to which he or she has a right. Conversely, justice is present in some community insofar as its members enjoy those goods that are due them, to which they have a right. Justice is present when no one is being wronged.

What we have then is this: the deliverance of which God speaks to Moses in the flaming unconsumed bush, and of which Zechariah speaks over his newborn son, is deliverance from injustice. And more generally: God's deliverance, God's redemption, is centrally deliverance from injustice. The story line in the biblical narrative that tells of God's deliverance speaks centrally of God's delivering people from injustice. There is, thus, no mystery as to why it is that in the redemptive story line of Scripture, God is over and over characterized as *just,* as *doing justice,* and as *loving justice.* The story line of the Trinitarian God as redeemer cannot even get going without the concept of justice. Of course one does not need the word; we have just noticed a cluster of words that all get at the same idea: "being wronged," "what is due one," "what one has a right to." They all get at the same concept, the concept of justice.

To fully understand the way in which justice and injustice figure in the scriptural story line of redemption, we must take a further step and distinguish between, on the one hand, what I shall call "doing justice," and on the other hand, what I shall call "seeking justice." Doing justice to someone will consist of not wronging that person, of not violating that person's rights, of not treating that person unjustly, of not being responsible for that person's not enjoying what is due him or her. By contrast, *seeking justice,* as I shall use the phrase, presupposes a case of injustice — presupposes that someone has been wronged, that her rights have been violated, that she has not received what is due her. To seek justice is to try to alter that situation so that it is no longer a situation of injustice. Of course, sometimes it is the *right* of a person who is being treated unjustly that I, a bystander, will try to eliminate that injustice. Even though I am not the one who wronged the person, nonetheless I would not be doing justice if I did not try to get rid of the injustice. I myself would be wronging him if I did not try to undo the situation in which he has been wronged by someone else. In such a case, my seeking justice would be a special version of my doing justice.

But sometimes one person's seeking to undo injustice done by another goes beyond what is due the victim; that is to say, sometimes one person's seeking to undo injustice goes beyond what justice requires, and is a case of supererogatory charity.

We have to distinguish, in turn — things are getting a bit complicated now! — between two sorts of justice that one can *seek;* that is to say, two sorts of justice that one can seek to bring about when confronted with a case of injustice. One can seek *retributive* justice; that is to say, one can seek to bring it about that the wrongdoer suffers some kind of retribution, pays some sort of "price," for his wrongdoing. When the retribution has been finished, then justice has been restored. Or one can seek what I shall call *liberating* justice; that is to say, one can seek to bring it about that the victim is freed from the injustice being perpetrated upon him.

Sometimes retributive justice is relevant but liberating justice is not; that happens when the act of injustice has already ceased, perhaps because the victim is dead. Sometimes liberating justice is relevant but retributive justice is not; that happens when somebody is being wronged and, though it is appropriate to seek their liberation, the cause of their being wronged is so diffused across some social structure that it is impossible to pinpoint responsibility.

When Scripture speaks of God as just, sometimes it has in mind that God does justice to God's creatures, that God treats them justly, and sometimes it has in mind that God executes retributive justice. What is intrinsic to the redemptive story line, however, is not God's doing justice but God's seeking justice — that is, God's working to undo injustice; and then, more particularly, God's seeking *liberating* justice. God liberated Israel from the injustice of her slavery in Egypt. And much later, speaking in Nazareth on a Sabbath morning, Jesus announced to his hearers that the following words were being fulfilled as he spoke:

> The Spirit of the Lord is upon me,
> because he has anointed me to preach good news to the poor.
> He has sent me to proclaim release to captives
> and recovering of sight to the blind,
> to set at liberty those who are oppressed,
> to proclaim the acceptable year of the Lord. (Luke 4:18-19)

Justice, when understood as enjoying what's due one, enjoying what one has a right to, has received a bad press from Christian thinkers in recent years. Better to think in terms of love and responsibility, they say. On this occasion I will have to forego considering why justice and rights have received this bad press, and content myself with observing that if one holds that there are no rights, then one will also have to hold that there are very few obligations. Those who are against rights regularly call them "subjective rights" — actually, I think, because this is a rhetorical way of snubbing them, but officially because a right is something that attaches to a subject. They are not against *right,* they insist, or *the right;* they are only against *subjective rights.* But if one insists on calling rights "subjective," on the ground that they attach to subjects, then, in all fairness, one must also call obligations "subjective," since they too attach to subjects. Using this terminology, my point is this: usually if one person is deprived of his or her rights, then another person has failed in his or her obligations. Hence, if there were no subjective rights, then also there would be very few subjective obligations.

It's time that we returned to hope. The Christian hopes for two things: she hopes for consummation, and she hopes for redemption; she hopes for a transformed mode of existence that goes beyond God's work as creator and sustainer — a new creation, a new age, not in any way brought about by "flesh and blood," that is, by the dynamics of creation; and she hopes for deliverance within this created order, within history, especially deliverance from injustice. Two distinct hopes, neither to be assimilated to the other: hope for a new creation, and hope for the just reign of God within this present creation.

IV

In the Gospel of Matthew we read that the last words spoken on earth by Jesus to his disciples began, "All authority in heaven and on earth has been given to me" (28:18). This theme, of all authority now belonging to Christ, is picked up at various points in the Pauline letters — most extensively in First Corinthians 15. Let me quote:

> Christ has been raised from the dead, the first fruits of those who have fallen asleep. For as by a man came death, by a man has come

also the resurrection of the dead. For as in Adam all die, so also in Christ shall all be made alive. But each in his own order: Christ the first fruits, then at his coming those who belong to Christ. Then comes the end, when he delivers the kingdom to God the Father after destroying every rule and every authority and power. For he must reign until he has put all his enemies under his feet. . . . When all things are subjected to him, then the Son himself will also be subjected to him who put all things under him, that God may be everything to every one.

What does this mean — that upon his resurrection, all authority in heaven and earth has been given to Christ, to be retained by him until such time as he has defeated all competing rule, authority, and power, at which time he will deliver the kingship to the Father? What does it mean that Christ is now king and will remain that until he has fully pacified the realm?

A fully adequate answer would require the careful elaboration of at least two lines of thought: an exegetical study of the line of thought in those New Testament passages where this proclamation of Christ as king comes to the surface, and a study of the Old Testament background, so as to discern the connotations of "king" and "kingship." This is obviously not the place to develop adequately either of these approaches. I confine myself to a brief indication of the relevant Old Testament background.

The Old Testament writers were well acquainted with bad kings. What they had to say about bad kings is much less relevant to our purposes here, however, than what they had to say about good kings. The *locus classicus* is the opening of Psalm 72. Let me quote part of it:

> Give the king thy justice, O God,
>   and thy righteousness to the royal son!
> May he judge thy people with righteousness,
>   and thy poor with justice!
> Let the mountains bear prosperity for the people,
>   and the hills, in righteousness!
> May he defend the cause of the poor of the people,
>   give deliverance to the needy,
>   and crush the oppressor!

. . .

> May all kings fall down before him,
>   all nations serve him!

. . .

> For he delivers the needy when he calls,
>   the poor and him who has no helper.
> He has pity on the weak and the needy,
>   and saves the lives of the needy.
> From oppression and violence he redeems their life;
>   and precious is their blood in his sight.

What comes through emphatically in this passage is that the business of the good king is justice. Prosperity is also invoked. But it is not from the king that one expects prosperity; one expects it, or hopes for it, from the favorable operations of the natural order, here symbolized as "the mountains" and "the hills":

> Let the mountains bear prosperity for the people,
>   and the hills, in righteousness!

The king's concern with justice is not so much *doing justice* as *seeking justice* — that is, struggling to undo *in*justice. The good king delivers the needy, defends the cause of the poor, and saves the weak and needy from oppression and violence.

Let's go back then to what Paul might mean when he says that all authority belongs to Christ until such time as all competing power and rule have been conquered, at which time Christ will hand the kingship over to God the Father. Given this Old Testament background, what else could he mean but that Christ is now at work in the world seeking justice — that is, working for the abolition of injustice? Paul's implicit thought must be that there are two kinds of kingship, the kind that consists in the administration of a polity in which there is no injustice, and the kind that consists in struggling to overcome the injustice present in the polity. Christ's kingship is of the latter sort. When Christ's conquest of injustice has been completed, that kind of kingship will no longer be needed, whereupon the Father will exercise the former kind.

I do not suppose I have to argue here that those over whom Christ has authority are not confined to the members of the church; Christ's authority extends to all humankind. There has been a powerful tendency in Christian political theology of the latter part of the twentieth century to place the church at the center of reflections on social justice and governmental authority. That seems to me a profound mistake. It is indeed as a member of the church that the Christian, including then the Christian theologian, speaks and acts. That is the Christian's location, epistemological and ontological. Only when standing in that location can one hear the totality of the story of the threefold way in which the three-person God relates to all that is not God. But the story heard when standing in that location is far more than a story about the church. It is — to speak now only of the redemptive story line — a story that tells the good news of Christ working to undo the wrongs that we inflict on each other, working to undo injustice.

Aquinas, as we saw earlier, distinguishes between the *object* of hope and the *ground* of hope. The object of the hope of those who believe the story line of redemption is that justice will some day reign. The basis of their hope is that this is Christ's cause — Christ being the second person of that Trinity which is God.

V

It is rather often said that whereas most of humanity has thought in terms of a cyclical view of history, Judaism introduced a linear view. I cannot speak to whether there are linear views of history to be found outside Judaism and its sphere of influence. What does seem to me indubitably true is the converse: Judaism introduced a linear view of history — though not in the way that this claim is generally understood. In the Wisdom literature of the Old Testament there is little if anything of the consummation and redemption story lines; God is understood almost exclusively as creator and sustainer. There is also little if anything of a linear view of history. The picture is that of nothing new under the sun. Everything comes around again: springtime and harvest, birth and death, dawn and dusk, poverty and wealth. It is in the redemptive and consummation story lines that one finds a linear view of history — not because the biblical writers narrating these story lines were ontologists of temporality, but rather because the redemption and consummation story lines are inherently linear. They are stories of new things happening and yet to happen, not stories of the same old things happening yet again.

Fundamental to modernity are a blending and secularizing of the story lines of Scripture in such a way that there is thought to be good ground within the natural order for expecting that society will someday be liberated from injustice and we will all enjoy well-being until we die. A few scientists have even speculated that eventually a technology will be discovered that halts aging, thereby eliminating death due to old age. Those who successfully dodge fatal accidents will be able to retain the vigor, the agility, the curiosity, the libido, of a twenty-five-year-old.

This is optimism, not hope, and it is grounded in creation, not God. The claim or assumption is that there are grounds within the natural order for expecting this happy turnout. Hope in the power of Christ to establish his kingdom of justice is replaced by optimism grounded in the powers of humankind and of nature to secure both justice and well-being.

Jean-Francois Lyotard's claim to fame is his announcement of the end of all the grand meta-narratives of modernity. Were it in fact the case that there are no meta-narratives left, our mentality today would be so different from the dominant mentality of the West over these past four centuries that there would finally be good reason for announcing the end of modernity and the arrival of its successor, postmodernity. In fact it is not the case. It is true that all those narratives have died which located the ground for hope in the potentials of central economic planning and non-democratic political regimes; a vivid telling of the dashing of those hopes can be found in the recent book by Jonathan Glover, *Humanity: A Moral History of the Twentieth Century*.[3] But the lesson drawn in most quarters of the West is not that we should give up on optimism but that our optimism should be grounded on the potentials for justice and well-being borne by a market economy combined with a democratic polity. This particular meta-narrative, so far from being dead, is flourishing as never before.

Christian theoreticians and laypeople in the modern world have regularly succumbed to the temptation to jump on the bandwagon of one or another of the optimistic meta-narratives of modernity, justify-

3. New Haven: Yale University Press, 2000.

ing the jump by declaring that those particular dynamics of creation identified by the narrative in question are the *means* whereby Christ is bringing about his just rule. After all, God does use secondary causes, does he not? Some have thought that Marxism successfully identified those dynamics, others that Nazism successfully did so; some have thought that American nationalism contained the crucial dynamics, many now think that market capitalism combined with political democracy does so.

These conflations of Christian hope with secular optimism are one and all heretical. Though they all propose keeping God in the picture as the principal cause of those secondary causes that they have identified, they nonetheless all conflate the story line of redemption with the story line of creation. Rather than redemption being seen as God's unexpected good news for a creation mysteriously haunted by wrongdoing, it is seen as the playing out of the potentials of creation. Let it be added that the currently popular meta-narrative is as implausible as all the others. Looking at global capitalism as it operates both within its core and at its periphery, is there really any reason for thinking that if only it is combined with a democratic polity, injustice will be on the way out? Is there even any reason to think that on the periphery, the combination with democracy is at all stable? Does not the increasing integration of economies around the globe into one capitalist system make ever more likely a truly calamitous worldwide economic collapse?

VI

If the hope that Christ will bring about his just kingdom is not to take the form of optimism concerning the potentials of one and another dynamic within creation, what form is it then to take? Let me begin my answer with what will, for a few minutes, seem like a diversion. On 15 June 1985, a large number of Christians in South Africa participated in a "Prayer Service for the End to Unjust Rule." It was of course to God that they addressed their prayer — not to the African National Congress, not to the South African government, not to anything at all other than God. The "Prayer of Petition" that they together uttered on that day went as follows:

This day O God of mercy
We bring before you all those
Who suffer in prison,
Who are oppressed,
Who mourn those who died in freedom struggles
    in places like Soweto, Cross Roads, Uitenhage,
    Sharpeville and many places not known to us.
Deliver us from the chains of apartheid, bring us all
    to the true liberty of the Sons and Daughters of God.
Confound the ruthless, and grant us the power of your kingdom.

In an open letter from prison issued on 23 March 2001, and addressed to Kader Asmal, the Minister of Education in the South African government, Allan Boesak wrote as follows about the place of prayer within the struggle to overturn apartheid:

> . . . prayer is not doctrinal formulations or the mumbling of magical formulas. Neither is it an escape from our earthly responsibilities. Rather it is a call to take up those responsibilities, not on our own, but in total dependence on the grace of God and in the power of God.
>
> Yes, for this very reason our prayers are sometimes political. They must be, because all the world is the Lord's, and there is no area of life, not a single inch, that is not subject to the lordship of Jesus Christ. So politics and politicians cannot consider themselves outside the demands of the gospel or outside the circle of prayer. We pray for politics, not because we feel so much at home there, in that world of intrigue and compromise, of betrayal and awesome responsibility, but because even there we must assume our positions as believers. Even there we must dare to name God, to confess God within the womb of politics, and so challenge every idolatry that seeks to displace God in the lives of God's people. And so we came together to pray for transformation, political and societal and economic; and we prayed for personal transformation, for conversion, so that people might be driven by inner conviction rather than by political expediency.
>
> We pray also because we believe passionately in the power of prayer. Prayer changes things, Christians say, and that is true. It is

that conviction, you will remember, that inspired us in 1985 to call for a day of prayer for the downfall of the apartheid regime. We prayed then in the midst of a storm too, and we were viciously condemned by all who felt themselves threatened by a God who listens to the prayers of the oppressed. We were vilified by those whose interests could not abide the changes we were praying for. But the thing is, God heard our prayers, things changed, and apartheid is no more.

And it is not as if this is something new. We have always believed this. God is a God of liberation and those deeds of liberation can be seen throughout history, beginning with the liberation of the people of Israel from slavery. And Christians have shared this faith with others in this country for so long as anyone can remember. My own participation in the struggle for liberation in this country was based on, and inspired by, my faith in Jesus Christ.

[Christians] come together to pray because they are deeply convinced that transformation that is only social, economic and political, however indispensable, is not enough. They believe that we need the power of God in our lives so that transformation can be fundamental. Let me be bold, Minister: South Africa would not be free today if there were not such people, and South Africa needs them today more than ever before. As you reflect on the history of South Africa as you did last Wednesday, please do not forget this. More than anything our struggle was sustained by prayer and faith. I know. I was there. Denying this historical truth will only exacerbate our already grave situation.

The occasion of Boesak's writing this letter was that two days before, on 21 March 2001, forty-five thousand Christians had gathered in the Newlands stadium in Cape Town to pray for peace, justice, and true reconciliation, while only about three hundred showed up for an ANC rally at which Kader Asmal was the main speaker. In a fit of pique, Asmal attacked the assembly of Christians as exclusivist.

I submit that Christian hope for liberating justice will take the form, among other things, of prayer. It will take the form of petitionary prayer: it will pray in hope for the undoing of injustice, not only for the undoing of injustice in general but for the undoing of particular injustices. It will have the courage to name injustices, and then to pray for the undoing of the injustices named. And if those named injustices are undone, Christian hope will then offer prayers of thanksgiving, not just for the undoing of injustice in general but for the undoing of the named injustices.

What this obviously presupposes is the courage to identify the hand of God in history. To name the injustices for whose undoing one thanks God in Christ is to identify the signs in history of Christ's liberating work.

In addition to taking the form of prayer, Christian hope for liberating justice takes the form of struggling for such justice. *Ora et labora* has always been the conviction of the Christian church. Not just praying and then, in addition, working — praying for one thing and working for another; rather, working for the very thing for which one prays. Which of course presupposes, once again, naming the injustice. One cannot struggle for the undoing of the injustice whose alleviation one has prayed for without naming it. The Christians of South Africa struggled for that for which they prayed; its name was, the overthrow of the apartheid regime.

You and I have been schooled to become extremely edgy when anyone proposes to identify the hand of God in history. And with good reason: some of the things that have been identified as the doings of that hand are appalling. We do not have any particular trouble naming some case of injustice and struggling for its elimination. But we become nervous when we name that same injustice in our prayers and pray to Christ that he will crown with success our efforts at alleviating that injustice. And we become *extremely* nervous when, upon the success of our endeavors, we thank Christ for the alleviation of that named injustice. For how else is this to be interpreted but as identifying the hand of Christ in history? To thank Christ for some named case of liberating justice presupposes, like it or not, identifying that as a sign of Christ's liberating work in history. And as I say, identifying Christ's work in history makes us nervous.

VII

Something more must be said on the matter of identifying Christ's work. But before I get to that, let me note that now that I have finally gotten around to speaking about you and me as struggling for justice, after thus far speaking only about God, I can hear someone saying that what you and I must practice is love, not justice. We must, admittedly, take account of all those biblical passages about your and my doing justice and struggling for justice, they say, but what takes priority is not that justice but what Jesus taught us: love your neighbor.

My response is that it all depends on what you mean by love. If by love and its synonyms — *caritas, agape,* and so forth — you mean active concern for the well-being of the neighbor, then I think it's false that we ought to prioritize love over justice. Here's why: sometimes one has to choose between trying to secure the well-being of the other, and wronging her; and though it may not always be the case that one should choose not to wrong her, often that will be how one should choose. History is littered with examples of Christians wronging others while loving them — loving them too much, as it were. For the sake of his or her moral or religious well-being the other was tortured. Love was given priority over justice. They were wronged for the sake of their well-being. That was wrong.

The fact that sometimes one has to choose between wronging the other and trying to secure his or her well-being has its counterpart in oneself: sometimes one has to choose between one's own moral excellence and one's well-being. It's a point Augustine already saw when, in his *City of God,* he observed that sometimes we are required to diminish our own happiness by sorrowing with the sorrowing.

VIII

To introduce the more that has to be said about Christian hope, let me refer to the quite extraordinary "Meditation on Inutility" that concludes Jacques Ellul's book on *The Politics of God and the Politics of Man.* Ellul raises what seems to me exactly the right question. "In spite of God's respect and love for man," he says,

> in spite of God's extreme humility in entering into man's projects in order that man may finally enter into his [God's] own design, in the long run one cannot but be seized by a profound sense of the inutility and vanity of human action. To what end is all this agita-

tion, to what end these constant wars and states and empires, to what end the great march of the people of Israel, to what end the trivial daily round of the church, when in the long run the goal will inevitably be attained, when it is always ultimately God's will that is done, when the most basic thing of all is already achieved and already attained in Jesus Christ? One can understand the scandalized refusal of modern man who can neither accept the inutility of what he has done nor acquiesce in the overruling of his destiny.[4]

Ellul's point is clear. Christian hope for liberating justice is not an optimism grounded in the potentials of creation but hope grounded in the promise that Christ will bring about his just and holy kingdom. That hope is to take the form, in part, of our participation in Christ's cause by ourselves working for liberating justice. But then we learn that God moves in mysterious ways, sometimes bringing our best efforts to naught, sometimes wresting liberation out of appalling evil. So what's the point, if we who faithfully seek justice are overruled while justice is wrested from the efforts of those who seek wrong? What's the point of working in someone's cause when he will bring about that cause in whatever way he pleases? Is it not all futile?

Ellul's response — not so much an answer, I would say, as a response — is, "Just obey." No matter what, obey.

There is a divine law, which is a commandment, and which is addressed to us. Hence we have to fulfill it to the letter. We have to do all that is commanded. The sense or conviction of the utter futility of the work we do must not prevent us from doing it. The judgment of uselessness is no excuse for inaction. . . . Pronounced in advance, futility becomes justification of scorn of God and his word and work. It is after doing what is commanded, when everything has been done in the sphere of human decisions and means, when in terms of the relation to God every effort has been made to know the will of God and to obey it, when in the arena of life there has been full acceptance of all responsibilities and interpretations and commitments and conflicts, it is then and only then that the judg-

---

4. Jacques Ellul, *The Politics of God and the Politics of Man,* trans. Geoffrey W. Bromiley (Grand Rapids: Eerdmans, 1972), p. 190.

ment takes on meaning: all this (that we had to do) is useless; all this we cast from us to put it in thy hands, O Lord; all this belongs no more to the human order but to the order of thy kingdom. Thou mayest use this or that work to build up the kingdom thou art preparing. In thy liberty thou mayest make as barren as the fig-tree any of the works which we have undertaken to thy glory. This is no longer our concern. It is no longer in our hands. What belonged to our sphere we have done. Now, O Lord, we may set it aside, having done all that was commanded.[5]

There is something profoundly right about this. Christian hope for liberating justice takes the form of working for such justice in the confidence that, in ways mysterious to us, Christ will make use of what we have done along with that which others have done, good and bad, for the coming of the rule of justice in his kingdom. What I find missing in Ellul, however, is the willingness to identify the signs of Christ's redemptive work. We do our work and then we say, "Make of it what you will, O Lord." That implies that our prayers of petition and of thanksgiving for Christ's redemptive work of righting the wrongs of the world must always remain general; they can never name a particular injustice that we petition Christ to remove; they can never name a particular injustice for which we give thanks to Christ that it has been removed. To discern whether this refusal to identify the signs is acceptable, I think we must look at what Christians who cried to God for deliverance felt compelled to do. The black South African Christians found themselves compelled to name the injustice that they petitioned God to remove, and compelled to name the righting of injustice that they thanked God for bringing about. To do that last, is to identify the signs of Christ's redemptive action.

The solution is not to refrain from identifying the signs of Christ's redemptive rule but to resist the arrogance of supposing that our identifications are indubitably correct and complete. Sometimes we miss the signs; sometimes what we took to be a sign proves not to be that. Likewise we must resist the arrogance of supposing that the signs of Christ's redemptive action coincide with the goals of our successful endeavors. Sometimes what we achieved proves, to our deep disap-

5. Ellul, *Politics of God,* pp. 195-96.

pointment, not to be very liberating at all; sometimes what seemed to us a failure proves to be surprisingly liberating. Christian hope for liberating justice is confident as to its ground in Christ, while at the same time it is humble as to our ability to discern the ways in which our endeavors contribute to the coming of Christ's rule of justice.

IX

A good many of Rembrandt's paintings were initially painted by apprentices in his workshop, Rembrandt then applying the finishing touches. Sometimes what a gifted apprentice handed over to the master was already so much like a Rembrandt that little remained for the master to do; on other occasions, though the preliminary painting came from the hand of the same gifted apprentice, and was again very close to being a Rembrandt, it nonetheless fell short in such a way that the master had to do a lot of repainting in order to bring it up to his standards. On other occasions, the apprentice was so incompetent that Rembrandt had to do a major re-painting in order to make it a Rembrandt; on a few occasions, though the apprentice was again very incompetent, he nonetheless somehow produced a painting that required only a bit of tweaking by the master to bring it up to standard.

The apprentices hoped that they would produce paintings that would require very little re-painting by the master; some even dared hope that someday the master would say, "It's right just as it is." Nonetheless, the master so regularly surprised the apprentices with what he did with their productions that they became quite tentative in their expectations as to what he would do. Though they did not entirely give up expectations, by and large they just stood back and expected once again to be surprised. And they became rather good at recognizing when the master had completed a painting and when it still needed his touch. The ability to recognize when a painting was a true Rembrandt was of course important for them; how else could they aim at producing such paintings?

Some of the apprentices, observing that sometimes a quite bad production on their part required just a bit of tweaking, while at other times a rather good production required massive repainting, asked Rembrandt about the point of their work: what's the point of our undergoing all this training and producing all these paintings if our best productions sometimes require a lot of reworking by you and our worst, sometimes almost none?

Rembrandt would have none of this. Do your best to paint a Rembrandt, he insisted. I've been at this a long time; trust me. I would much rather have you try your best than have you just slack off. What you do is important for my work. Trust me, it is.

The Crossing of Hope, or Apophatic Eschatology

KEVIN L. HUGHES

Let human voices be silent; let human thoughts repose. To things in-comprehensible they stretch out, not as if to comprehend them, but only to share in them. And share in them we shall.

St. Augustine of Hippo[1]

In other words, it depends on us
To make sure that hope does not deceive the world.

Charles Péguy[2]

---

1. Augustine, *Enarratio in Ps. 146*, 11, in *Patrologia Latina*, vol. 37, ed. Jacques-Paul Migne (Paris: Petit-Montrouge, 1844-55).
2. Charles Péguy, *The Portal of the Mystery of Hope*, trans. David Schindler (Grand Rapids: Eerdmans, 1996), p. 66.

This essay is the fruit of the constructive conversations I have shared with the participants in Calvin College's 2000 Seminar in Christian Scholarship, "Modernity, Postmodernity, and the Future of Hope," led by Miroslav Volf and funded by the Pew Charitable Trusts, and with those who attended the conference by the same title at Calvin the following Spring. While my topic was somewhat controversial in the group (or perhaps because of this), I benefited greatly from the comments of my seminar colleagues, and I offer them my thanks. Thanks, too, to two anonymous readers and to my friends and Villanova colleagues Anthony Godzieba, Martin Laird, and William Werpehowski for helpful comments along the way. My title and the wordplay on "crossing" it implies is a tip of the hat to Jean Luc Marion, *God without Being*, trans. Thomas A. Carlson (Chicago: University of

One striking element of the turning of the millennium and the recent World Trade Center tragedy is the way in which the language of Christian eschatology is never far from the discussion. The Y2K worries and fabricated Nostradamus predictions of the events of September 11 that circulated worldwide on e-mail testify to the degree to which the language and symbols of the "End of the World" still capture the Western imagination. And this is fitting, in a sense. Eschatology, or the theological understanding of the end of the world, is traditionally a way in which Christians have come to terms with history, both in its terrors and in its transformative possibilities, and thus it should be no surprise that Christians continue to interpret historical events in these terms today. If this is true of the "person in the pew," it is true as well for theologians. In fact, much fruitful theological work in the twentieth century has made use of eschatology to speak precisely about the social, political, and historical import of Christian faith,[3] largely in response to the historical disaster of the Shoah. We continue to live, and live fruitfully, in the "shadow of the second coming."

And yet, the destruction of the Branch Davidian cult in Waco, Texas, in 1993, the Heaven's Gate cult suicide, and perhaps even the eschatological motivation of extremist terrorists like the "martyrs" of September 11 testify as well to the dangers of eschatological thinking. A certain perverse kind of hope for an end that is all too determined can give permission for acts of violence, against oneself or against others or both. So, when, as Christians, we are called upon to "give an account of the hope that is in us" (cf. 1 Peter 3:15), we are, and should be, a bit reticent. We know how dangerous hope can be.[4] Yet hope we must.

---

3. The most significant of these in the twentieth century are Jürgen Moltmann, *A Theology of Hope* (London: SCM, 1967), and *The Coming of God: Christian Eschatology* (Minneapolis: Fortress, 1996); Johann Baptist Metz, *Faith in History and Society: Toward a Practical Fundamental Theology* (New York: Seabury, 1980); and Wolfhart Pannenberg, *Theology and the Kingdom of God* (Philadelphia: Fortress, 1969). All of these authors have spoken of the place of Auschwitz in their thinking.

4. On this political point of caution, I have learned from Nicholas Lash, "The Church's Responsibility for the Future of Humanity," in *Theology on the Way to Emmaus* (London: SCM, 1986), pp. 186-201.

Chicago Press, 1991), chap. 3, "The Crossing of Being," and passim. Unless otherwise noted, biblical quotations in this essay are taken from the New American Bible.

In the light of such dangers, the challenge of Christian hope remains that of opening oneself to a hope that is not wish fulfillment or thinly veiled ideology. In other words, Christian eschatology must strive for a disciplined hope. But how can one say neither too little (and risk despair) nor too much (and risk an overdetermined ideology)? My argument is that such discipline is available to eschatology from a related field of study, mystical theology, and more specifically, from what is called the *apophatic* tradition. *Apophasis,* literally the "flight from speech," is "the name of that theology which is done against the background of human ignorance of the nature of God."[5] Often called "negative theology," it is theology that struggles to remain aware of what we do not and cannot know or say about God and the mysteries of faith. It is the disciplined speech of "unknowing" and "learned ignorance" before the mysterious presence of God. By making use of apophatic methods of disciplined speech, eschatology may learn to speak of hope without overdetermination, to navigate between the presumption of claiming to know too much and the emptiness of knowing nothing at all. An apophatic eschatology seeks to preserve the "learned ignorance" that follows from the fact that our hope is not fundamentally in any particular social or political arrangement, but in the infinite mystery of God.

The Future of Hope: Some Current Strategies

Deconstructive Hope without Hope

The dangerous face of eschatology has led some postmodern philosophers to worry that *any concrete hope* contains the threat of violence. In the words of John Caputo, "For determinable faiths — as the history of all the fundamentalisms, Jewish, Islamic, and Christian, instruct[s] us — are uncommonly dangerous to everybody's health, that of their own members as of everyone else, a threat to everyone's safety. . . ." Caputo asserts that it is the act of determination itself that sows the seeds of violence. The deconstructive alternative is "religion without religion," "faith without faith," and hope in "what is not and never will be pres-

---

5. Denys Turner, *The Darkness of God: Negativity in Christian Mysticism* (Cambridge: Cambridge University Press, 1995), p. 19.

ent, what is structurally to come (à venir)."[6] For Caputo (reading Derrida), hope can only be a limit concept, the projecting of our desires upon something that will never, ever come. "[The] very idea of the Messiah would be destroyed were the Messiah, to everyone's embarrassment and consternation, to have the indiscretion to show up and actually become present."[7] Such a strategy may succeed in removing the violent consequences of certain fundamentalist accounts of hope, but it also seems to erase hope itself altogether.[8] One is left crying endlessly *"Viens, oui, oui" to* one knows not what *for* one knows not what. One is called to hope in nothing at all.

Theological Hope: To Speak or Not to Speak?

The trials of the recent past have made this sort of "hope without hope" politically salutary, and one could argue that it is theologically healthy as well. One might argue that if we attempt to capture our hope too concretely in formulas and images, we risk theological *hubris,* claiming to know more than we can and to comprehend the incomprehensible mystery that lies at the center of existence and the end of history. If we believe that the world to come will be where we see God "face to face" and where God will be "all in all" (1 Cor. 13:12; 15:28), then the object of our hope is the fullness of the presence of God and is thus, finally, ineffable. For who can conceive of the infinite abundance and the immediate presence of the living God? What we see now is "as in a glass, darkly." At St. Paul's own admission, we do not know what we shall be. Flesh and blood cannot inherit the kingdom of God. To describe too clearly the order and nature of the world to come is, as one friend of mine has said, to try to glean from the brown, papery tulip bulb what the brilliant tulip will be. Much recent theology has been at-

6. John D. Caputo, *The Prayers and Tears of Jacques Derrida: Religion without Religion* (Bloomington: Indiana University Press, 1997), p. 73.

7. Caputo, *Prayers and Tears of Jacques Derrida,* p. 78.

8. James K. A. Smith's essay in the present volume, "Determined Hope: A Phenomenology of Christian Expectation," points to the necessity of an intentional object in anything we might call "hope." I cannot "hope" without hoping "in" or "for" something. The burden of this essay will be to show that an apophatic hope still meets this criterion while protecting eschatology from idolatry or illusion.

tracted to the negative, swept up in the "apophatic rage." But if the apophatic tradition is understood as wholly "negative," one wonders if the hunger to negate leaves anything left over for faith.[9]

That is, if we carry this theological reticence to its apparent conclusion, then it seems that we empty our hope of any substance, any concrete stuff, and we are left with a deconstructive "hope without hope" in a theological key. For example, one senses a sort of emptiness in theologian Nicholas Lash's "nescience" (or "knowing nothing") of hope, whereby he asserts that "the Church alone knows that we know absolutely nothing about our absolute or ultimate future except that we *have* a future in the mystery that we call God."[10] If we know only that, if we must only fall silent at any suggestion of what the character of that future will be, it is not clear that we can succeed in following 1 Peter's exhortation to "give an account of the hope that is in us." As Jean-Luc Marion says, "Silence, precisely because it does not explain itself, exposes itself to an infinite equivocation of meaning."[11] Our silence of awe at the ineffable God too easily can be taken for the silence of the void, of the fact that there's simply no "there" there to hope in. So we must speak, however chastened, halting, and "unknowing" this speech will be. And one wonders if "having *a* future," whatever that future may be like, is enough to sustain true hope.

Our challenge, then, is to learn to speak of hope *for God's reign* without slipping into the idolatrous claim that *God's reign is our reign.* Christian hope in God is hope *for us* and *for our life in God,* so we cannot be satisfied with Caputo's hope in "what never will be present." But neither can we accept an account of the eschaton that speaks too easily or too clearly of the heavenly "ineffable things, which no one may utter" (2 Cor. 12:4). The challenge of eschatology is to articulate a hope that is neither presumptuous nor empty.[12]

---

9. On the relationship between this "negativity" and the fullness of the apophatic tradition, see Martin Laird, "Gregory of Nyssa and the Mysticism of Darkness: A Reconsideration," *Journal of Religion* 79 (October 1999): 592-616.

10. Lash, *Theology on the Way to Emmaus,* p. 194.

11. Jean-Luc Marion, *God without Being,* trans. Thomas A. Carlson (Chicago: University of Chicago Press, 1991), p. 54.

12. One attempt to meet the challenge is found in Paul Griffiths, "Nirvana as the Last Thing?" *Modern Theology* 16 (January 2000): 19-38. For Griffiths, any narrative construction of "final eschatology" is analytically mistaken and theologically idolatrous. Grif-

One recent salutary effort is found in a book by Richard Bauckham and Trevor Hart. Bauckham and Hart explore the role of the imagination, the fantastic, and the image in eschatology. They acknowledge both sides of our dilemma, and their reading of the Book of Revelation shows how images both reveal and obscure the heavenly realities they portray. The One seated on the throne in Revelation is not depicted but is known only as the source of glory. Even the images of the beasts in the heavenly court seem to defy depiction through the very abundance of their description — four faces, eyes all around, and so on. Other examples from the New Testament abound. Yet a certain risk remains in employing the theological imagination in such a fashion. While the flourishing use of the human imagination is an asset to theological thinking in general, and to eschatology in particular (consider, for example, the rich, deep resource of Dante's *Divine Comedy*), one must ask what controls or disciplines this imagination? How does one use the imagination in a disciplined, critical theology? If we are to take up the challenge of disciplined hope, we must reach beyond the faculties of the imagination, and perhaps beyond images. Such a move brings us into the realm of mystical theology.

The Apophatic Dimension of Eschatology: Paul, Augustine, Gregory of Nyssa

Mystical Theology in Brief

Mystical theology is the field of formal Christian theological reflection that concerns the preparation for, the consciousness of, and the reaction to what can be described as the immediate or direct presence of God.[13] It

---

fiths proposes an analytic solution of asserting logically contrary propositions. But it is difficult to imagine that this inspires any hope in the believer. So while the suggestion makes sense formally, I'm not sure it offers sufficient promise as a theological practice.

13. This is my adaptation of Bernard McGinn's definition of *mysticism* in *The Foundations of Christian Mysticism: Origins to the Fifth Century*, vol. I of *The Presence of God: A History of Western Christian Mysticism* (New York: Crossroad, 1991), p. xvii. My adaptation is only in making the definition specific to theological reflection and thus removing it from the all-encompassing "-ism." This definition has been much discussed since the work was published, but McGinn has stuck with it in the more recent volumes.

is a tradition that goes back at least to the second century with Origen, but its roots can be found in the New Testament. Paul's journey to the "third heaven" where he was "caught up into Paradise and heard ineffable things, which no one may utter" (2 Cor. 12:2-4) and John's visionary journey into heaven as he is "caught up in [the] spirit" (Rev. 4:1ff) are emblematic instances in the canon of the "consciousness of the immediate presence of God." Origen, Augustine, and the Cappadocian Fathers, among others, applied the interpretive schema of Platonic and Neoplatonic thought to make sense of just such an experience of the God whose immanence is guaranteed by his transcendence.[14] The conviction of these fathers of the church was that an encounter with the living God was not reserved only for Paul or John but was open to anyone. In fact, one might argue that such a sense of "encounter" is properly speaking an element essential to all Christian life. "The mystical life, at its source, is nothing other than the Christian life,"[15] said Marie-Dominique Chenu, to which Nicholas Lash adds the following: "If . . . the 'mystical element' in Christianity is a matter of preparing for, becoming conscious of and reacting to, the ever deeper sense and recognition of God's presence, then it is — in vastly varying degrees of actualization — an element in *every* Christian life."[16] The tradition of mystical theology, then, is not the search for "special revelations" or esoteric ecstasies, but is properly that part of theology specifically devoted to developing one's "senses" for the recognition of the presence of the living God.[17]

---

14. This apparent paradox is such only if "transcendence" is spatialized and made into an "otherworldly" place of "heaven." But if God were limited to inhabiting a "transcendent" place "up there," then he would not, in fact, be *transcendent* at all. This "spatialization of knowledge" has been described as a peculiarly modern phenomenon, but it is one that Augustine struggled with in his early years as well (cf. *Confessions*, bk. VII). God's transcendence is precisely the possibility of his being *everywhere* without being *everything* (pantheism). See Thomas Weinandy, *Does God Suffer?* (Notre Dame, Ind.: University of Notre Dame Press, 2000), and Kathryn Tanner, *God and Creation in Christian Theology: Tyranny or Empowerment?* (New York: Blackwell, 1988).

15. M.-D. Chenu, O.P., "Une théologie de la vie mystique," *La vie spirituelle* 50 (1937): 49.

16. Nicholas Lash, *The Beginning and the End of 'Religion'* (Cambridge: Cambridge University Press, 1996), p. 171.

17. Of course, many mystical writings describe ecstasies and revelations. See, e.g., *The Book of Margery Kempe* and Angela of Foligno, *Memorial,* in the *Collected Works,* ed. Paul LaChance (Mahwah: Paulist, 1993). But the mystical doctors of the Catholic church

The classical example of how this is done in mystical theology is in the writings of the one we know only as Pseudo-Denys[18] the Areopagite, a sixth-century Christian whose real identity has been lost in the historical record. Denys and the tradition that follows from him are devoted to working out the logic of Christian speech about the ineffable God. Mystical theology is thus "the name of that theology which is done against the background of human ignorance of the nature of God."[19] Denys's apophatic theology, as a particular kind of mystical theology, offers a method or form of speech that aims to navigate between presumption and nothingness.

Denys's theology is not simply intended to affirm one's ignorance, however. He does not merely acknowledge (as if after the fact) the inadequacy of our concepts and constructions in speaking of God, as if struck with a fit of philosophical scruples. His purpose is far more practical than that: he intends to speak of the way in which the soul, and all creation, is led to return to God. Early in his *Mystical Theology,* Denys describes his task:

> In my earlier books my argument traveled downward from the most exalted to the humblest categories. . . . But my argument now rises from what is below up to the transcendent, and the more it climbs, the more language falters, and when it has passed up and beyond the ascent, it will turn silent completely, since it will finally be at one with him who is indescribable.[20]

(e.g. Bonaventure, Teresa of Avila, John of the Cross) and classical mystic texts (*The Cloud of Unknowing,* the writings of Meister Eckhart) are profoundly critical of such "experiences" of God. On this point, see Turner, *The Darkness of God.*

18. Or "Pseudo-Dionysius." For the sake of convenience, I will refer to the author as "Denys," following Turner, *The Darkness of God,* and Andrew Louth's introduction to *Denys the Areopagite* (London: Geoffrey Chapman, 1989). The texts are available in English translation in *Pseudo-Dionysius: The Complete Works,* trans. and ed. Colm Luibheid and Paul Rorem (Mahwah: Paulist, 1987). For a helpful beginner's introduction, see Paul Rorem, "The Uplifting Spirituality of Pseudo-Dionysius," in *Christian Spirituality I: Origins to the Twelfth Century,* ed. Bernard McGinn and John Meyendorff (New York: Crossroad, 1987), pp. 132-51.

19. Turner, *The Darkness of God,* p. 19.

20. *Mystical Theology* 3, translation from Luibheid and Rorem's *Pseudo-Dionysius,* p. 139.

So the "unknowing" of mystical theology is the result of the approach to God in contemplation and, for Denys, in liturgy. In the ever-deepening encounter with the living God, language fails. This much is a truism of Christian theology — the finite struggles to define the infinite and cannot. But Denys's apophatic method strains to articulate his theology in such a way that this principle of humility inheres in the structure of the language itself. In a sense, mystical texts like those of Denys echo the journey of the soul from confident claims about what it can understand to struggling to speak of the awesome presence of God, in which it can only participate (as Augustine's quote, at the head of the essay, suggests).

Critics such as Eberhard Jüngel have suggested that so wholly negative a theological project does not attend sufficiently to our confession of faith in the Word of God. God is not silence, but Word, and this means that *negative theology* is a method that does not quite fit the revelation of God in Christ.[21] But it would be premature to describe Denys's theological project as simply negative. For Denys, a negation is still a claim about what is — it still claims to have enough of a grasp upon a reality to say, "that's not it." Thus, even negations must be overcome and surpassed, as the following sequence of predicates indicates: *God is knowable; God is unknowable; God is neither knowable nor unknowable; God is more than knowable or unknowable.* For Denys, all of these statements are true, but none is sufficient. The first is true metaphorically; the second is true anagogically — as a truth which leads to union with God; and the third is what Denys Turner calls "second-order apophatic," and is true in the sense that Pseudo-Denys calls "unitive." The last sense breaks down grammatically — how can something be more than a negation? — and, as such, it uses language to propel the soul beyond language. Like a catapult, language is used to set the soul

---

21. Eberhard Jüngel, *God as the Mystery of the World* (Grand Rapids: Eerdmans, 1983), pp. 250-61. A response to Jüngel is found in Michel Corbin, "Négation et transcendance dans l'oeuvre de Denys," *Revue des sciences philosophiques et théologiques* 69 (1985): 41-76. Jüngel's critique risks overlooking the distinction made by John the Solitary: "How long shall I be in the world of the voice and not in the world of the Word?" (cf. Sebastian Brock, "John the Solitary, *On Prayer*," *Journal of Theological Studies* n.s. 30 [1979]: 84-101). The Word of God cannot be identified with the words of theological discourse, and theological language can be an obstacle. Apophatic theology is a discipline of words that prepares and opens one to the Word.

upon a trajectory — the ascent to God — but then cannot proceed itself. Language is left behind. Apophasis does, in fact, point *toward* something; it does not leave one in a void.[22] This is, after all, why deconstructionists like Derrida and Caputo finally reject this mode of discourse after a long courtship — it actually intends toward that of which it cannot speak.[23] The "unsaying" of apophatic theology is not "saying nothing," since that would only *positively* signify absence. It is not an articulation of the absence of God, but an unsaying of the concepts of "presence" and "absence," rooted in the superabundance of God's presence intimately encountered.[24]

Denys's method of dialectical negation offers the clearest and best insight into the logic of apophasis, but it is not the only apophatic style in the tradition. Julian of Norwich's theology tends toward the same apophatic goal through an overabundance of images, deploying what Vincent Gillespie and Maggie Ross call an "apophatic image." For them, the mystical writer "must seek to create what [Roland] Barthes called an 'orgasmic text' which 'dislocates' the reader's historical, cultural, and psychological assumptions, the consistency of his tastes, values, and memories, and brings to a crisis his relation to language." Julian's showings overflow with images, from the graphic images of the suffering Christ to the coincidence of masculine and feminine in speaking of Jesus as mother, to the rich deployment of parable. But all of these center upon the pre-eminent Christian apophatic image, the Crucified, "a sign of contradiction, allowing the creative tension between its conflicting significations to generate a precious stillness, a chink in the defensive wall of reason that allows slippage into apophatic consciousness."[25]

22. Cf. Jean-Luc Marion, "In the Name: How to Avoid Speaking of 'Negative Theology,'" in *God, the Gift, and Postmodernism,* ed. John D. Caputo and Michael J. Scanlon (Bloomington: Indiana University Press, 1999), pp. 20-53; Martin Laird, "'Whereof We Speak': Gregory of Nyssa, Jean-Luc Marion, and the Current Apophatic Rage," *Heythrop Journal* 42 (January 2001): 1-12.

23. Caputo, *Prayers and Tears,* chap. 1.

24. On the distinction between "signifying absence" and apophatic unsaying, see Denys Turner, "The Darkness of God and the Light of Christ: Negative Theology and Eucharistic Presence," *Modern Theology* 15 (April 1999): 143-58.

25. Vincent Gillespie and Maggie Ross, "The Apophatic Image: The Politics of Effacement in Julian of Norwich," in *The Medieval Mystical Tradition in England,* Exeter Symposium V, ed. Marian Glasscoe (Cambridge: D. S. Brewer, 1992), p. 57.

Mystical theology, whether through Denys's tripartite logic of affirmation, negation, and negation-of-negation or through the superabundant and paradoxical images of Julian, aims to speak of the encounter with the living God which lies at the heart of Christian life. It demands, as Michael Sells says, "a rigorous and sustained effort both to use and free oneself from normal habits of thought and expression."[26] Knowing that God is no thing to be comprehended, it pushes speech and concept to the breaking point, the point beyond which the ineffable God is encountered intimately.

Sells, Gillespie, and Ross employ these terms in the context of mystical theology, not eschatology. But I suggest that there are deep connections, both historical and theological, between the two disciplines, and that the one might learn fruitfully from the other. Historically, the roots of eschatology and mystical theology drink from the same streams in the apocalyptic visions of Second Temple Judaism.[27] Later, the medieval tradition unites both of these categories under the "anagogical" sense of Scripture, that which speaks of "for what we are intended" or "where we are headed."[28] The combination is not accidental; rather, it manifests a certain logical connection. For St. Bonaventure, for example, the soul is the microcosm to the world's macrocosm — both are engaged upon the journey into God.[29] His vi-

---

26. Michael Sells, *Mystical Languages of Unsaying* (Chicago: University of Chicago Press, 1993), p. 217.

27. See Jonathan Z. Smith, *Map Is Not Territory* (Chicago: University of Chicago Press, 1993), chap. 3. Bernard McGinn has also made this argument in "Apocalypticism and Mysticism: Aspects of the History of Their Interpretation," *Zeitsprünge: Forschungen zur Frühen Neuzeit* 3 (1999): 292-315.

28. I refer here to the famous Latin distich on the four senses of Scripture: *littera gesta docet, quod credas allegoria/moralia quod fecit, quo tendas anagogia.* The anagogical sense of Scripture was in no way univocal in the history of exegesis, but such a joining of mystical and eschatological union can be found in Bonaventure, *Collations on the Six Days,* and there are other such examples pointed out by Henri de Lubac in *Exégèse Mediévale: les quatre sens d'écriture,* 4 vols. (Paris, 1963-67), especially pt. 1, chap. 10, "Anagogy and Eschatology." See also his *Theological Fragments* (San Francisco: Ignatius, 1989). See also my "Henri de Lubac, the 'Fourfold Sense,' and Contemporary Scholarship," *The Heythrop Journal* 42 (October 2001): 451-62.

29. "For the contemplative Church and the soul do not differ, except that the soul has within itself that which the Church has within many" (Bonaventure, *Collations on the Six Days* 23.4, *Opera Omnia* V [Quarrachi: Collegium S. Bonaventurae, 1882-1902], p. 445). Bonaventure also describes the ascent of the soul into God as a sort of death: "Let us

sion of history ends in mystical union, and his notion of mystical union in this life is as a foretaste of the eschaton. As Henri de Lubac says, "the doctrinal and spiritual exegesis practiced by the great Christian tradition could be defined neither by the establishment of a simple 'historical progression' nor by a pure 'vertical symbolism.' . . . The joys of the eternal realm are, as Saint Gregory says, 'the secret joys of the interior life.'"[30] The testimony of the mystical tradition shows that the experience of God's presence in contemplation is the foretaste of the fullness of God's presence in the eschaton. Mystical theology and eschatology are thus united in the ineffable presence to which they point. While the two remain distinct elements of theological reflection, it is a distinction between taste and fulfillment or metonymy and full presence. As such, each is an important corrective to the other. For our purposes, mystical theology provides the resources for disciplining our images of the kingdom of God, for retrieving a disciplined hope.

Eschatology and Mystical Theology: The "Twin Sisters"[31]

Eschatology is the branch of theology that seeks to recognize and describe the presence of the living God as promise, as the future fullness of the soul's life in God, and as the New Jerusalem "where God will be all in all." It is constituted as a field precisely in its speculation about the future fullness of God's presence (or "final eschatology"), the path to that fullness ("transitional eschatology"), and the difference all of this makes to the world. Put in mystical terms, eschatology concerns

---

then die and enter into this darkness. Let us silence all our cares, our desires, and our imaginings" (*Journey of the Mind into God* 7.5, in *Opera Theologica Selecta* [Quarrachi: Collegium S. Bonaventurae, 1964], p. 213). I am citing from the English translation of the *Journey* by Philotheus Boehner, O.F.M, in the *Works of St. Bonaventure*, vol. 1 (St. Bonaventure: Franciscan Institute, 1956), unless otherwise noted.

30. Henri de Lubac, *Medieval Exegesis*, vol. 2, trans. E. M. Macierowski (Grand Rapids: Eerdmans, 2000), pp. 186-87.

31. This essay was completed prior to my reading of Rowan A. Greer, *Christian Hope and Christian Life: Raids on the Inarticulate* (New York: Crossroad, 2001). Although the Reverend Greer's focus is somewhat different from my own, I am delighted and grateful to see similar insights into the three figures I discuss below in his discussion of the relationship between the "there and then" and the "here and now."

the world's preparation for (transitional eschatology), consciousness of (final eschatology), and reaction to ("the difference it makes") the immediate presence of God. What is proleptically *present* to the mystic, and expressed rhetorically in mystical traditions, is *anticipated* in eschatology, and expressed in images of the fullness of the kingdom of God that is yet to come. In other words, the productive tension between mystical theology and eschatology is none other than the tension between presence and anticipation, between the "already" and the "not yet," that inheres in the parables of Jesus and the preaching of St. Paul.[32]

St. Paul

Thus, when St. Paul, who according to apophatic tradition "knew God in unknowing,"[33] struggles to articulate his eschatological teachings, concepts seem to fail and language breaks open in a fashion that anticipates the great mystical theologians, such as Denys and Bonaventure. Though he lacks a self-conscious apophatic method, Paul already struggles to "say and unsay" the truth of the resurrection and the kingdom of God.

In 1 Corinthians 13, Paul caps his discussion of spiritual gifts with the famous "love chapter." Here Paul mounts both a moral and an eschatological critique of the spiritual gifts he has discussed in chapter 12. The moral dimension is perhaps most familiar: "If I speak in human and angelic tongues but do not have love, I am a resounding gong or a clashing cymbal" (1 Cor. 13:1). The eschatological critique follows from it:

32. For the classic statement of the "already" and "not yet" in the parables of Jesus, see Oscar Cullmann, *Christ in Time: The Primitive Christian Conception of Time and History* (Philadelphia: Westminster, 1964), and Norman Perrin, *The Kingdom of God in the Teaching of Jesus* (Philadelphia: Westminster, 1963). For discussion of this theme in Paul and ancient and medieval theology, see Kevin L. Hughes, "The Apostle and the Adversary: Paul and Antichrist in Early Medieval Exegesis," Ph.D. diss., University of Chicago, 1997; and Kevin L. Hughes, "Eschatological Union: The Mystical Dimension of History in Joachim of Fiore, Bonaventure, and Peter Olivi," *Collectanea Franciscana* 72, nos. 3-4 (2002): 105-43.

33. Denys the Areopagite, *Letter 5,* in *Pseudo-Dionysius,* ed. Luibheid and Rorem.

> Love never fails. If there are prophecies, they will be brought to nothing . . . if knowledge, it will be brought to nothing. For we know partially and we prophesy partially, but when the perfect comes, the partial will pass away. . . . At present we see indistinctly, as in a mirror, but then face to face. At present I know partially; then I shall know fully, as I am fully known. (1 Cor. 13:8-10, 12)

Paul's celebration of love becomes in verse 8 a critique of knowledge and prophecy. Whatever spiritual gifts we may have in this life cannot be anything more than "partial." And such partial knowledge will not be completed by the perfect, but will pass away when the perfect comes. Paul signals his inability to describe the eschatological reality with concepts or visions. He can only point toward it with images that suggest transparency and fullness. The chapter thus supplies the beginnings of a negative hermeneutic: knowledge and prophecy are inevitably partial and thus inadequate to the description of the fullness and immanent presence ("Then I shall know even as I am known") of God's reign. While Paul's emphasis on the potential fulfillment of knowledge in the eschaton keeps his discussion from being fully apophatic in the technical sense, 1 Corinthians 13 speaks *toward* the ineffable intimacy of divine presence.

In 1 Corinthians 15, Paul displays an apophatic inclination in his discussion of the resurrected body. Faced with opponents who deny the resurrection of the dead, Paul quickly defends its centrality to any faith in Christ. "For if the dead are not raised, neither has Christ been raised, and if Christ has not been raised, your faith is in vain; you are still in your sins" (1 Cor. 15:16-17). But immediately after this affirmation, Paul turns to address what the nature of the resurrected body will be, and here, he practices a sort of negation: "what you sow is not the body that is to be but a bare kernel of wheat, perhaps, or of some other kind" (v. 37). This seed is transformed in death. "It is sown corruptible; it is raised incorruptible. It is sown dishonorable; it is raised glorious. . . . It is sown a natural body; it is raised a spiritual body" (vv. 42-44). Scholars have argued over the meaning of Paul's phrase "spiritual body," contending variously that he means "psychosomatic unity,"[34]

---

34. Oscar Cullmann, *Unsterblichkeit der Seele oder Auferstehung der Toten?* (Stuttgart: Kreuz, 1964).

"the self,"[35] a "disembodied person,"[36] or even a "community."[37] But this wrangling over definitions misses the heart of Paul's argument. Paul deliberately constructs a paradox with "spiritual body," using terms which are conventionally opposed to break open convention and point beyond conceptual knowledge. This apophatic strategy becomes clear in the verses that follow: "For that which is corruptible must clothe itself with incorruptibility, and that which is mortal must clothe itself with immortality" (1 Cor. 15:53). Almost anticipating later mystical theology's affirmation, negation, and transcendence of opposites, Paul posits the resurrection body as corruptible incorruptibility and mortal immortality. Both eschatological continuity and change are affirmed, but only in apophatic paradox.

St. Augustine

The passage from Augustine with which I began the essay makes this apophatic dimension of eschatology more explicit. In his sermon on Psalm 146 (Vulg.), Augustine ponders verse 5: "Great is our Lord, and great is his power. His wisdom cannot be numbered."[38] This last phrase, he says, expresses the ineffability of God, who himself is the source and author of "number." He cannot be measured by a measure less than himself; thus, reason falls silent: "Let human voices be silent; let human thoughts repose. To things incomprehensible they stretch out, not as if to comprehend them, but only to share in them. And share in them we shall."[39] The mind "stretches out" beyond the limits of its own reason, not to understand, but to "share in" the ineffable presence of God. Thus far, Augustine has given a fair statement of the

---

35. John Perry, *A Dialogue on Personal Identity and Immortality* (Indianapolis: Hackett, 1978).

36. Paul Gooch, *Partial Knowledge: Philosophical Studies in Paul* (Notre Dame, Ind.: University of Notre Dame Press, 1987).

37. James A. T. Robinson, *The Body: A Study in Pauline Theology* (London: SCM, 1952).

38. Ps. 145:3 (Revised Standard Version).

39. "*Conticescant humanae voces, requiescant humanae cogitationes; ad incomprehensibilia non se extendant quasi comprehensuri, sed tamquam participaturi; participes enim erimus*" (*Enarratio in Ps. 146*, 11, in *Patrologia Latina* 37:1906).

apophatic ascent to God. But then he concludes in an eschatological key, with the promise of fulfillment: "Share in them we shall." Augustine's thought flows seamlessly from the mystical to the eschatological – from "learned ignorance" to hope. The "share" of the presence of God to which the mind stretches in the present is a foretaste, the proleptic presence, of the "share" that is the object of our hope, "when God will be all in all."[40] For Augustine, as for Paul, eschatology holds out the promise of fulfilled vision. But even so, eschatology is present language about that future fulfillment, and thus it is subject to the limits of finite language struggling to articulate the infinite and ineffable. What remains is the promise of a share, but what the nature of that "share" is, Augustine believes we cannot say. The appropriate response is silence and repose, but it is not the repose of quietism. Rather, it is the repose of "human thought," of the discursive mind's striving to circumscribe the uncircumscribable. What is left is the nondiscursive longing for that share in divine presence. It is the silence of love.

St. Gregory of Nyssa

In Gregory of Nyssa, we may see the logic of apophatic eschatology worked out most carefully. Like Paul and Augustine, many Christian writers recommended negative theology based upon the epistemological limitations of mortality. The imperfect vision of this life will be perfected in the beatific vision, where we shall truly behold the glory of God. But the negations of apophatic theology result from the infinite mystery of God more than from the epistemological limitations of finitude. Thus, Gregory of Nyssa concludes that life with God in the eschaton will never cease to be ineffable. This ineffability is due not to the distance of God, or to finitude or sin, but to the very abundance of the gift of God's presence, whose sweetness is always more than we can digest. Divine presence will remain mysterious eternally, since it is by

40. Richard Bauckham's interpretation of Revelation 21 is relevant here. For Bauckham, the New Jerusalem symbolizes the fact that "God's creation reaches its eschatological fulfillment when it becomes the scene of God's immediate presence," and "He will be 'all in all' (1 Cor. 15:28), not through the negation of creation, but through the immediacy of his presence to all things" (*Theology of the Book of Revelation* [Cambridge: Cambridge University Press, 1993], pp. 140-41).

its very divinity beyond all knowledge, whether of this life or the next. "The soul grows by its constant participation in that which transcends it; and yet the perfection in which the soul shares remains ever the same, and is always discovered by the soul to be transcendent to the same degree," says Gregory.[41] For him, even after death life is the infinite progress of the soul deeper and deeper into the mystery of God.

> [In] our constant participation in the blessed nature of the Good, the graces that we receive at every point are indeed great, but the path that lies beyond our immediate grasp is infinite. This will constantly happen to those who thus share in the divine Goodness, and they will always enjoy a greater and greater participation in grace throughout all eternity. . . . Thus they never stop rising, moving from one new beginning to the next, and the beginning of ever greater graces is never limited of itself.[42]

Even in heaven we shall always, and without end, have to transcend our own conceptions progressively, in light of the ever deeper mystery of God. To extend Augustine's argument, we shall indeed share in those divine realities, but we will never be sated by them. Rather, the experience of each "moment" of eternal life will spur desire for even more of the infinite depths of God. For Gregory, then, the ineffability of God promises that eternal life is formally much like our own here and now — that mystical theology is *very closely* allied with eschatology, as both describe the movement of the soul "from glory to glory," ever deeper into the ineffable presence of God.

Apophasis, Image, and Eschatology:
St. Bonaventure and Julian of Norwich

Thus far I have demonstrated some biblical and patristic points of contact between eschatology and mystical theology, but what is to be

41. Gregory of Nyssa, *Commentary on the Song of Songs*, Sermon 5, in *From Glory to Glory*, ed. Jean Daniélou, trans. Herbert Mursurillo (London: Charles Scribner, 1962), p. 190.

42. Gregory of Nyssa, *Song of Songs*, Sermon 8, *Patrologia Graeca* 941C, ed. Jacques-Paul Migne, pp. 212-13.

gained from these family resemblances? More specifically, how might one perform the insights of mystical theology in an eschatological key? To begin to answer these questions, I will examine a classic work of mystical theology, Bonaventure's *Itinerarium mentis in Deum,* first summarizing and drawing out its mystical elements, and then offering an eschatological reading.

St. Bonaventure's *Journey of the Mind into God* is a mystical work in which images abound and are seldom negated explicitly. Bonaventure's worldview is sacramental; every creature is a symbol that communicates the presence and activity of the living Creator. He offers an itinerary of the soul, wherein the intellect proceeds from the consideration of natural things, to the consideration of humanity as the *image of God* (which we retain even after the fall), to its reality as the *likeness of God* (humanity restored by grace), and finally to the contemplation of God as "Being" and as "Goodness," and beyond. Despite these abundant affirmations, Bonaventure's work is an exercise in apophatic theology. One thus ascends from "natural philosophy" to "anthropology" to "theology," and then into God Himself, seeking to speak with ever greater specificity of the reflections of the Creator in the material, anthropological, and conceptual dimensions of the created order, but always acknowledging that the divine reality infinitely exceeds those reflections. In this ascent, theological eloquence and precision are essential, but they are not the end. They are only the means through which the soul reaches its limits and breaks them open. Bonaventure lacks Denys's dialectical method of "saying and unsaying," but he follows the plan of Denys's *Mystical Theology* according to which "the more [the mind] climbs, the more language falters, and when it has passed up and beyond the ascent, it will turn silent completely, since it will finally be at one with him who is indescribable."[43] The ascent of the soul reaches the limits of the intellect and must pass over into silence.

"In this passing over, Christ is the way and the door, Christ is the ladder and the vehicle, being, as it were, the Mercy Seat above the Ark of God. . . . He who turns his full countenance toward this Mercy Seat . . . beholds Christ hanging on the Cross."[44] Just as one reaches the limits of

---

43. *Mystical Theology* 3, trans. from Luibheid and Rorem's *Pseudo-Dionysius,* p. 139.

44. Bonaventure, *Journey of the Mind into God* 7.1-2, in *Opera Theologica Selecta* (Quaracchi: Collegium S. Bonaventurae, 1964), p. 212.

description and expects to be released into the dark abyss of God, Bonaventure confronts the reader with what is perhaps the most concrete, vivid, and bracing image in the Christian tradition — the bleeding image of the Crucified. Placing the cross at the apophatic end of the journey of the mind into God, in Turner's words, "dramatise[s] with paradoxical intensity the brokenness and failure of all our language and knowledge of God."[45] Precisely when the reader's intellect expects the most abstract, hazy description of a "cloud of unknowing," she is confronted with an image that defies the intellect: the Crucified God. This is the "apophatic image." The cross represents the "crossing out" of human wisdom (cf. 1 Cor. 1.18), and thus of all intellectual understanding and theological predication. The darkness of incomprehension is one and the same as the darkness that "came over the whole land" (Mark 15:33) on Good Friday. The mystical silence of Denys's Christian Neoplatonism is for Bonaventure identical with the silence of awe before the self-emptying love of God in Christ, a love which invites, even demands in its weakness, imitation.[46] Bonaventure's apophaticism is therefore not faith, hope, and love in *nothing*, but the disciplined use of language and image to point to the fullness of the presence of God, whose deepest revelation is, paradoxically and ineffably, upon the cross.

Bonaventure's image of the Crucified has eschatological as well as mystical consequences. He elsewhere describes the highest state of contemplation as "the common boundary between the way and the fatherland."[47] The mystic enjoys a taste of the fatherland, as contemplation bridges the gap between mortal life and the life to come: "Let us, then, die and enter into this darkness," he says. "Let us silence our cares, our desires, and our imaginings. With Christ Crucified, let us pass out of this world to the Father."[48] Mystical death anticipates mortal death, and the flash of mystical passing "out of this world" anticipates the New Heaven and New Earth. But the path to such anticipation is the self-emptying love of the Crucified.

---

45. Turner, *Darkness of God*, p. 132.

46. For a discussion of the cross in Bonaventure, see Ilia Delio, O.S.F., *Crucified Love: Bonaventure's Mysticism of the Crucified Christ* (Quincy, Ill.: Franciscan, 1998), and Elizabeth Dreyer, ed., *The Cross in Christian Tradition: From Paul to Bonaventure* (Mahwah: Paulist, 2001).

47. Bonaventure, *Collations on the Six Days* 3.30, in *Opera Omnia* V.348.

48. Bonaventure, *Journey* 7.6, p. 214.

What if one were to read eschatology through the lens of Bonaventure's mystical itinerary? If the mystic's sense of the presence of God is in fact the anticipation of the eschaton, then the implication is that, as one stands on the "boundary of the fatherland" and peers into the New Jerusalem, precisely when one expects to find the unmediated presence of God, one still sees the cross. This suggestion is disquieting, as it may conjure an image of "eternal Crucifixion" that suggests some divine masochism. But such is not my intent. Rather, if we think of Bonaventure's image of the border, the Crucified stands on that boundary between the terrors of history and the fullness of the reign of God, and we cannot overlook it. We can only look through it. While the promise of resurrection and the kingdom of God is offered in the paschal mystery of Christ, we have only finite human language and concepts with which to describe it. Whatever images of the fatherland we may see will then be "crossed," that is, marked with the folly of the cross as merely human wisdom. They will have the cross of Christ superimposed upon them. Whatever hopes we may have are not obliterated, but are nonetheless marked with the cross, that is, with the paradox of ineffable, boundless love expressed in a world of sin as "obedience to the point of death, even death on a cross" (cf. Phil. 2:8).[49]

In *The Crucified God*, Jürgen Moltmann speaks of the cross as "the negation of everything which is religious . . . of all deification, all assurances, all images and analogies and every established holy place which promises permanence. . . . It does not invite thought but a change of mind."[50] The image of the Crucified *crosses out* whatever assurances one has about the world and its permanence. Through the cross, Christian theology comes to what Moltmann calls a "critical theory of God."[51] I suggest that, in like fashion, the apophatic image of the Crucified in Bonaventure's *Journey* might be called a critical theory of hope. But Moltmann *contrasts* this "critical theory" with an analogical theology

---

49. The object of hope in and of itself is, and must be, beyond the cross and thus in the mode of resurrection. But we cannot see it *as such*. The Risen One appears not with scars, but with wounds that are still open (John 20:27), and the resurrection appearances themselves show a sort of narrative apophaticism of recognition and lack thereof (Matt. 28:17; Luke 24:13-32, 36-43; John 20:15-16). Thanks to Miroslav Volf for helping me clarify this.

50. Jürgen Moltmann, *The Crucified God* (Minneapolis: Fortress, 1993), pp. 38-40.

51. Moltmann, *Crucified God*, p. 69.

that is strikingly like Bonaventure's *Journey:* the "pure, self-forgetting contemplation of God . . . [wherein] he who loves wisdom, through the *eros* for wisdom which has taken hold of him, himself becomes wise. . . . The steps by which [participation in God] is imported can here only be the likenesses of God in nature, history, and tradition, which indirectly reflect and reveal something of God himself."[52] This seems to make theology all negation, the signification of God's absence from "nature, history, and tradition," which would seem to problematize any speculation about the object of our hope. In contrast, what Bonaventure offers is an analogical theology that ends dialectically at the foot of the cross. As an apophatic theologian, Bonaventure refuses to choose between affirmation and negation, between analogy and dialectic, since the reality of God is beyond both.

Bonaventure's placing of the cross at the summit of contemplation reveals that the resurrection of Christ, the "first fruits" of the eschaton, does not undo the cross, but rather completes and crowns his self-emptying kenotic love which it displayed (cf. Phil. 2:6-11, especially v. 9). There is no resurrection but through the cross. Resurrection stands for us as the pledge and promise of the time "when God will be all in all," the source of Christian eschatological hope, but we cannot contemplate "life in the kingdom" without "crossing" our hopes with the unsettling image of the Crucified as the revelation of divine love. The apophatic image of the Crucified is the "image and analogy" through which all other images and analogies must pass. In this way, eschatology is not a pure theory of the eschaton, but a critical theory. What we find represented in Bonaventure is a theology confident in its predications, sensitive to the sacramental power of image and imagination, but never without the disciplines of unknowing, never without a relentless turning back upon itself. For Bonaventure, this discipline is given in the cross itself, the "apophatic image" of the invisible God.

To say that eschatology is apophatic is not to suggest that all our hopes must be denied, for that would only signify "absence," making "absence" present. Rather, it means that whatever hopes we have and whatever hopes we deny must all be "crossed" with the cross of Christ. So when we articulate our hope in the kingdom of God, we cling to this by faith but relentlessly turn back upon ourselves and confess the lim-

---

52. Moltmann, *Crucified God,* p. 69.

its of our own conception. So every hope for the kingdom must be at one and the same time a confession that it is no "kingdom" such as we can conceive, that it is neither God's reign nor not God's reign; it is beyond all reigns. It is a reign where power is made perfect in weakness, as on Good Friday. And thus the hope is crossed.

The lesson of Bonaventure's apophatic theology of the cross is that the Crucified One is the apophatic image that lies beneath, above, and within all of our theological predications. The "image of the invisible God" is none other than Christ on the cross.[53] Our eschatology cannot hope to fill its images with more than this. Julian of Norwich, as she beheld a vision of the bleeding body of Christ crucified, heard a voice telling her to look up to heaven for her comfort. Even though she thinks that the voice is trustworthy, she refuses and tells Christ on the cross,

> No, I cannot, for you are my heaven. I said this because I did not wish to look up, for I would rather have suffered until Judgment Day than have come to heaven otherwise than by him; for I well knew that he who bound me so painfully would unbind me when he wished. Thus I was taught to choose Jesus as my heaven, though at that time I saw him only in pain. I was satisfied by no heaven but Jesus, who will be my bliss when I go there. And it has always been a comfort to me that I chose Jesus for my heaven, through his grace, in all this time of suffering and of sorrow. And that has been a lesson to me, that I should do so for evermore, choosing Jesus alone for my heaven in good and bad times.[54]

For Julian, as for Bonaventure, the cross is the deepest hope, the "only heaven" that she can see and should see in this life, "in good and bad times." This side of the End, in a world of brokenness and sin, we are as "bound" as she, and the articulation of our hopes must embody this. Our gaze toward heaven — if we dare to make it — cannot bypass the cross. The judgment of grace in the presence of God — and only that — will "unbind us" when it is his will, freeing us to see, at least in part,

53. Karl Barth, *Church Dogmatics* II.2, cited in Moltmann, *Crucified God,* p. 69.
54. Julian of Norwich, *Revelations of Divine Love,* trans. Elizabeth Spearing (Harmondsworth: Penguin, 1998), p. 69.

what "God dwelling in our midst" will truly mean. Julian herself knows with confidence that it will be "bliss" in the eschaton. But she knows this only from contemplating the "divine love" displayed upon the cross. Divine love, and thus our hope for now, "in all this time of suffering and of sorrow," is cruciform.

In the early stages of preparing this essay, I wondered if I was perhaps a bit too maudlin, if I was too much a "Good Friday Christian." Was I dwelling too long on the cross, without the corrective hyphenated cross-and-resurrection? Was this evidence of a medievalist's piety for the suffering of God? But in the end, I decided that both the theological and the political import of this work — inasmuch as there is import — was in resisting the hyphen.[55] The story of Jesus is not, and cannot be made, a "comedy," with the resurrection as the "happy ending" that erases the scandal of the cross. Theologically, this would blunt the critical power of the cross of Christ. Rather, I think that *in this life* the resurrection is necessarily the "Redemption of tragedy."[56] The statement of Christian hope is not "all's well that ends well," but Julian of Norwich's assertion, *while gazing on the Crucified,* that "all shall be well, and all shall be well, and all manner of things shall be well." To posit our eschatological hopes too concretely or too confidently (a) makes human life and history comic, risking the erasure of suffering, and (b) runs the risk of making that comedy into "our comedy," a scenario of which Derrida is perhaps rightfully afraid. Such a comedy would be manipulable and idolatrous.

Hope is a *crossing.* Hope is that by which we *cross over* from the "already" to the "not yet," from foretaste to fullness. But such a *crossing over* can happen only if hope itself is *crossed* — that is, *crossed out* but left on the page, asserted paradoxically as both true and untrue, in the acknowledgment that the fullness we seek is more full than our hope can express. The language of our hopes thus breaks open, leaving us with a hope that is deeper than language or concept or symbol. In the end, the infinite God is our hope, and life in the unknowable God will shatter even our most profound eschatologies. As a French poet wrote, "hope is the anxious waiting of the good sower; it is the longing of those who

---

55. See n. 46 above.

56. Cf. Katherine Brueck, *The Redemption of Tragedy: The Literary Vision of Simone Weil* (Albany: State University of New York Press, 1995).

are candidates for heaven. Hope is the infinity of love."[57] Hope, then, is the longing that remains when we have crossed our hopes, where we are vulnerable at the foot of the cross in unknowing longing for the resurrected union with the Bridegroom. Hope is not the object of our desire, even so grand a desire as the kingdom of God or the "new heavens and new earth," for as soon as we say these we bring our own limited vision of what these things are. Hope is the longing itself for the deeper reality of a love that is beyond all loves, for the beauty that lies beneath, before, behind, above, and within those symbolic, evocative visions, for the time when "God will be all in all." Such longing is not quietism, but is in itself a "critical theory of hope" which allows us to recognize and proclaim all utopian dreams as false idols. "In other words, it depends on us," as Charles Péguy says, "To make sure that hope does not deceive the world."[58] With Julian,[59] we cling humbly to the Crucified, the image of self-emptying love, and wait in joyful hope for the time when we will be unbound and Christ will be our bliss in the heavenly kingdom of God.

---

57. From Charles Péguy, *The Portico of the Mystery of the Second Virtue,* cited by John Paul II in his "General Audience of January 24, 2001," available at The Holy See Online, at http://www.vatican.va/holy_father/john_paul_ii/audiences/2001/documents/hf_jp-ii_aud_20010124_en.html. 25 July 2002.

58. See n. 2 above.

59. For the sociopolitical implications of Julian's theology, see Frederick Christian Bauerschmidt, *Julian of Norwich and the Mystical Body Politic of Christ* (Notre Dame, Ind.: University of Notre Dame Press, 1999).

Natality or Advent: Hannah Arendt and Jürgen Moltmann on Hope and Politics

DAVID BILLINGS

*Because the same One, who is begotten and born of God the Father,
without ceasing in eternity, is born today, within time, in human
nature, we make a holiday to celebrate it. St. Augustine says that
this birth is always happening. And yet, if it does not occur in me,
how could it help me? Everything depends on that.*

Meister Eckhart

Introduction: Bringing Arendt and Moltmann into Conversation

The cataclysmic events of the twentieth century have precipitated un-
precedented challenges to both political thought and action. How can
we work toward political ends and ideals when the unintended consequences of such action so often have been violence and terror? The
weight of recent history can paralyze action. The darkness of the recent
past can dim our comprehension of present challenges. Yet a flight
from the life of action to a life of pure contemplation is not a responsi-

I wish to thank the Pew Charitable Trusts and Calvin College's Seminars in Christian
Scholarship for their support of this project. Thanks also goes to Miroslav Volf, whose
comments on an earlier draft of this paper were quite helpful.

ble choice. This would leave the modern proclivity for totalitarianism and calamity unopposed and ill-comprehended. Hannah Arendt and Jürgen Moltmann, both of whose lives were disrupted by such events, confront these challenges.[1]

Although they responded to similar challenges, the task of bringing these thinkers into conversation with each other has unique difficulties. The common realm of concern that I will explore is politics. My strategy will be to examine aspects of Arendt's theory of action and Moltmann's eschatology — each of which has significant ties to the political realm.[2] More specifically, I will examine Arendt's idea of "natality" and Moltmann's idea of "advent" as resources for a hope that can become politically engaged.[3] In the end I find that each has something important to teach us about political hope. In addition, I find that Arendt's notion of natality can be useful in the context of Christian eschatology.

1. While the events leading to and surrounding World War II had the greatest personal impact upon both, each responds to a variety of contemporary challenges. Both are sensitive to the impact of the battlefields of the First World War and the beginning of the atomic age, which concluded the Second. In addition to her highly controversial analyses of the Holocaust (most notably her report on the Eichmann trial), Arendt responds to, for example, Stalinism, Western imperialism, radical student movements, the Vietnam conflict, and even Sputnik. Moltmann mentions Auschwitz and Hiroshima as representative twentieth-century challenges, but also, for example, Chernobyl and the fall of Eastern European Communism.

2. Arendt restricts her use of the term "action" to what we might call mutual or coordinated action. It is for Arendt a specifically political term. Moltmann has always been concerned about the political implications of eschatology (Richard Bauckham, *The Theology of Jürgen Moltmann* [Edinburgh: T&T Clark, 1995], pp. 99-108).

3. The thematic comparison I undertake in this chapter could be enriched by considering ties of intellectual genealogy. Moltmann acknowledges the influence on his own thinking of certain twentieth-century Jewish thinkers (Jürgen Moltmann, *The Coming of God: Christian Eschatology,* trans. Margaret Kohl [Minneapolis: Fortress, 1996], pp. 29-30). This community of thinkers constituted one part of the landscape of Arendt's early intellectual development. Of those specifically mentioned by Moltmann in this passage, Walter Benjamin and Gershom Scholem were particularly important for Arendt. The theme that Moltmann appropriates from these thinkers (the revival of messianic thinking), however, does not appear to have impressed Arendt in the same way.

Arendt on Natality

Hannah Arendt concludes her monumental work *The Origins of Totalitarianism* with a striking and unanticipated expression of hope:

> But there remains also the truth that every end in history necessarily contains a new beginning; this beginning is the promise, the only "message" which the end can ever produce. Beginning, before it becomes a historical event, is the supreme capacity of man; politically, it is identical with man's freedom. *Initium ut esset homo creatus est —* "that a beginning be made man was created" said Augustine. This beginning is guaranteed by each new birth; it is indeed every man.[4]

These words are striking — even scandalous — because of their context. They come at the end of her analysis of the historic and ideological roots of Nazism and Stalinism. This analysis uncovers a potential for totalitarianism very deep within human nature and a unique capacity to develop that potential within the conditions of modernity. What then can one make of these closing words?

The reference to birth reveals that Arendt locates a capacity for hope in an aspect of the human condition she calls "natality." Natality primarily points to the fact that we all begin this life in birth and that each birth represents something radically new — a new beginning — a newcomer and an individual that the world has never seen before.[5] For Arendt, birth (natality) and death (mortality) together constitute "the most general condition of human existence."[6] Human mortality has motivated serious philosophical inquiry at least as far back as Plato's *Phaedo*. Arendt's focus on natality, by contrast, is uncommon in Western thought.[7] In her most

---

4. Hannah Arendt, *The Origins of Totalitarianism* (San Diego: Harcourt Brace, 1973), p. 479.

5. This meaning of the term "natality" is of Arendt's own coinage. ("Natality" otherwise is a statistical term that refers to rates of birth.)

6. Hannah Arendt, *The Human Condition* (Chicago: University of Chicago Press, 1958), p. 10.

7. Arendt's employment of this idea is novel, but not entirely without precedent or parallel. It is not difficult to find scattered reflections in various philosophers that touch upon what Arendt calls natality (although without employing her distinctive idiom). Arendt is unique, however, in giving natality such importance.

striking and creative use of the concept, Arendt argues that natality grounds the possibility of political action:

> the new beginning inherent in birth can make itself felt in the world only because the newcomer possesses the capacity of beginning something anew, that is, of acting. In this sense of initiative, an element of action, and therefore of natality, is inherent in all human activities. Moreover, since action is the political activity par excellence, natality, and not mortality, may be the central category of political, as distinguished from metaphysical, thought.[8]

Also:

> With word and deed we insert ourselves into the human world, and this insertion is like a second birth, in which we confirm and take upon ourselves the naked fact of our original physical appearance. . . . [This insertion's] impulse springs from the beginning which came into the world when we were born and to which we respond by beginning something new on our own initiative.[9]

In these passages, Arendt weaves together several distinct notions: birth, (political) action, and beginning/initiative. While the connection between action and beginning may not be difficult to understand, bringing *birth* into this mix seems curious. After all, nothing in the concept of birth logically entails a capability of political action or initiative.

To understand her position, we must see Arendt as working within the methodological tradition of existential phenomenology, particularly showing the influence of her teachers, Heidegger and Jaspers.[10] Natality is an existential category which can be seen as a supplement (or perhaps an alternative) to Heidegger's notions of "Being towards death" and "thrownness."[11] Arendt's use of "natality" in reference to the fact of human birth is not a definition that will be sub-

---

8. Arendt, *Human Condition,* p. 9.

9. Arendt, *Human Condition,* pp. 176-77.

10. Patricia Bowen-Moore, *Hannah Arendt's Philosophy of Natality* (New York: St. Martin's, 1989), pp. 6-9.

11. See Martin Heidegger, *Being and Time,* trans. John Macquarrie and Edward Robinson (San Francisco: Harper and Row, 1962), pp. 174, 277.

jected to analysis. Rather, it is a way of pointing to an aspect of the human condition that can acquire meaning for human existence. Arendt is not concerned with the physical characteristics of giving birth (characteristics we share with other mammals), but with something unique to human beings: our capacity to enter into the human world as a unique and irreplaceable individual. This human world should be thought of as a cultural and political space, not a physical location. It is the human nature of the world we come into that distinguishes natality (as a characteristic of human existence) from the births and beginnings of other living beings. Because human beings have the power of initiation (beginning something new in a way that brings the recognition of a community), they exist fundamentally as individuals rather than as members of a species. When a person enters the human world through speech or action, she discloses who she is in a way made existentially possible by natality. Arendt explains:

> Action and speech are so closely related because the primordial and specifically human act must at the same time contain the answer to the question asked of every newcomer: "Who are you?" This disclosure of who somebody is, is implicit in both his words and his deeds. . . .
>
> In acting and speaking, men show who they are, reveal actively their unique personal identities and thus make their appearance in the human world, while their physical identities appear without any activity of their own in the unique shape of the body and sound of the voice. This disclosure of "who" in contradistinction to "what" somebody is — his qualities, gifts, talents, and shortcomings, which he may display or hide — is implicit in everything somebody says or does.[12]

Birth and political action are connected by the ideas of beginning and disclosure. As a creature capable of beginning something new, it is natural that I understand my capacity to begin in terms of my own beginning (that is, my birth), or in terms of the beginnings I see around me in my own community (the new generation). As a creature capable of

---

12. Arendt, *Human Condition*, pp. 178-79.

disclosing myself, it is natural that I understand this capacity in terms of my own original disclosure.

Natality does not refer to pagan or neopagan notions of fertility or the cycles of birth and death. In fact, Arendt believes that natality reveals the human capacity to enter into a linear history and break free from the cycles of returning sameness. Eternal cycles of birth and death are appropriate ways to understand nonhuman animals, but not human beings.

> Nature and the cyclical movement into which she forces all living things know neither birth nor death as we understand them. The birth and death of human beings are not simple natural occurrences, but are related to a world in which single human individuals, unique, unexchangeable, and unrepeatable entities, appear and from which they depart. . . . Without a world into which men are born and from which they die, there would be nothing but changeless eternal recurrence, the deathless everlastingness of the human as of all other animal species.[13]

Natality and Hope

What can natality teach us about hope? In the reflections that follow, I take Arendt's ability to find hope in natality as a point of departure, but the point of view expressed here should not be attributed to Arendt. Her treatment of natality centers on its application in a theory of political action, and she does not explore the link to hope that I examine.

Hope looks to the future. In holding a newborn baby, one's thoughts are drawn toward the horizon of the future. One considers the possibilities latent within this small wonder who cannot even conceive of them yet. As there is a difference between hope and assurance, however, a parent may feel fear as well as joy in contemplating the future possibilities of the new child.[14] Authentic hoping cannot be prop-

---

13. Arendt, *Human Condition*, pp. 96-97.

14. Notice that I am here approaching natality from the perspective of a parent. This is a perspective that I find only obliquely mentioned in Arendt's writings, but that I find helpful in exploring the existential meaning of natality. Human beings have their

erly separated from taking risks. One who is no longer willing to risk disappointment must also reject hope. Yet this is not an excusable attitude for parents. They must hope for their children. They must accept the risk of pain and disappointment contained in hope.

In birth, we recognize an *opening up* of the horizon of future possibilities — in fact, the opening of a new horizon entirely (the horizon of the child). An instructive contrast with the *hope* of natality may be the idea of *barrenness,* which may be extended metaphorically to mean the constriction and cutting off of future horizons. There has been some discussion among the contributors to this volume concerning what the "opposite" of hope may be (e.g., despair, malaise, or something else). I propose that any compelling candidate will have the character of barrenness.[15] Consider the way Abram viewed his situation when God first proposed a covenant: "After these things the word of the LORD came to Abram in a vision, 'Do not be afraid, Abram, I am your shield; your reward shall be very great.' But Abram said, 'O Lord GOD, what will you give me, for I continue childless'" (Gen. 15:1-2 NRSV). Even the rewards and gifts of God seemed to be without significance to Abram because the future horizon was constricted and barren. Next consider the extravagance of God's response: "He brought him outside and said, 'Look toward heaven and count the stars, if you are able to count them.' Then he said to him, 'So shall your descendants be'" (Gen. 15:5 NRSV). The horizon has been opened wider than the imagination can grasp. Hope has been reborn.[16]

Consider how natality provides hope in the face of death and mortality. Pascal provides a famous image in his *Pensées:*

> Let us imagine a number of men in chains, and all condemned to death, where some are killed each day in the sight of the others, and

---

beginnings in birth, and we begin in such a way that we are born to parents. The possibility of our becoming parents (or teachers or caregivers) can affect the way that we understand our own births and thus our own beginnings.

15. This does not mean that barrenness is the opposite of natality. For human beings (who all have the characteristics of natality), barrenness and fertility are contrary possibilities.

16. This example is merely intended to illustrate the natural affinity between hope and natality. I do not wish to imply that human beings can be hopeful only when they have descendants.

those who remain see their own fate in that of their fellows, and wait their turn, looking at each other sorrowfully and without hope. It is an image of the condition of men.[17]

For all of Pascal's insight, the present discussion should make clear a significant point of dissimilarity between the plight of the prisoners and the human condition in general. The future horizons of the prisoners are constricted to an extreme degree; this need not be the case for all human beings. With natality, we have an opening of future horizons and the possibility of hope. This understanding of hope prods me to look beyond merely the satisfaction of my own desires. The coming of a new generation can give a committed and consistent egoist (if there is such a creature) no comfort. He still will die and may see himself as one of Pascal's prisoners. We can see here a glimpse of a political dimension that natality may help us recognize.

Natality without Eschatology: Arendt on History

While the language of natality has a natural affinity with the expression of hope, I see difficulties with Arendt's apparent conviction that natality is sufficient to give us an adequate hope. These difficulties can be seen if we compare Arendt's view of history to that of Augustine. This comparison is instructive because Arendt's thoughts about natality were inspired by her work on Augustine.[18] While natality is a distinctive and important idea, I am not convinced that it can provide adequate hope when it is radically detached from an eschatological context.

In dealing with natality, Arendt frequently quotes a passage from *The City of God:* "that a beginning be made man was created."[19] This

---

17. Blaise Pascal, *Pensées,* trans. W. F. Trotter (New York: Modern Library, 1941), sect. 199.

18. Bowen-Moore, *Arendt's Philosophy of Natality,* pp. 9-10.

19. This is how she translates the passage in *The Origins of Totalitarianism.* She quotes the Latin as *"Initium ut esset homo creatus est."* This quotation is not, however, precise. The Loeb Classical Library edition renders the passage ". . . *quod initium eo modo antea numquam fuit. Hoc ergo ut esset, creatus est homo, ante quem nullus fuit"* (*The City of God Against the Pagans: Books XII-XV,* Loeb Classical Library [Cambridge: Harvard University

passage comes at the end of a chapter in which Augustine refutes two theses which he takes to be related. The first thesis is that human souls exist in eternal cycles of reincarnation; the second is that "there is nothing new in nature which has not previously existed."[20] Here we find the concern for beginning and the new which Arendt wishes to utilize — although Augustine uses the language of creation rather than that of birth.

Beginnings were only half of Augustine's concern, however; he also dealt with what may be called the *end* (in the sense of both final stage and purpose) of human life: a state where "the redeemed souls abide in most certain bliss without any return to misery."[21] Augustine finds the denial of true beginnings repulsive precisely because it eliminates the possibility of a redemptive end. If there is nothing new in the natural order (and if everything that has existed cycles back to exist again), then we will truly never escape the "great calamities" and "frightful evils" of the present life. Augustine finds this view so disturbing and hopeless that were it true, he thinks that the greater wisdom would be to remain ignorant of it. Readers today may notice that Augustine's argument disputes a view strikingly similar to Friedrich Nietzsche's notion of the eternal recurrence. Whereas Nietzsche insists that we must come to embrace the eternal recurrence if human existence is to be meaningful, Augustine views the idea with horror and disgust. On this point of fundamental difference, Arendt seems to cast her lot with Augustine rather than with Nietzsche. There is a formida-

---

Press, 1966], XII/21). (I have added a phrase immediately before the passage to show why Arendt uses the term *"initium."*) R. W. Dyson translates the passage as "In order that there might be this beginning, therefore, a man was created before whom no man existed" (Augustine, *The City of God Against the Pagans,* trans. R. W. Dyson [Cambridge: Cambridge University Press, 1998], p. 532). In *The Human Condition,* she quotes the passage in the Latin more accurately as "[*Initium*] *ergo ut esset, creatus est homo, ante quem nullus fuit*" (brackets in original) and translates it as "that there be a beginning, man was created before whom there was nobody" (p. 177). In another place she quotes the passage in Latin without translating (this time as "[*Initium*] *ut esset, creatus est homo, ante quem nullus fuit*") and then explains it saying, "Because he *is* a beginning, man can begin; to be human and to be free are one and the same. God created man in order to introduce into the world the faculty of beginning: freedom" (Arendt, *Between Past and Future* [New York: Viking, 1968], p. 167).

20. Augustine, *City of God,* trans. Dyson, p. 531.
21. Augustine, *City of God,* trans. Dyson, p. 528.

ble irony to this alignment, however. Nietzsche believes one should embrace the eternal return (in part) because the meaning of existence cannot be derived from transcendent sources. Augustine would have seen Nietzsche's attempt to find meaning without transcendence as a project doomed to failure. Yet Arendt, like Nietzsche, finds herself in a situation where she cannot appeal to the transcendent ideals of a God directing the world in providence, the final redemption of the individual after death, or an eschatological end (divine or human) to history.[22] Instead she must affirm Augustinian beginnings without Augustinian ends (something that Augustine would have found pointless and perhaps incoherent), translate the Augustinian idiom of creation into her more neutral idiom of birth, and then transfer the context of the discussion from eschatology to politics.[23]

The hope that Arendt finds seems to be contained within the expanding horizon of the new generation (and coming future generations). Within this horizon is the possibility that the totalitarian era may come to an end. After the Nazi era, Germany may enter into a stable democratic stage. After Stalin, one like Gorbachev may emerge. Yet it is naive to focus on these possibilities. The expanding horizons, as Arendt never forgets, also involve the possibilities for ever-worsening evils. After the fall of Communism in Eastern Europe, ethnic hatred and genocide may return. Hope involves an irreducible element of risk. Risk does not constitute hope, however, and (it seems) hope cannot be reasonably sustained when the risks are too great. Taken by itself and stripped from a context of eschatological ends, natality provides little hope. Yes, the future may be different because of the implicit promise of "the new" in each new birth; this difference may, however, be evil. Even in the darkest

---

22. I do not wish to overstate the force of this argument. "Transcendent" turns out to be a rather slippery term. In fact, for Arendt, there is a kind of transcendence implicit in human birth and realized through political action. This is because the *human* world of politics and culture is not reducible to the natural world (it transcends the natural). Yet Arendt cannot accept the stronger forms of transcendence that Augustine requires for his concept of history. Arendt does not affirm an end (final purpose) for human history or even a belief in historical progress.

23. I do not think that it is wrong for Arendt to do this. In fact, there is great value both in Arendt's idiom and in the application of this language to politics. My point here is that these moves can serve to obscure the original eschatological context of these ideas and cover up an apparent incongruity that I hope to highlight.

days of World War I, there was the possibility — within the context of human natality — that the next generation would invent and employ even more horrible ways of killing. We cannot apply a law of averages here, expecting good fortune after bad. A bad situation may improve, but it also may get worse. This extreme uncertainty of outcome, it seems, would most likely result in either cynical fatalism or stoic detachment — not robust hope. Even if one can find some degree of hope in bare natality, it is questionable whether such hope will be strong enough to sustain and inspire dedicated political action in dark and uncertain times. The conviction that natality without eschatology can cultivate political hope requires qualification or more explanation if it is to be plausible. Arendt draws her idea of beginnings from Augustine but then attempts to divorce these beginnings from the idea of ends. Yet for Augustine, the rationale for beginnings is clearly wrapped up in ends. As far as I can see, Arendt fails to explain how Augustinian beginnings provide hope separated from their original context.

In spite of these difficulties, Arendt's position still has value. Her language of natality provides significant insight into the human condition and the experience of hope and gives us a compelling way to express that hope (as the section on "Natality and Hope" indicated). Moreover, there are weaknesses in Augustine's position that Arendt can help us overcome. As Arendt argues in her doctoral dissertation, Augustine cannot develop an adequate view of politics because loving the world for its own sake is idolatry and secular (worldly) events cannot attain true significance.[24] In other words, while Augustine's eschato-

---

24. Arendt's dissertation was published in English in a modified form as *Love and Saint Augustine* (Chicago: University of Chicago Press, 1995). Arendt takes this anti-worldly stance to be an essential part of a Christian understanding of history and politics, although paradoxically in tension with the essentially Christian ethics of neighbor love (Arendt, *Between Past and Future*, p. 66; Ronald Beiner, "Love and Worldliness: Hannah Arendt's Reading of Augustine," in *Hannah Arendt: Twenty Years Later*, ed. L. May and J. Kohn [Cambridge: MIT Press, 1996]; Hauke Brunkhorst, "Equality and Elitism in Arendt," in *The Cambridge Companion to Hannah Arendt*, ed. D. Villa [Cambridge: Cambridge University Press, 2000], pp. 190-93). It is significant for this discussion that Moltmann can provide a fundamentally different view of history and politics which is nonetheless thoroughly Christian. For example, he writes, "Revelation was not written for 'rapturists' fleeing from the world, who tell the world 'goodbye' and want to go to heaven; it was meant for resistance fighters, struggling against the godless powers on this earth . . . out of love for this world of God's" (*Coming of God*, p. 153).

logical ends do provide a kind of hope, they do not provide political hope — i.e., a hope that can sustain and enrich political action. Augustine offers a hope against the world (with its great calamities and frightful evils) rather than for the world. A concern with natality, on the other hand, can help us to recognize that we are born into this world, and that as parents or educators, we must take responsibility both for the world and for our children.[25] Taking responsibility for the world requires political action. When we act we open up new possibilities, and these possibilities are interlaced with both risk and promise. We also disclose ourselves as irreplaceable individuals. Our hope may be sustained by a larger eschatological context (here I part company with Arendt), but it must work itself out in striving for justice and identifying with the poor and the oppressed here and now.

Moltmann on Advent and Time

To the present conversation I bring yet another voice. Jürgen Moltmann provides an eschatological vision quite distinct from that of Augustine and a subsequent concern for the world that grounds a sophisticated political theology. Moltmann positions his eschatology in contrast to both a "presentative" (or "now already") eschatology and a "futurist" (or "not yet") eschatology.[26] The issue is whether the promise of the kingdom of God is yet to be fulfilled in the future or whether it is already now being fulfilled in the lives of Christians. (Although Moltmann here is in dialogue with modern theologians, I take it that Augustine provides a futurist eschatology.) Both views, Moltmann believes, presuppose a concept of linear time. Against this presupposition, Moltmann presents his eschatology of the coming God and a new concept of time:

> The eschaton is neither the future of time nor timeless eternity. It is God's coming and his arrival. In order to express this we shall take an *Advent-like* concept of the future that springs from the history of God, from the experiences and expectations of God as these are re-

25. Arendt, *Between Past and Future,* pp. 185-86.
26. Moltmann, *Coming of God,* p. 6.

corded in the biblical writings. . . . We shall take the category of the *novum* — the new thing — as the historical category which characterizes the eschatological event in history.[27]

Moltmann explains his point by referring to the common biblical formula for speaking of God. For example, "Grace to you and peace from him who is and who was and who is to come."[28] One would expect the third description to be "who will be" rather than "who is to come." There must be some reason for this grammatical shift. For Moltmann, this coming (advent) breaks through the linear concept of time and ultimately opens up "categories for eschatology."[29] Thus Moltmann distinguishes two different concepts of time which correspond to two different ways of speaking of "what is ahead": *futurum* (what *will be,* but does not yet exist) and *adventus* (what *is* coming, but is not yet here).[30] The idea of advent in turn can influence the way we understand God. "God's future is not that he will be as he was and is, but that he is on the move and coming towards the world. God's being is in his coming, not his becoming."[31] The ultimate culmination of this coming is the redemption of the world and history: from transience and death as well as from sin and evil.[32] This indwelling of God alters the transcendental conditions of both time itself and the world.[33] This end is really a new beginning: the beginning of "eternal time." This end transforms, fulfills, and completes time; it does not repudiate time. Creation's "temporality is itself the true promise of its eternity, for eternity is the fullness of time, not timelessness."[34]

Yet if this eschatological vision is to cultivate a political hope, we must be able to find consequences of this advent *before* the ultimate re-

27. Moltmann, *Coming of God,* p. 22.

28. Rev. 1:4; see Moltmann, *Coming of God,* p. 23.

29. Moltmann, *Coming of God,* pp. 23-26.

30. This discussion might be confusing in English because Moltmann identifies the term *Zukunft* with *adventus,* but in translation it appears as "future."

31. Moltmann, *Coming of God,* p. 23.

32. Richard Bauckham, "Eschatology in the Coming of God," in *God Will Be All in All: The Eschatology of Jürgen Moltmann,* ed. Richard Bauckham (Edinburgh: T&T Clark, 1999), p. 17.

33. Moltmann, *Coming of God,* pp. 26, 272.

34. Moltmann, *Coming of God,* p. 264.

demption. This is where the practical differences between Moltmann and the futurist eschatology emerge. Advent breaks into history as *novum* — a radically new thing that could not have been anticipated on the basis of past history. "It evokes unbounded astonishment, and transforms the people whom it touches."[35] This transforming, astonishing change (which Moltmann insists is not a mere "interruption" but a "conversion") frees us from the paralyzing influence of the past. Because advent comes into history, the significance of our present struggles is not swallowed up by the final end.[36] Rather, this conversion "make[s] present the ultimate in the penultimate, and the future of time in the midst of time."[37] Thus for Moltmann the purpose of apocalyptic literature is to "awaken the *resistance of faith* and the *patience of hope*. [Apocalypses] spread hope in danger, because in the human and cosmic end they proclaim God's new beginning."[38] Also, the memory of Christ's resurrection "lets us look beyond the horizon of our own death into the wide space of eternal life, and beyond the horizon of this world's end into God's new world. Life out of this hope then means already acting here and today in accordance with that world of justice and righteousness and peace, contrary to appearances, and contrary to all historical chances of success."[39] Finally, Moltmann posits a millenarian "kingdom of peace" in history as a mediation or transition between present world history and the new world. This millenarian hope, he thinks, provides a "powerful motivation" for "consistent discipleship" as well as a way to articulate a contrast between "the community of Christ" and society.[40] This is Moltmann's vision for a hope that is eschatologically situated and politically engaged.

---

35. Moltmann, *Coming of God,* p. 28.

36. Arendt expresses a similar concern in a different context when she argues that the Marxian end of history (the classless society), far from giving meaning to the prior struggles, actually robs all history prior to its culmination of true significance (*Between Past and Future,* pp. 79-80).

37. Moltmann, *Coming of God,* p. 22.

38. Moltmann, *Coming of God,* p. 203.

39. Moltmann, *Coming of God,* p. 234.

40. Moltmann, *Coming of God,* p. 201.

Interactions

When we bring Arendt and Moltmann into conversation with each other on the topic of political hope, both surprising similarities and instructive differences emerge. I now turn to a critical comparison between Arendt and Moltmann concerning the ways that their ideas address both political and eschatological issues.

The New in Natality and Advent

Both Arendt and Moltmann locate political hope in the experience of the new. Only through some radical sort of newness can the tyranny of past events be overcome. At least formally, the new in natality and advent have many common features. Both elicit astonishment. Neither could be predicted on the basis of prior events. Arendt writes, "The new always happens against the overwhelming odds of statistical laws and their probability, which for all practical, everyday purposes amounts to certainty; the new therefore always appears in the guise of a miracle."[41] Moltmann writes, "The new thing is the surprising thing, the thing that could never have been expected."[42] Despite the similar spirit of these statements, however, they do reveal a fundamental difference. *Novum* (the new associated with advent) is the historical manifestation of something not "against the overwhelming odds of statistical laws" but absolutely impossible apart from the coming of God. Moltmann's understanding of the eschaton (a redeemed world without transience or death) has no analogue in Arendt's thought. The new for Moltmann is grounded in God's coming; for Arendt it is grounded in an aspect of the human condition. (This difference reflects two fundamentally different worldviews. While the resulting senses of the new are distinct, however, I argue below that they are not incompatible.) Nevertheless, this difference does not eliminate the fact that within human history the new of natality and *novum* look quite similar. This side of the eschaton, no historical event (no matter how surprising or even miraculous in Arendt's sense) is obviously or

41. Arendt, *Human Condition*, p. 178.
42. Moltmann, *Coming of God*, p. 28.

indisputably the work of God rather than of human agents acting in their world.

In spite of these similarities, Moltmann seems wary of using the language of birth. For example, he criticizes the idea that the present is "pregnant with future." This view, he thinks, lacks the capacity to astonish (there is no *novum*) and consequently it lacks a principle of hope.[43] Should this be taken as a criticism of the new in natality? Not at all. On this point, Arendt and Moltmann agree. As I explained above, the genesis of the idea of natality (in Augustine) is in opposition to a view that denies the possibility of what is radically new. The position rejected by Augustine and the position rejected by Moltmann deny the radically new (although for different reasons). The new of natality and the new of advent are substantially similar in this sense. Why then does Arendt employ the language of birth while Moltmann here rejects it?

This difficulty can be resolved by making a distinction between birth and *giving* birth. Moltmann rejects the view that could be expressed metaphorically as the present continually giving birth to the future. During labor, birth is both inevitable and imminent. During labor, there is nothing astonishing about a birth occurring. If this is our dominant metaphor for the future, then the future can contain nothing "new" in the sense Moltmann believes political hope and Christian eschatology require. For Arendt, however, labor and natality are distinct (although not unrelated).[44] The birth occurs when the process of giving birth ends. It is the new, utterly unique life inaugurated by birth that can astonish us, not the mere fact that a birth follows labor.

So the new in advent and the new in natality have both substantive and formal similarities, and at least one crucial substantive difference (i.e., the divine or human origin of the new). To what extent could either Arendt or Moltmann appropriate the insights of the other on this issue? First of all, I see no convincing way for Arendt to adopt an advent sense of the new, for God plays no part in her thinking. As I have already argued above, this significantly weakens the hope that natality by itself can provide. Some attention to the new of natality could, however, be incorporated into Moltmann's thought.

To speak merely of "the new" can be extremely abstract and for-

---

43. Moltmann, *Coming of God,* p. 25.
44. See Arendt, *Human Condition,* pp. 8-9, 105-6, 115.

mal. Moltmann's *novum* seems to have this character. In contrast, natality implies a more particular and embedded kind of new beginning. This is a new beginning that faces the future but that is not entirely without ties to the past. The newborn needs parents in order to survive, and part of the job of parents is to provide a context in which the newcomer can grow and thrive — to link the new to the past with bonds of tradition and love. No human society could survive if each new generation was not linked to some degree to past patterns of living. Arendt writes, "the child requires special protection and care so that nothing destructive may happen to him from the world. But the world, too, needs protection to keep it from being overrun and destroyed by the onslaught of the new that bursts upon it with each new generation."[45] Natality's newness comes from within. The newcomers that form the new generation are always *our* children; they are not simply strangers that come to us from outside. Even the most xenophobic society welcomes newcomers when these newcomers are their own children. On the individual level, a mother brings her child into the world. The child does not come to her from the outside. The child is already within. In contrast, the animating force of *novum* is coming toward us. It is outside, coming in. This new is unexpected precisely because it is outside the sphere of our expectations.

Although I would not dispute the usefulness of *novum,* the situated sense of the new is, politically, crucial. If there is to be a political realm at all, then at some point *we* (human beings) must act and realize the potential for the new that is already within us. The coming of God may be important, but we must do more than just wait for this coming. Moltmann obviously believes this already. My sense is that natality can help us express this imperative more forcefully. In addition, we should not forget that this action — this making new — is always embedded in a web of contexts and traditions, a human world formed from the actions of prior generations. At times Moltmann emphasizes the break with what is past: "What is new announces itself in the judgment on what is old. . . . it makes the old obsolete."[46] While there are situations in which this stance is appropriate, in the realm of politics this could be dangerous if applied without discrimination. At the same time,

45. Arendt, *Between Past and Future,* p. 186.
46. Moltmann, *Coming of God,* p. 27.

Moltmann does not obliterate all ties to the past. Indeed, the very idea of redemption involves maintaining what is to be redeemed. The creation is not annihilated and replaced; rather, the creation is gathered up and created anew.[47] Moreover, the eschatological category of conversion implies some kind of continuity with the past. It is striking that in his discussion of this idea Moltmann uses the phrase "rebirth to a new life."[48] This may be a sign of an implicit sense of natality.

Even in the realm of eschatology, both concepts of the new are useful and important. On one hand, Christians affirm that the new age is brought into being by the power of God. Speaking of the return of Christ as a "thief in the night" is in line with a concept of the new that is coming from outside (cf. Matt. 24:43). Here, the *novum* is expressive and insightful. We must not forget, however, that this coming of God is a *return*. The one who is returning is the one who was *born* unto us. A stranger is not coming but one of us, a part of the human community.

The Concept of Time

At first glance, the time concepts associated with natality and advent seem to provide a striking contrast. Natality makes a linear time possible in the form of human history but advent rejects the linear time concept. This difference, however, is more apparent than real. It turns on the meaning of the term "linear." For Arendt, the term more or less means non-cyclical. In other words, a linear concept of time allows that singular, non-repeatable events can acquire significance. This idea is contrasted with the cycles of nature. The human world, grounded in natality, does not merely move in cycles.[49] In *this* sense of linear, Moltmann's *adventus* concept of time is also linear. In a strictly cyclic notion of time, nothing new is possible because everything (significant) is a return. When Moltmann rejects a linear concept of time, he has in mind "time as a linear, homogeneous continuum, free of surprises."[50] The past produces and determines the future, so the future

---

47. Moltmann, *Coming of God,* p. 29.
48. Moltmann, *Coming of God,* p. 22.
49. Arendt, *Human Condition,* pp. 96-98.
50. Moltmann, *Coming of God,* p. 30.

contains nothing that was not already implicit in the past. *This* sense of linear time is clearly incompatible with Arendt's understanding of natality.[51]

Two basic differences remain between Arendt and Moltmann on the concept of time. First, Arendt does not develop an *adventus* concept of time or anything quite like it. (I see no incompatibility between natality and Moltmann's concept of time; it may be possible to affirm both.) Second, Arendt has no concept of eternal time to begin in the eschaton. This again exhibits the fundamental point of difference between the two thinkers already mentioned above.

Mortality

The issue of human mortality reveals instructive differences between Arendt and Moltmann. First consider Arendt's striking but cautiously stated suggestion (quoted fully in the "Arendt on Natality" section) that identifies natality as the central category of political thought and implies an association of mortality with metaphysical thought. Arendt does not explain or justify this association, but we can suppose she is thinking along the following lines: Death presents us with a problem that admits of no practical solution. We cannot overcome death politically, ethically, or technologically. (We do talk about saving lives, but actually we postpone death, which remains inevitable.) The metaphysician's response to mortality is to leave this transient realm of death behind by means of thought and enter the realm of eternal (timeless) truths. Arendt does not deny the value of thought's timeless character, but would insist (I think) that any system of thought principally motivated by the challenges of mortality will remain "metaphysical" (in the sense of having no practical or worldly application). On the other hand, natality presents us with a variety of challenges that demand practical and political responses. There is always a new generation to introduce to the world and integrate into our common social life. We must learn to

---

51. Arendt evidently was unsatisfied with the metaphor of a mere straight line for time. In a different context, she struggles to devise an alternate metaphor: a pair of vectors (past and future) that meet at an angle and produce a new vector from the resulting "parallelogram of forces" (*Between Past and Future*, pp. 11-12).

live together with those who are born to us, or we will not be able to live at all. *If* we accept Arendt's double identification on this point (and Moltmann might find reason to reject it), then we should be concerned about the role of mortality in Moltmann's thought. Clearly, Moltmann wants his eschatology to be in the realm of praxis rather than theoretical speculation.[52] But if transience and mortality are our *fundamental* concerns, there is very little that *we* can do, other than wait for the coming God and speculate about what this coming will be like. In Arendtian terms, Moltmann's concern with what is new and even his insistence that eternity is *not* timeless hint at a place for natality already at work in his thinking (although not recognized as such). What remains is to explore more thoroughly what insights an attentiveness to natality could reveal for Moltmann. As I have said before, I see nothing that prevents Moltmann from critically incorporating some of Arendt's ideas on this subject.

At the same time, there is a sense in which Moltmann could turn this objection concerning mortality back on Arendt. While it is true that mortality influences and motivates (to a degree) Moltmann's thought, at least he envisions a kind of solution to the problem it poses. In *overcoming* the power of mortality through the redemption of time (past, present, future) Moltmann opens up a space for hopeful (political) action. For Arendt, however, mortality must remain a kind of open wound and the past must remain unredeemed. She cannot anticipate a change in the transcendental conditions of time itself. The permanence of death is exhibited in the unchangeableness and unredeemability of the past. Nothing can be done for the victims of past crimes (at least, crimes of a certain sort). The Nazi and Stalinist regimes "discovered" radical (or absolute) evil with their "crimes that men can neither punish nor forgive."[53] Then what can we do? It seems that we either must turn our backs to the victims, in order to move on to something new, or look back with paralyzing horror. Moltmann envisions a way to overcome this tyranny of history. The fact that Arendt would not have found Moltmann's solution plausible (since it is based in the coming of God) does not mitigate the dilemma that she faces.

52. Miroslav Volf, "After Moltmann," in *God Will Be All in All*, p. 252; see Moltmann, *Coming of God*, p. 146.
53. Arendt, *Origins of Totalitarianism*, p. 459.

Conclusion: Natality within Eschatology

What have Arendt and Moltmann to teach each other? What have both to teach us today? Both perspectives are valuable and important, yet some choices must be made. I have found it more plausible to incorporate Arendt's insights into Moltmann's framework of thought than the other way around. This should not be surprising. Moltmann's ideas about God have no foothold in Arendt's view of the world, but Moltmann can have no objection to any genuine insights into the human condition. But how can a hope based upon God be reconciled with a hope grounded in the human condition? The answer to this question has already been suggested though not stated explicitly. The divine and the human come together in the incarnation, which exhibits a unity of the new of natality and the new of advent. This grounds my claim that a recognition of natality is compatible with Moltmann's general position. Moltmann's christological perspective[54] should be able to accommodate both natality and advent, and each may be transformed by the other. When natality is understood in the context of a christological eschatology, the new thing of which I am capable may be a reflection of the birth of Christ within time and within me. As Meister Eckhart says, everything depends upon that.

54. Bauckham, "Eschatology in the Coming of God," pp. 2-10.

Christian Hope and Postmodernity

The Gospel of Affinity

JOHN MILBANK

What is postmodernity — not simply postmodernism as a set of theories, but also postmodernity as a set of cultural circumstances? And what is the place of the Christian church amidst this postmodernity? How is the church to manifest itself and how are Christians to articulate its position in these new circumstances? To work through these questions, we need to think in terms of the gospel and the unavoidable, albeit cautious, affinity that exists between postmodernism and Christianity. If we do so, we can perhaps with better understanding and new hope live as pilgrims among the empires of our time and in the city of God.

Postmodernity

Above all, postmodernity means the obliteration of boundaries, the confusion of categories. In the postmodern times in which we live, there is no longer any easy distinction to be made between nature and culture, private interior and public exterior, hierarchical summit and material depth; nor between idea and thing, message and means, production and exchange, product and delivery, the state and the market, humans and animals, humans and machines, image and reality; nor between beginning, middle, and end. Everything is made to run into everything else; everything gets blended, undone, and then re-blended.

There are no longer any clear centers of control, and this means that new weight is given to plurality and the proliferation of difference. None of these differences ever assumes the status of a distinct essence, however; rather, they are temporary events, destined to vanish and be displaced.

Let us consider some of the main instances of boundary confusion. First of all, there is the blurring of the distinction between nature and culture. One important aspect of modernity was the sense that human beings could make and remake their own cultural universe. This was usually seen as being done against the backdrop of fixed laws of nature, however. To some extent, because humans were also recognized as natural, such laws were seen as impinging on the human sphere as well — limiting the range of freedom for human self-making. Thus humans were sometimes seen as by nature fundamentally self-preserving, fear-avoiding, happiness-seeking, sympathetic, and productive creatures. But just recently, all this has changed. First of all, people no longer seem to find any need to identify a human essence — no longer is human auto-creation operating within essential parameters. Humans, it seems, might make anything of themselves. We are our own anarchic laboratory. We can manipulate ourselves into a million shapes. Perhaps the only figure of essence which remains here is the idea that humans are productive. But we are as much the *result* of productive processes as agents *in command* of production. In consequence, the asymmetrical teleological and hierarchical aspects of human existence tend to get flattened out into degrees of intensity along a quantitative scale. For example, no longer are there firm characteristics of childhood, middle age, or old age; no longer are there clear differences (other than the biological ones) between men and women; and no longer is there much heterosexuality as opposed to a single, univocal (and therefore transcendentally "homosexual") proliferation of multiple desires.

At the same time, the frontier of culture has so invaded nature that culture appears to be amidst nature; it is no longer like a mind or fortress surmounting it. We can now intervene, technologically, in the organic realm, and the hybridization and manipulation of the natural fruit, vegetable, and even animal forms are increasing exponentially. Here, also, boundaries are being transgressed. But already, in the AIDS epidemic and the phenomena of global warming, the unintended consequences of human intervention involve natural forces becoming much more palpable actors within the cultural sphere. And no doubt genetic manipulation will lead to many more instances of this uncomfortable rebound.

But at a more profound level, our perceptions of nature and culture seem to be merging. Accounts of supposedly "material" realities become more and more ethereal: increasingly, with the decay of any sense that we as humans are governed by natural law, we come to wonder whether "laws" are not a projection by humans upon nature in general. Modern physics, for a long time now, has tended to think in terms of irreversible temporal processes, engendering not so much laws as relatively fixed habits. And such habits are not really the habits of material items; it is much more that the material items are the deposits of highly abstract depositions. Likewise, in the sphere of biology, the talk of "codes" and "codings" is not intended in any merely metaphorical sense — if there is metaphor involved here, then it is in the very operation of biological metamorphoses themselves.

Conversely, however, human mental life is increasingly thought of as an embodied life, manipulable in terms of all sorts of narcotic stimuli and regimes of gymnastic exercise. While nature is viewed in terms of the communication of signs, human thought is seen in terms of the processing of electronic impacts in the endlessly complex patterns of plus and minus signs — which point our way through the garden of forking paths, whose only sure fatality is the arrival of the next proximate intersection.

In these circumstances, it is not surprising that, once again, Baruch Spinoza enjoys a huge vogue, for he was the philosopher who proclaimed that there is a dual aspect to all phenomena: that the "order and connection of things" is also "the order and connection of ideas." Ideas already inhabit things; but conversely, for us to think is to rearrange reality — not to mirror it, but actively to alter its characteristics.

After the blurring of the boundary between nature and culture comes the new confusion of interior and exterior. And there is a deep connection, for in modern times the private self guarded the boundary between culture and nature — a man went from public work to the sanctum of his home, with his supposedly "natural" family, and looked out upon his cultivated back garden with its intimation of wilderness. Today, however, there is no sanctum. The home, most of all, is invaded by the public voices of the media, with their scarcely veiled instructions and commands. And the computer terminal now gives domestic access to the global public space — not a real space, but a new, virtual spatiality. Meanwhile, what has happened to the old, real public space — the space for promenading, for civility and courtship? In the United States, it has already largely vanished. Instead of the public piazza we have the interlocking of semi-private spaces — such that one walks from shopping mall into hotel foyer into office complex and so forth. Increasingly, houses are situated within gated or even guarded enclaves.

Of course, in this situation, most of our modern "liberal" political discourses start to appear completely meaningless, for they are all predicated on a mutual agreement to protect the right to do what one likes with one's own, so long as this does not interfere with the rights of the other. How can this criterion any longer apply to the real interlocking "rhizome" of material spaces, or to the fluid highway of virtual space? The shared covered walkway is pragmatically negotiated, not constructed according to general formal requirements of universal association, while the telephone and e-mail give license to endless mutual intrusion and surveillance. "My" website, my informational contribution, has already decided certain things for others, in a space that is theirs as well as mine, like a common grazing ground. No wonder that, for some people, the information highway seems like a simulated communist utopia. This perspective, nevertheless, is deluded, for what is "shared" here is only the immediate proximity of everywhere to everywhere else, which lacks in affinity, or inherited communality — it is therefore only a place without place of total estrangement. The difference from a liberal organization of discrete spaces is really but the self-implosion of a hyper-liberalism: I can choose anything anywhere, but these choices will always be for the choices of others, selecting me. Since anything can now be mine, nothing at all will really be mine. Liberalism always depended upon the principle that the inalienable private possession is in principle alienable — that is, sellable. But now, everything is entirely possessed as inalienable, and already is enacted in its constitutive possible alienability all at once.

The new interfolding of inside and outside is exhibited also in a third set of confusions, that between all the traditional modern economic categories. It is this confusion which produces the age of *information*. We still find it hard to believe that the production of abstract and ephemeral signs pointing to other signs can have become the driving force of the economy. In the United Kingdom, many still refuse to recognize that the almost total collapse of the automobile industry there may actually now give Britain a certain advantage over Germany, where a relatively up-to-date automobile industry still thrives. Backwardness in one phase is an advantage for the next — as Germany, which missed out on the phase of steam, once discovered. In that early industrial era, most people insisted that the production of food must always be the driving economic motor. Instead, as we know, agriculture became subordinated and was itself mechanized. Today, manufacturing is being subordinated and itself informationized. Areas like Los Angeles or London that work on the most abstract sectors of the economy thus are the most booming areas and also the new foci of global command.

In the age of information, production often consists (and sometimes entirely so) in the *exchange* of the product. Likewise, the consumption of the product can already be a type of laboring, while promotion and marketing become themselves the prime generators of profit, rather than its secondary accomplices. And expenditure of informational capital can be equally an investment of such capital in future production. Furthermore, there is no longer any clear disciplinary structure operating between management and worker within a real distinct site, like a factory or an office, nor within a clearly demarcated firm or company. Instead, one has networks of intellectual workers dispersed through real-space, working somewhat for themselves, and somewhat for varying others. These workers are auto-controlled through the pressures of the need to compete, or the desire for knowledge and influence. No one is telling them how many hours they must labor, but they increasingly feel forced to work without ceasing. Furthermore, the boundary between this work and their leisure time is becoming more and more hazy, since the seeking out of "contacts" is increasingly vital to work performance.

Alongside this sphere of the production of signs, however, it is important to mention also the increased importance of "service industries" — such as catering, medicine, education, transport, beauticians, and so on — which cater more directly to the needs of minds and bodies. These services, however, also are increasingly operated through levels of higher abstraction, which allow them to benefit from global expertise and fashion.

In these spheres also, deregulation ensures that hours worked tend to multiply. Meanwhile, in the older manufacturing industries, longer hours are directly enforced, because globalization and informatization have destroyed the bargaining power of manufacturing workers. Thus we can glimpse sight of a gigantic paradox: the increased freedom, deregulation, and differentiation of work in the postmodern era nonetheless permit capital, and in particular the multi-national corporations, to reap vastly increased profits from the vastly increased amount of surplus labor that is now being expended in every sphere of production. The times of postmodernity are in no sense post-capitalist times, but rather times of capital writ still larger. Indeed, capital has always been a force of abstraction; today it reaps even larger material benefits from increased abstraction. And even from its inception, capital produced and marketed signs and fashions; it would not have engendered a new abstract equivalence between commodities if it had not done so. It is, in a way, simply that something always latent in modernity is now much more clearly in the foreground.

Perhaps more drastically novel than informatization is a fourth mark of postmodernity, namely, globalization. This has to do not with the blurring of divisions within the economic realm, but rather with a merging of this realm with the political sphere. For a long time, the sovereign nation-state assisted the extension and regulation of the free market, but it nonetheless tended to subordinate the making of profit to military strength and ethnic or national unity. Capitalism always tended to overflow state boundaries, and today it can operate far more effectively by its capacity to shift human, material, and financial resources swiftly, right across the globe. This does not mean, however, that the state and politics have come to an end. To the contrary, more than ever the market requires the international state-ordering of virtual reality, international legal checks on financial speculations, and international policing of popular, ethnic, and religious dissent. Alongside the global market is emerging a kind of global empire — a new sort of postmodern empire, which, as Michael Hardt and Antonio Negri argue, continues a specifically American project of neo-Roman Republican empire.[1] This is not, like the old British and French empires, an empire of center and subordinated colonies, but instead an empire of endlessly expanding fron-

1. See Michael Hardt and Antonio Negri, *Empire* (Cambridge, Mass.: Harvard University Press, 2000). The present essay is heavily indebted to their analyses throughout.

tiers, an empire of inclusion, not remote control, and an empire able to distribute power to its peripheries. But this more invisible, distributed power is all the more a controlling power. Within this empire, the United States, the United Nations, and various nongovernmental agencies and multinational corporations all tend to share and blend functions of dominion. The political and the economic are by this means fusing.

So far, then, we have seen that postmodernity can be characterized in four ways, all of which have to do with the dissolving of fixed limits. These ways are: (1) the blurring of the nature/culture divide, (2) the merging of public and private, (3) the use of the information economy, and (4) economic and political globalization. But before one asks, "How is the church to conduct its mission and articulate its intellectual vision on this postmodern terrain?" we must first ask, "Does postmodernity, of itself, possess anything like a religious dimension?"

Here we should note that the blurring of boundaries has a cultural presupposition. That presupposition is one of *immanence*. An ordering of the world in terms of essences and relative values is linked in some way to teleology and hierarchy, or else, alternatively, to spatialization. In pre-modern times it was a matter of the former — everything had its appointed goal and relative value in relation to a distant, transcendental source, which was equally foundation and finality. Both thought and social nature mirrored this assumption. In modernity, by contrast, from about 1300 onward, the world was gradually accorded full reality, meaning, and value in itself, without reference to transcendence. Thus, what Gilles Deleuze called "the plane of immanence" was born. In modern times this plane was seen as contributing a kind of fixed spatial grid. Although height had been lost, depth displaced height and there still persisted fixed natures, especially human nature. In postmodernity, however, neither height nor depth remains, but only a shifting surface flux, because immanence is now conceived in terms of the primacy of time, not space. Possibility, productivity, and change have been set free, for both nature and culture, which, as a result, are increasingly indistinguishable. It follows, of course, that both modernity and postmodernity are relentlessly secular, meaning that (1) they evaluate and explain without reference to transcendence; (2) they see finite reality as self-explanatory and self-governing; and (3) they see this finite reality which is the *saeculum* — the time before the eschaton for Christian theology — as being all that there is.

In these senses, postmodernity is no more open to religion than was modernity — indeed, as more emphatically immanentist, it is really less so. Nevertheless, just as there were strange modern modes of religiosity, so there are strange postmodern modes of religiosity. Two of these are worth mentioning. First of all, academic exponents of relatively Marxist versions of postmodernism are fond of giving a Spinozistic twist to their atheism. The plane of immanence is seen as the sphere of active, productive forces, which manifest themselves in human terms as desire and love. The still-beckoning communist future is seen as an apocalyptic refusal of negative, resentful, tragic, and death-obsessed emotions. These emotions are unnecessary, and hitherto were imposed upon us by alien oppressors. Something of Spinoza's "intellectual love" or his *Deus Sive Natura* persists in all of this — there is to be a joyful reception and active contemplation of the immanent totality. For indeed, once oppression is surpassed, liberated nature-going-beyond-nature fully appears.

The second example is at a far more popular and widely dispersed level, and at first sight seems quite different and perhaps not at all postmodern. This is the phenomenon of "new age" religions. These religions all stress that salvation is to be located in a higher self, above the social, temporal, remembered self. This self can put one in harmony with everything, with the whole cosmos. This seems unpostmodern to the extent that it takes modern individualism to an extreme and seems to advocate retreat within an absolutely private, interior space. But this position shares with the Spinozistic one an assumption of immanence — of a self-regulating cosmos. Moreover, its higher-self-merging-with-the-cosmos is really rather like the ironic remove of the Spinozistic subject from its own process in flux. It is akin also to the Wittgenstein of the *Tractatus,* able to speak of what belongs to the subject as somehow standing impossibly outside the "all" of things that can be spoken of. There are also parallels to Emmanuel Levinas's and Jean-Luc Marion's tendency to demote the graspably visible world as the regime of totality, and to Michel Henry's proclamation of a world counter to this totality, which consists in the pure, never visible interior of matter manifest as auto affection.[2] Thus, in post-

2. See John Milbank, "The Soul of Reciprocity: Parts One and Two," *Modern Theology* 17 (July and September 2001): 335-91, 485-507.

modernity, alongside the stress of fluid and permeable boundaries, we have a new affirmation of the sanctity of an empty mystical self, a self able to transcend, identity with, and promote, or else refuse, the totality of process in the name of a truer "life" which is invisible. It will be apparent that even organized religion gets infected today with this kind of "spirituality."

Thus we need to add the linked notions of immanence, self, and life to nature merging with culture, inside merging with outside, information era, and global regime if we are to envisage the full dimensions of postmodernity.

Evaluating Postmodernity

Now that we have sketched out these five dimensions, we can ask how the church is to evaluate these new circumstances (which will lead us to the even more crucial question of how the church is to manifest itself and articulate its position in these new circumstances). In answering these questions, I want, in general, to suggest that we regard postmodernity, like modernity, as a kind of distorted outcome of energies first unleashed by the church itself. If that is the case, then our attitude is bound to be a complex one: not outright refusal, nor outright acceptance, but more an attempt at radical redirection of what we find. In recommending such a redirection, I suggest that neither a reiteration of Christian orthodoxy in identically repeated, handed-down formulas, nor a liberal adaptation to postmodern assumptions, will serve us well. The latter response would clearly be a betrayal, but the former might well be a betrayal of a more subtle kind, one that allows us the illusion of a continuation of the faith in merely formal, empty terms. Such terms would discover no real habitation for faith in our times. Instead, we must allow a very critical engagement with postmodernity to force us to re-express our faith in a radically strange way. Such an expression will carry with it a sense of real new discovery of the gospel and the legacy of Christian orthodoxy.

My assertion here is not intended as a general, methodological remark about Christianity in relation to culture, which might easily be taken as no more than another mode of liberalism. Instead, it is based upon the inevitable, if wary, affinity that must exist between Christianity and postmodernism. As I have said, postmodernism is the obliteration of boundaries. And Christianity is the religion of the obliteration of boundaries. Secular commentators like Hardt and Negri assume, in all too modern and essential a fashion, that there is some sort of "natural" human desire that demands de-territorialization without end. More cautiously, I suggest that Christianity itself invented a discourse and tradition of living beyond the law, and argue that the West is still thinking through and living with this idea. For Christianity did, indeed, explode all limits: between nations, between races, between the sexes, between the household and the city, between ritual purity and impurity, between work and leisure, between days of the week, between sign and reality (in the sacraments), between the end of time and living in time, and even between culture and nature, since Jesus advised us to follow the mute example of the lilies of the field. Indeed, the very category "creature" enfolds and transcends both the natural and the cultural. Culture, for the Gospels, is only a higher and more intense "life," while, inversely, all of nature is the divine artifact. But above all, with the doctrine of the incarnation, Christianity violates the boundary between created and creator, immanence and transcendence, humanity and God. In this way, the arch taboo grounding all the others is broken.

There is an apparent problem here, however. Judaism, the religion of the Old Testament, is *not* the religion of the obliteration of boundaries. Indeed, it is perhaps the very opposite: the religion of the reassertion of boundaries. Most "primitive" cultures are marked by a rigid marking out of limits, often described as "taboos."[3] In postprimitive times, when societies began to be captured by state formations, taboos were removed, or else subordinated to more abstract laws, which are imposed from outside, not inscribed in ritual practice. Ancient Israel, however, appears to have reacted against state formations, such as Egypt and Babylon, by making a kind of half-return to the primitive and inventing a new system of more universalized ritual boundaries. Primitive tribal boundaries typically had to do with restricting complexity, confusion, and thus conflict. But while they are thus comprehensible in functional terms, the actual instances of taboo

---

3. See Franz Baermann Steiner, *Selected Papers: Taboo* (New York: Berghahn, 1998), and *Selected Papers: Orientalism, Value and Civilisation* (New York: Berghahn, 1998). I am indebted greatly to conversations on these matters with Michael Mack.

can often seem utterly arbitrary. The provisions of the *Torah*, by contrast, although often strange-seeming, exhibit a more cosmic scope and a more unrestricted interest in limiting the shedding of blood and the confusion of categories, both of which could lead to instability and struggle. It is as if the Jewish people took up, in a more universal mode, the instinctive sense of primitive peoples that barriers must be erected against future danger and the augmentation of human and natural power.

Are we to take it, then, that Christianity really reverses this mission of Israel to the world? No. Such an interpretation is forbidden to us by all patristic teaching. To take this view would be to side wholeheartedly with postmodernity and, at the same time, refuse, as the work of a demiurge, the revelation of the old covenant. Postmodernity, not Christianity, is the final refusal of all taboo, and it is worth mentioning here the suggestion by the Jewish anthropologist Franz Steiner, that the Jews were destroyed by the Nazis not in the name of totality (as for Emmanuel Levinas), but rather as the people of the limit, in the name of the transgression of every limit, by immanent crowned power.

So, are we here presented with some sort of clue to the riddle of our times? Some thread through the postmodern labyrinth? Is postmodernity the misreading of the gospel beyond the Law? Does it overstress passing beyond boundaries at the expense of the virtue of boundaries? And does the cure for our postmodern condition lie in a healing of the rift between the seemingly opposed Christian and Jewish principles? Or, rather, does it lie in rediscovering that the Christian going beyond-the-Law nonetheless preserves and elevates the Law? This would mean nothing less than discovering a hidden mean between process and limit, between movement and stasis. In theological terms this would mean the co-belonging of grace with Law, not a dialectical duality of Law and gospel.

Responding to Postmodernity

It is this clue I now want to follow up, in terms of the church's response to the five aspects of postmodernity. First of all, then, the question of the merging of nature and culture.

Religious people, like many others, tend, instinctively, to feel uneasy in the face of a general collapse of all that was once regarded as natural. They are tempted to fall back on an insistence that God has made the human species and all others to be as they should be, and that either nature, or God's positive law, has given clear and firm guidance for the conduct of human relations. The trouble, though, with this approach is that an open-ended transformation of the natural world has always been regarded by Christian theology as proper to our *humanum,* and even as intrinsic to the redemption of humanity and the cosmos, looking toward the eschaton. Already, throughout history, we have drastically altered both nature and our bodies, and questions of right and wrong in such matters have never been decidable *merely* in terms of what has been pre-given by divine design. Certainly, that must be ceaselessly attended to, but questions of right and wrong in those instances more ultimately require a discernment of teleology, and a ceaseless discrimination of what is good in itself.

Here it needs to be said that the unleashing of a sense of human creativity in the Renaissance — and along with it a sense of the undeveloped potential of natural forces — did not automatically go along with a loss of a sense of teleology and of participation in God. The new sense of creativity and power was not at all simply the counterpart of Scotist univocity, which encouraged thinkers to speak, for the first time, of finite being *qua* being without reference to God, as Gilles Deleuze and Antonio Negri tend to claim. Instead, one can see that alternative interpretations were offered of human creativity, in terms *either* of univocity *or* of analogy. In terms of univocity, human creativity is taken to mean that, in a certain domain — for example, politics, or mathematics, or even physics, as with Galileo — human beings have, univocally, the same kind and extension of power as God has. It is *this* interpretation that engenders what Hans von Balthasar called "Titanism." In terms of analogy, however, as worked out especially by Nicholas of Cusa, who thought still within a Dionysian perspective, human creative power and natural power are never equal to God, and yet in its very creative exercise, such power participates in the divine *Logos* or *Ars,* and thus registers "conjecturally" a sense of how things should develop toward their proper goals. Even in its originating, creativity remains discerning.

When it comes to contemporary practical examples, we need to continue to exercise this power of discernment. Consider, for example, reproduction and sexual relations. Surrogate fatherhood or motherhood is not wrong because it violates the pre-given process of repro-duction. Rather, we have to ask complex questions about what such procedures will do to human identity — and whether the different iden-tities which may thereby emerge are richer or weaker identities, more viable or more unstable and threatened. Ultimately, we must ask whether the co-belonging of sex and procreation alone sustains human beings as more than commodities, because children are thereby the outcome of personal encounters at once accidental and yet chosen, in a fashion that is irreplaceable and essential to an ontological grammar that we should continue to elect. (I believe the answer is yes.) But such reflections involve not a refusal of choice, nor a mere postmodern res-ignation to choice, but a kind of higher-level "choice about choice." At present, of course, we woefully lack cultural practices that might medi-ate our intersubjective meta-choices.

At present, the postmodern fusion of nature with culture is more like the collapse of nature into culture. The Christian question here might be as to whether this emphasis should be reversed; in other words, while we accept and embrace the revisability of the given world, such dynamism needs and should not refuse notions of nature and es-sence, not as what is exhaustively given but as what may eventually be disclosed with and through time, rather than despite it. Certain trans-formations and graftings may develop and unfold more of a partially pre-given and desirable identity; certain others, the reverse. Certain hy-brids should find their place; certain others not. Certain interventions within the rhythms of nature still permit and uphold them; certain others run a clear if incalculable risk of upsetting them. Each case is a matter of discernment, according to no pre-written rules, precisely be-cause we have faith that we do live in a creation where discernment is possible. In this sense, the transgression of boundaries is not antinomic, but is, rather, the ceaseless extension of the book of the Law in real positive enactments.

The contesting of the postmodern thus lies precisely in this trust in discernment and the discrimination among resting places. Postmodernity inscribes, tyrannically, only one law: produce, alter, or make different, such that yesterday's transgressive innovation is today's crime of stasis. In this sense its antinomianism enacts a new law and is not, like the gospel, really beyond the Law at all. For if there is truly no essence or nature, truly no "proper way" for anything to be, then nothing should be attended to, nothing should be regarded in its hidden possibilities for its *own* development. Instead, every possibility must imply that its realization requires an act of arbitrary (and not at all creative) destruction. Certain Spinozistically inclined postmodernists are fond of speaking of the extension of the bonds of love and solidarity on the basis of compatible emotions and understandings.[4] But this is to invoke the primacy of *affinity,* and there can be affinity only between things that, in some fashion, can be *characterized,* even if such characterization is provisional. Otherwise there are only affinities of accident, whose instances convey no freight of enacted truth, and which instantiate no proleptic hope of a final chain of affinities with no exterior of exclusion. (Indeed, given the Spinozistic rooting of passive resentment in the limited perspectives of the finite modes, there must always be exclusion, save for the privileged attainment of the active perspective of the absolute by a fated few.) Furthermore, without the *convenientia* of analogy, the binding of differences under affinity can be no more than merging and coalescence into a single super-difference.

Above all else, for us today the gospel concerns this issue of affinity. Christians believe that God became a human being and denied the division between creator and creation. In doing so, however, God also preserved it. In becoming human, God in no way changed in himself, in no way entered within time. Nor was anything that Christ did in any way "mixed" with his divinity — except at one point, namely, that of personality, or of character. Jesus was God because his *affinity* with God was so extreme as to constitute identity — but an identity not of substantial nature, but of character, *hypostasis, persona.* And Jesus communicated to his disciples not simply teaching but precisely this *character,* which they were to repeat differently, so constituting a community of affinity with Jesus — not a community of nature (a family), nor a coerced association (a *polis*), nor yet a postmodern marketplace of proliferating differences; rather, a community of differences in identity — but an identity diffused through the non-identical repetition of character, or of affinity. Affinity is the absolutely non-theorizable, the ineffable. Affinity is the sacred. And it is the beyond-the-ethical which alone gives us the ethical, for without affinity love can be only the

---

4. See, for example, Michael Hardt, *Gilles Deleuze* (Minneapolis: University of Minnesota Press, 1997).

merely ethical and immanent command to put the other first — that is, a self-abasement before the rival egotism of the other, which the other would in turn have to renounce. Instead of modern selfishness, one would then have a kind of postmodern endless postponement of egotism (Levinas and Derrida). By contrast, there can be more than egotism, there can be *love,* only if there are ecstatic reciprocity and an interplay of characters who naturally "belong together." In this way, the network of affinity, beyond nature, discovers a higher nature (the supernatural, the gift of grace). It is for this reason that, in the Bible, loving God involves not just our being well disposed toward God, but being "like" God, akin to God, made in God's image. This image does not fundamentally consist in any single human property — such as our reason alone, abstracted from all other aspects — but rather in the whole person (even if this be specifically a whole rational person). Thus we cannot say *in what respect* we are like God. The image of God that we bear, or are, simply is an ineffable likeness: an affinity.

I think that a lack of trust in affinity, and a lack of the mediation of affinity through the church, might, to a degree, explain the *sexual* crises and confusions of our time. Christians can only say this with fear and trembling, however, because throughout much of their history, especially in the period since the Reformation, they have failed to realize that affinity puts the erotic at the heart of *agape,* which cannot be merely the empty and nihilistic gaze of well-wishing. Because affinity, having a liking for someone, and falling in love with someone seem uncontrollable — as indeed they are — we have tended to think they are nonmoral or unmoralizable spheres. To the contrary, however, these phenomena are the very pre-conditions for morality. Without ontological kinship — without a kind of aesthetic co-belonging of some with some, and so ultimately of all with all — not formally and indifferently (as if every person is equally near every other, as on the Internet, which not accidentally is awash with prostitution in multiple guises) but via the mediation of degrees of preference — there can be no possibility of real peace and reconciliation, only a kind of suspension of hostilities.

For these sorts of reasons, I think, we are totally wrong to approach contemporary sexual issues as primarily moral matters, or as matters of what should and should not be done. On the whole, disagreements about sexual morality are a farcical unreality, masking a grotesque depth of hypocrisy. "Liberals" always seek more fidelity and security than they own up to, and "conservatives" in practice usually will put life before principle. In this realm, the sham of argument is forever overshadowed and defeated by anxiety. So the church should cease its participation in these unedifying disputes. Marriage is a matter not of morality, but of the basis of morality in occurrence. It is either there or not there — entirely willed by the partners and by them alone, only because God himself has joined them together. This is Christ's teaching, and like him we should keep ironic and blushing silence about everything else, leaving it to the discernment of individuals and pastoral guidance. Also horrendous are the conservative attack on "sex outside marriage" (with no real warrant in Christian tradition — especially lay tradition) and the "liberal" slandering of fidelity, which is a slandering of sexuality itself and its deeply ethical jealousies. This same slandering often fails to observe the increasing displacement of erotic affinity by a general system of market competition for sexual conquest that is entirely complicit with the pursuit of economic power and advantage (as the French novelist Alain Houillebecq has demonstrated). Both liberals and conservatives also tend to perpetuate the ludicrous untruth that erotic excitement and fulfillment increase with the new and the altogether strange, and lapse with time and familiarity. Yet to the contrary, common experience proves that sex is impossible save in the relaxed presence of the ever-different-familiar, even if familiarity can descend from the outset, like a miracle. Freedom, innovation, and passion grow here most surely with custom alone, as much as in the exchange of words, musical notes, or witticisms. It is not that sex outside marriage is wrong, simply that it is impossible, and never what anyone wants in the slightest.

It should also be said here that modernity (ever since the Renaissance) has always oscillated in sexual matters, between a disciplinary puritanism unknown to the Middle Ages, on the one hand, and a promotion of a death-obsessed and narcissistic eroticism, on the other. Postmodernity often accentuates the latter path, but here once again it privileges entirely the flow of difference over the fertile pools of relatively constant essence. In particular, it tends to despise the mystery of the general difference of masculine and feminine in favor of a supposedly more exciting dispersed and unpolar differentiation. Yet this ungeneric, ungendered, and so of course unsexual differentiation cannot then truly allow any arrival of the event of affinity in its most intense sexual mode, since it thereby lacks any vehicle of mediation. Male/female sexual difference, while it is indeed mysterious and sublimely ineffable, nevertheless does not entirely escape articulation — or else it would be a vacuous difference that made no difference. In general, the clichés truly do hold, although they must be further nuanced: men are more nomadic, direct, and abstractive; women are more settled, subtle, and particularizing — though the sexes are equally innovative, legislative, and conservative within these different modes. A preponderance of counter-instances could of course be held to disprove this assertion, yet equally they could be held to witness to the abolition of gender by a ruthless postmodern capitalism which wishes to engender only "individuals," who are turned narcissistically to themselves and to the abstract center, never to the embodied other who displays a radical generic otherness that truly unsettles our ego. The same abolition requires the ideal synthesis of "masculine" autonomy and self-control with "feminine" compliance and sociability (these traditional qualities being somewhat more culturally induced, one might argue). It desires neither men nor women. None of this can be "proved," but it is often important to state boldly what one sees and cannot in the nature of the case demonstrate: this is the real crux of responsibility. And, in the end, the issue concerns not bald fact but rather the question of what is really desirable, teleologically and eschatologically — an equality of the sexes without sexual difference (and an *entirely* inexpressible difference really is no difference, even if one must struggle forever to articulate it), or a new equality of the sexes which seeks to enhance a sexual difference that it also affirms.

We must think in terms of the equality of difference. This is so because without the settled, abstraction is not an abstraction but only another, arbitrary, settled view. Inversely, without abstraction the settled is not settled, but another abstraction in its very fixity, one that is immune to the specific shifts of life and time. (Here also Christian abstraction is necessarily betrothed to Jewish specificity.) Instead, without this marriage, we are speaking of multiple narcissisms and purely active and so self-expressive desires, without need and lack (for lack can persist non-negatively within fulfillment). This kind of sexuality is "transcendentally homosexual," and this must be the outcome where male-female relations are not seen as paradigmatic of the sexual as such. There need be no problem whatsoever with the idea that homosexual practice is part of the richness of God's creation. Indeed, its often parodic and ironic character (which springs at once from its need to mimic sexual difference, and its non-heterosexual logic, for which two enamored partners may share a desire for a third)[5] can hint toward the life of angels.

But where homosexuality is seen as equal in sacramental significance to the unity in difference of man and woman (where it is supposed that people of the same sex can "marry"), then as a matter of logic, one has chosen the superiority of homosexuality over heterosexuality, and denied the place of the non-angelic within the cosmic and erotic order. If both are "the same," then, indeed, "the same" triumphs: transcendentally speaking, there are simply many "persons," all in theory potential sexual partners. It thus seems that there can be no neutral characterization of sexuality as such.

In fact, it is heterosexuality and sexual difference which the church finds *really* difficult to accept — though it lies at the very heart of its mystery. Thus it was persecuted by old puritanism, and now it is denied by the new pious indifference toward gender, for which all that matters is "friendship." Far too easily and with a sham radicalism, the churches and especially clergy tend to degenerate into secret gay cults: the gnosis of campdom. After all, the homoerotic has dominated them for centuries. What is new, exciting, or radical about any of this? Today, past patriarchy and misogyny are simply writ larger and more explicitly within circles of gay hegemony (with which lesbianism is often simply complicit). In addition, the production of a normative "homosexual" subjectivity serves, as Theodor Adorno rightly foresaw, the deepest purposes of capitalism: thereby the production of children can be increasingly commodified, and handed over to state and market regulation, so that human beings may be better subordinated to the increase of profit and the stockpiling of abstract power. No, the test of its real embracing of incarnate mystery will come when the church is able to accept and no longer trivialize human sexuality in its most shocking and vivid and defining (heterosexual) guise.

In the face of the fusing of nature and culture, therefore, the church should proclaim the "gospel of affinity." It is the church of all marriages and quasi-marriages, the church of all natural and spiritual

---

5. Howls of protest here are futile: these things are again and again observable.

offspring. Appropriate responses to other aspects of postmodernity then follow from this central insight. In the face of the blending of private and public, the church needs to accentuate the private pole as the underplayed one, as earlier it identified that of nature. Since the church fuses *oikos* and *polis,* values of nurture and reconciliation — not locked doors and barren highways — need to constitute our interweavings. We must learn to take literally the idea that we are "grafted" onto Israel, that we now belong with Israel in one spiritual blood-group, and we must think of all our human relations in terms of extended family. The computer screen makes us equally near the whole world, but we need to resist the illusion that this is possible. We are finite and cannot love all equally, except in loving God and trusting that all are loved by others. We need rather to love properly those that we are destined to love. And such extensions of family must invade also the entire realm of law and punishment. The church should promote the sense that such processes must be processes of penance and reconciliation as well as of justice. It must dispense forever with Luther's two kingdoms, and with the notion that a state that does not implicitly concern itself with the soul's salvation can be in any way legitimate.

Therefore reconciliation needs to be added to affinity. And, third, in the face of the information age, the church needs to be wary of the secular tendency to promote the abstract, and should come to realize that only Christianity fully celebrates the concrete and bodily. If the immanent world is all there is, then it tends to reduce to our abstract grasp of it, and we come to believe that it consists in abstractions that we can rearrange. For this outlook, there is neither being nor knowledge, nor the affinity between them, but rather a shifting flux of the semi-concrete and the semi-abstract (the realm first located by Duns Scotus in terms of the formal distinction).[6] By contrast, we are able to acknowledge a depth in things only when we see them as surpassing our finite grasp, and as grounded in God the Creator. In this way, only recognition of participation in God gives bodies their solidity, because to grant them this we need to see how in God bodies persist as eternal. Likewise, we have true knowledge of them only when we share something of God's insight into how he wished them to be. So if an over-abstracting secular world has lost bodies and truth in favor of informa-

---

6. See Catherine Pickstock, *After Writing* (Oxford: Blackwell, 1998), pp. 121-67.

tion, we need to reclaim both those realities. With Spinoza this time, we need to develop a less ascetic spirituality, which insists that to participate more in God we need always to enter further into true, temperate, corporeal pleasures. The insinuation of both puritans and atheists, that one must choose either sensual pleasure *or* God, and always sacrifice either one or the other, must be exposed as a reduction of God to the ontic — that is, as considering God as if he were a finite recompense for the loss of something finite.

So we now have affinity, reconciliation, and embodiment. In the face of globalization and the new American empire, we must counterpose Augustine's counter-empire, the city of God. We may do this alongside many secular brothers and sisters (for example, socialists, communists, and anarchists). We should not refuse their co-operation, but yet we should insist that they have little real grasp of the counter-empire, since, for them, it is still a matter of simply unleashing more undifferentiated liberty, going yet further beyond the law. For us, rather, it should seem that the impossibility of pure flux and unmediated difference will inevitably bring with it an arbitrary, oppressive de-territorialization. In the end, the only way to escape restricting terrain is to refuse the categorical opposition of territory and escape. If there *is* any human nature, perhaps it resides in the desire to be at once at home and abroad. But this is possible only where one admits the lure of transcendence. Then both immanent dynamism and immanent stasis are outplayed. Then the flux is not itself an immanent god — the pure space of pure movement — but consists merely in the relay stations, the open but identifiable essences along its course. Then we are not postmodern nomads, but ecclesial pilgrims.

Thus, to affinity, reconciliation, and embodiment we can now add not only the city of God but also transcendence. Immanence appears to be democratic and mobile, but it always re-erects a hierarchy of self-government that sunders the totality between the static and the mobile, or else the other way around. If the mobile is on top, as in postmodernity, then of course its truth can never arrive in the world, and the postmodern or new-age self that perceives this truth is ironically removed from the world, and from its real self-hood of memory and hope. We can then never be liberated or redeemed. No gift will ever be given. Instead, since pure flux, pure de-territorialization, will never be manifest, the urge toward this illusion will always engender the surrogate of formal, arbitrary, and oppressive control of flux by a sovereign empire. By contrast, transcendence appears hierarchical and fixed, but its ontological height is beyond all immanent heights, and therefore is as close to ontic depths as to ontic elevations. For this reason, its truth *can* be mediated to us and we *can,* one day, be liberated. For this reason, transcendence offers us its gift of affinity through reconciliation, in our bodies on pilgrimage within the city of God below.

Wounded Vision and the Optics of Hope

ROBERT PAUL DOEDE AND PAUL EDWARD HUGHES

Introduction

Sensationalism. Pornography. Pedophilia. These words describe critics' disapproving responses to fashion photographer Steven Meisel's photographs shot for Calvin Klein's 1995 controversial and highly sexualized "shock advertising" campaign, featuring scantily clad and .extremely young-looking models in compromising poses. One of the images shows a young blonde in her mid teens wearing a small sleeveless shirt and cut-off shorts that show her panties; she sits spread-eagled on a basement floor (reminiscent of — critics have suggested — cheap pornographic sets) with a look of surprise on her face and a clear message of sexual availability given by her body language. Such exploitation and objectification permeate our visual culture, making it more and more difficult for us to see the humanity of the other.

Is it possible that the human gaze — trained by such ads to be objectifying, marginalizing, and corrosive of subjectivity — can be reconfigured into a benevolent and loving gaze? Can the enterprise of photography, often an institutionalization of this gaze, and photographic images, in particular, be sources of hope and transformation in a postmodern culture saturated with exploitative imagery?

Through an integrative deployment of the disciplines of biblical theology, philosophy, and photography, we will suggest that vision and visuality can promote hope. Contrary to the often numbing and objectifying effects of images today, we argue that images do not have to function with or embody such negative effects. Instead, we will attempt to re-legitimize the visual by re-envisioning photography, and sight generally, through critical cultural and theological lenses. Ultimately, we will outline an aesthetics of photography and an ethics of vision that grounds hope in the sacramental disclosure of the human soul via the face.[1]

At the outset, a few words must be given to framing our discussion of hope. We believe that Christian hope must be grounded on a theological reading of human temporality, a reading that is narrative and whose plot includes four essential elements: transcendence, imagination, indeterminacy, and community.

Christian hope depends upon a transcendence that repudiates immanently grounded myths of hope and embraces a future that comes from God — in an eschatological re-envisioning of the fallen created order. This divinely promised future provides the impetus for our critique of the present order and its injustices, prevailing ideologies, and regimes of oppression.[2] It also provides a Christian vision of hope.

Hope cannot exist without the ability to imagine otherwise. In *Hope against Hope: Christian Eschatology at the Turn of the Millennium,* Richard Bauckham and Trevor Hart describe St. John's use of symbol in the book of Revelation as "an imaginative vision in which the dominant way of seeing things (both present and future) is fundamentally challenged and an alternative picture painted of the potentialities and pos-

---

1. Many of the points made in this paper are germinal, and will be developed in our forthcoming book contracted with Brazos Press, provisionally titled *Virtuous Vision: A Holistic Theology of Seeing.*

2. As Moltmann states, "Those who hope in Christ can no longer put up with reality as it is, but begin to suffer under it, to contradict it. Peace with God means conflict with the world, for the goad of the promised future stabs inexorably into the flesh of every unfulfilled present" (*Theology of Hope* [London: SCM, 1967], p. 21). Gabriel Marcel, the French Christian existentialist, says, "The only genuine hope is one based on what does not depend on us" ("Concrete Approaches to Investigating the Ontological Mystery," in *Gabriel Marcel's Perspectives on the Broken World,* trans. Katharine Rose Hanley [Milwaukee: Marquette University Press, 1998], p. 187). For a more comical perspective, see Walker Percy's *Lost in the Cosmos: The Last Self-Help Book* (New York: Pocket Books, 1983), where he, with wit and stunning insight into the human need for transcendence, explores the human predicament.

sibilities inherent in God's future."[3] This process encapsulates the role of the Old Testament prophets, who were called to see things otherwise.[4] We believe that eschatology is a form of countercultural global imagination, and *hopeful* eschatology narrates imaginatively all things in light of God's promises.

The *telos* and content of hope (an inherently futural verity) remain largely indeterminate — even within the Christian eschatological vision. Historically, violence and oppression usually have accompanied any hope that is defined by an overly determinate *telos*. When humans believe they know the precise shape of the good, they feel obliged to realize it by *any* means possible. Although Christianity has not consistently reflected the indeterminacy of the shape of hope's realization, we are convinced that Christian hope lives in the filtered light of a future justice whose adumbration is faint and contested — we do see through a glass darkly.

Finally, hope is communal. Gabriel Marcel writes that "there can be no hope which does not constitute itself through a *we* and for a *we*. . . . all hope is at bottom choral."[5] Or, as he writes elsewhere, "I hope in thee for us."[6] Bauckham and Hart agree: "Real hope is essentially rooted in the qualities and capacities of otherness, of that which lies beyond itself in other people."[7] The self-absorption arising out of Enlightenment individualism is called into question by this feature of hope.

It is this Christian sort of hope — constituted by conditions of transcendence, imagination, indeterminacy, and community — that we are considering with respect to vision in general, and photography and the photograph in particular. Can objectification be surmounted within these visual institutional practices, so that at least slight glimmers of such hope can shine through? With these principles of the eco-

---

3. Richard Bauckham and Trevor Hart, *Hope against Hope: Christian Eschatology at the Turn of the Millennium* (Grand Rapids: Eerdmans, 1999), p. 197.

4. On the prophets and their re-envisioning, imaginative task, see Walter Brueggemann, *The Prophetic Imagination* (Minneapolis: Fortress, 1978), and Abraham J. Heschel, *The Prophets* (New York: Harper and Row, 1962), particularly his introduction.

5. Gabriel Marcel, "The Encounter with Evil," in *Tragic Wisdom and Beyond*, trans. Peter McCormick and Stephen Jolin (Evanston, Ill.: Northwestern University Press, 1973), p. 143.

6. Gabriel Marcel, *Homo Viator: Introduction to a Metaphysic of Hope*, trans. Emma Craufurd (New York: Harper and Row, 1962), p. 60.

7. Bauckham and Hart, *Hope against Hope*, p. 62.

logical conditions necessary for the nourishment and proliferation of hope in mind, we turn now to the problem of exploitative vision — or, in theoretical terms, the phenomenon of "ocularcentrism."

The Problem of Ocularcentrism

Ocularcentrism is the technical philosophical term used for a fascination with the power that vision has — whether it is the vision of the physical eye or of the mind's eye — to get us in contact with reality. It is the placing of the eye and its accompanying metaphorics of image and luminosity at the center of our commerce with reality. But why has the charge of ocularcentrism become so scandalous in recent history? Why have American pragmatists, certain hermeneutical philosophers, and most post-structuralist cultural critics maligned the centrality of vision in contemporary Western culture? To answer this question we will outline the historical roots of visual primacy in the West and identify the features of vision that established its sensorial supremacy in antiquity and that have, subsequently and somewhat ironically, also come to be the targets of its contemporary vilification.

As far back as the historical record of metaphysical speculation goes, vision seems to have been the darling of sensory modalities. One can find reference to the supremacy of sight over the other senses in the pre-Socratic writings of Heraclitus and Parmenides.[8] Plato's "myth of the cave" highlights the unparalleled epistemic virtues of the pure vision of the mind's eye.[9] And, of course, for Aristotle vision is the noblest of senses.[10] A corollary of this privileging of vision is the metaphysics of light, wherein clarity and distinctness are valorized as sacred features of truth, while shadows, ambiguity, and vagueness are associated with illusion and error.

8. Kathleen Freeman, *Ancilla to the Pre-Socratic Philosophers: A Complete Translation of the Fragments in Diels,* Fragmente der Vorsokratiker (Cambridge: Harvard University Press, 1966).

9. Plato, *Republic,* trans. G. M. A. Grube (Indianapolis: Hackett, 1982), bk. VII. Notice here how already the metaphorics of vision has permeated the discourse of cognition.

10. Aristotle, *De Anima* and *Metaphysics,* in *The Complete Works of Aristotle,* trans. Jonathan Barnes (Princeton, N.J.: Princeton University Press, 1984); see especially *Metaphysics* A980a25.

Western culture has sustained many different discourses of vision. The form that this privileging of vision has taken has not been constant across its pre-modern, modern, and postmodern embodiments. All Western expressions of ocularcentrism have, however, used vision and its metaphorics to schematize conceptions of reality (ontology: essence as *eidos*, or form, or image), knowledge (epistemology: truth as clarity, or illumination), and behavior (ethics and politics: goodness as light). In the discussion that follows, we will use the theoretical work of Hans Jonas to explore the experiential grounds from which the primacy of vision arose to formulate the beginnings of a phenomenology of vision. Once we are familiar with ocularity's tendencies and potentials, we will be in a position to appreciate its current standing.

Jonas and the Nobility of Sight

Why has vision rather than touch, taste, or hearing been given such elevated status in the traditions of the West? What is it about vision that makes it stand out as more closely related to truth and reality than any other sense? Hans Jonas's seminal essay "The Nobility of Sight: A Study in the Phenomenology of the Senses"[11] helps us to answer this question. Jonas argues that the most basic concepts informing the Western worldview have their phenomenological roots in the virtues of sight. As he puts it, "the mind has gone where vision pointed."[12] He identifies three primary features of sight that supply the experiential grounds for schematic concepts that have become fundamental to the metaphysics of the West. Foregoing the details of Jonas's intriguing work, we can summarize his findings with a diagram of arrows pointing from the three most important experiential features of vision to concepts they have given rise to and underwrite.

simultaneity of image	$\rightarrow$	eternity
dynamic neutralization	$\rightarrow$	objectivity
spatial distance	$\rightarrow$	infinity

11. Hans Jonas, *The Phenomenon of Life: Toward a Philosophical Biology* (Chicago: University of Chicago Press, 1982).

12. Jonas, *The Phenomenon of Life*, p. 152.

Vision's *simultaneity of image* gives us in *an instant* sense of "a world of co-present qualities spread out in space,"[13] an image of a temporal slice, a moment out of time, a field of objects freeze-framed in various spatial relations. Arguably, all of the other senses have a temporal seriality built into their disclosures, such that the content of these senses is "never simultaneously present as a whole, but always in the making, always partial and incomplete."[14] Jonas says that sight is the only sense that "provides the sensual basis on which the mind may conceive the idea of the eternal, that which never changes and is always present,"[15] and thereby elevates "static Being over dynamic Becoming, fixed essences over ephemeral appearances."[16]

The ability of sight to remain anonymous in its instantaneous information-uptake of a whole field of objects is what Jonas means by its *dynamic neutralization*. The subject's interaction with the object of sight is kept at a minimum, because information is neutrally transmitted at the speed of light to the observer. Seeing requires no perceptible activity either on the part of the object or on that of the subject — they each let "the other be what they are and as they are."[17] Vision's "peculiar causal 'indifference,'" claims Jonas, provides the phenomenological grounding of the concept of objectivity, of an object as it is in itself as distinct from the object as it affects me or I or it.[18] Herewith essence seems to become separable from existence as the abstraction of the visual image is idealized into conceptual thought.

Finally, addressing the third feature, *spatial distance,* Jonas points out that neither simultaneity of presentation nor dynamic neutrality would be possible if sight was not "the ideal distance-sense."[19] By this he means that taste, touch, smell, and hearing all require and gain precision through proximity with the information source, while sight, in

---

13. Jonas, *The Phenomenon of Life,* p. 136.

14. Jonas, *The Phenomenon of Life,* p. 136.

15. Jonas, *The Phenomenon of Life,* p. 136.

16. Martin Jay, *Downcast Eyes: The Denigration of Vision in Twentieth-Century French Thought* (Berkeley: University of California Press, 1994), p. 24. As we shall see below, Heidegger's notion of the alethic gaze might well be a significant exception to this tendency.

17. Jonas, *The Phenomenon of Life,* p. 148.

18. Jonas, *The Phenomenon of Life,* p. 147.

19. Jonas, *The Phenomenon of Life,* p. 147.

contrast, improves through proper distance. "The best view is by no means the closest view," Jonas observes.[20] Sight co-presents the focal object with all of the intervening space that separates it from the viewer, as well as the background space from which the figure stands out. In fact, he suggests that the "and so on" with which visual space is imbued constitutes the experiential grounds of our idea of infinity: "The unfolding of space before the eye, under the magic of light, bears in itself the germ of infinity — as a perceptual aspect."[21] Much more than the other senses, vision's uncommitted route through space gives it a tremendous survival value, and offers its bearer a measure of time for adaptive behavior in response to the import of the sight, a sort of foreknowledge of future probabilities.

The metaphorics of vision have infiltrated our thinking because, if Jonas is right, our minds are rooted in our senses, and vision is the sense whose deliveries are most responsible for catapulting *Homo erectus* into transcending the immediacy of its commerce with otherness, and thus vision is the sense most responsible for *Homo Sapiens*'s distinct way of being in the world. If Jonas's speculations are correct, mind has indeed gone where sight points,[22] and this surely helps us to understand why vision typically has been considered the noblest of the senses. But, as we noted above, vision has fallen from grace in the assessment of many cultural theorists and philosophers today. After we examine the claims of two recent critics of vision's supremacy — Michel Foucault and Jean-Paul Sartre — we will be in a better position to appreciate why the privileging of vision is now strongly contested.

Foucault on the Social Expression of Visual Hegemony in Modernity

In 1791, Jeremy Bentham published his plans for the all-seeing prison architecture that he designated a panopticon, described by David Lyon as a prison whose center was an inspection lodge where prison guards "would be able to keep an eye on prisoners, whose cells fanned out in a

20. Jonas, *The Phenomenon of Life*, p. 147.
21. Jonas, *The Phenomenon of Life*, p. 151.
22. Jonas, *The Phenomenon of Life*, p. 152.

circular pattern around the central tower. Through careful use of lighting, prisoners' every movement would be clearly visible to the guards, although they, skillfully concealed behind wooden blinds, would be out of the prisoners' sight."[23]

Bentham's panoptic aspirations are early signs of modernity's tendency to transform vision into *supervision*[24] and are paradigmatic expressions of the social biases harbored in modernity's privileging of vision.[25] According to Foucault, the panopticon was, except for minor details, an ideal microcosm of the transparent and shadowless society that Enlightenment philosophes hoped the light of reason would produce.[26] If vision was the valorized sense of the Enlightenment, if knowledge was a supreme form of sight (and insight), and if knowledge and power are inseparable, then vision is supreme power. As Foucault put it, "The gaze that sees is the gaze that dominates."[27]

The panopticon harnessed this power to produce individuals whose socially aberrant subjectivity was to be disciplined out of them. These "subjects" were, in effect, "objects," docile bodies produced as the prisoners internalized the omniscient gaze of the wardens at the centered, normative eye of the inspection lodge. Over time, the panoptical relation of nonreciprocal visibility would engender a severe self-objectification in the prisoners: "as the prisoner subjects himself to the dissociative manipulation of surveillance. . . . he simultaneously experiences his body as abandoned, *as an object rather than a subject.*"[28] Under the constant objectifying gaze of otherness, prisoners would internalize the disciplines of the prison and begin to live their subjectivity as objects, conforming to the panoptic machine's microphysics of power. Foucault suggests that our late-modern society has itself be-

---

23. David Lyon, "Bentham's Panopticon: From Moral Architecture to Electronic Surveillance," *Queen's Quarterly* 98, no. 3 (Fall 1991): 597.

24. David Michael Levin, ed., *Modernity and the Hegemony of Vision* (Berkeley: University of California Press, 1993), p. 281.

25. Michel Foucault, *Discipline and Punish: The Birth of the Prison,* trans. Alan Sheridan (New York: Vintage, 1979), pt. 3.

26. Foucault, *Discipline and Punish,* p. 207.

27. Michel Foucault, *The Birth of the Clinic: An Archaeology of Medical Perception,* trans. A. M. Sheridan (London: Vintage, 1973), p. 166.

28. Lorna Rhodes, "Panoptical Intimacies," *Public Culture* (Winter 1998): 3 (emphasis ours).

come carceral: "We are . . . in the . . . panoptic machine, invested by its effects of power, which we bring to ourselves since we are part of its mechanism."[29] The dominant order today exercises its powers of normalization by making its subjects experience themselves as objects of its omnipresent gaze. Foucault believes that Bentham's panopticon epitomizes the social trajectory of modernity's dominant "scopic" regime. (Consider, for example, the omnipresence of surveillance cameras in public and private spaces.)

Sartre and the Ocular Breakdown of Intersubjectivity

Sartre, the man who says he thought with his eyes,[30] was somewhat of a paradox. On the one hand, he was an unrepentant voyeur, always watching others from a distance. For example, in his *War Diaries* he even refers to himself as an aerial plant[31] and claims that his natural place in life was a sixth-floor apartment in Paris that overlooked all the neighboring apartment buildings.[32] But, on the other hand, he suffered from ocular-phobia; his writings are filled with experiences of ocular violations. For instance, in his autobiography he recounts how he felt only once that God existed. While playing with matches, as a child, he accidentally burned a small rug. In the process of covering up this crime, God suddenly saw him. "I felt his gaze inside my head and on my hands," Sartre writes. "I whirled about in the bathroom, horribly *visible*, a live target. Indignation saved me. I flew into a rage against so crude an indiscretion, I blasphemed, I muttered like my grandfather: 'God damn it, God damn it, God damn it.' He never looked at me again."[33] Had it not been for God's ocular intrusion, "there might have been something between us,"[34] Sartre suggests. This mishap profoundly textured the rest of Sartre's life. As he says, "My truth, my character, and

29. Foucault, *Discipline and Punish*, p. 217.

30. Jean-Paul Sartre, *The War Diaries of Jean-Paul Sartre*, trans. Quintin Hoare (New York: Pantheon, 1984), p. 15.

31. Sartre, *The War Diaries*, p. 293.

32. Jean-Paul Sartre, *The Words*, trans. Bernard Frechtman (New York: Vintage, 1964), pp. 59-60, 293.

33. Sartre, *The Words*, p. 102.

34. Sartre, *The Words*, p. 103.

my name were in the hands of adults. I had learned to see myself through their eyes. . . . When they were not present, they left their gaze behind."[35] It also marked his later writings, where he read all social relations in the light of this experience, as if visual oppression were an essential feature of the human condition.

With Sartre we begin to recognize that the objectification Foucault identified in conditions of nonreciprocal visibility (Bentham's panopticon) may be a dimension of reciprocal visibility as well. In fact, Sartre's play *No Exit*, his biography of Jean Genet, and his magnum opus *Being and Nothingness* suggest that human identity is born in the objectifying gaze of the other — not through an intersubjective gaze into or along with the eyes of others, but through the violent staredown [*le regard*] of objectification.

Without getting lost in the welter of technical jargon and the paradoxical assertions through which Sartre paints his vision of human Being, let us simply say that his "thinking with his eyes" produced a rather dark understanding of human possibilities. Sartre depicts the eyes of others as drain holes in Being that seek to suck one's transcendence, one's freedom, into their own nothingness, where it congeals into a objectified image.[36] The other is "the subject who is revealed to me in that flight of myself toward objectification."[37] Only through the eyes of the other do I have a nature; whatever objective essence I have is found in the other's solidified image of me. So if I am to be the foundation of my own identity, I must possess the other through whose eyes my transcendence has been objectified into some thing. As Sartre puts it: "I attempt to lay hold of the Other so that he may release to me the secret of my being."[38] Little wonder that he asserts that "conflict is the original meaning of being-for-others."[39] When the Sartrean eye turns on itself, all it can see is an impossible upsurge of sheer nothingness from opaque and absurd Being.[40] When it turns to nature, all it can feel

35. Sartre, *The Words*, p. 83.

36. Sartre, *Being and Nothingness*, trans. Hazel Barnes (New York: Washington Square, 1966), p. 343.

37. Sartre, *Being and Nothingness*, p. 345.

38. Sartre, *Being and Nothingness*, p. 387. Further on, Sartre writes, "Thus my project of recovering myself is fundamentally a project of absorbing the Other."

39. Sartre, *Being and Nothingness*, p. 387.

40. Sartre, *Being and Nothingness*, p. 784. Here Sartre refers to the human reality as

is nausea at the dizzying spectacle of superfluous existences.[41] And, when it turns to others, all it can accomplish is conflict, a hellish battle of wounded and wounding gazes,[42] each seeking to transcend the transcendence of the other.[43]

Postmodernity's anti-ocularcentrism perhaps now begins to make a bit more sense. Foucault surveys the historical sites of power-knowledge that structure the sociopolitical dynamics of our civilization and indicts the carceral society that he sees for its ocularcentrism, its ominous display of how the microphysics of visuality gravitate toward objectification, control, and normalization. Sartre's pitiless eye looks deep into interpersonal dynamics and sees nothing but fragile subjectivities violently oppressing each other as each seeks impossibly to possess itself in the other's objectified image of it. Both Foucault and Sartre recognize that power and visuality are inseparable. But our question here is whether this power must always be of nefarious import. Can visuality not sometimes be redemptive as well?

Re-envisioning Ocularity

Redeeming Philosophical Insights

So are we doomed to an alienating visual primacy? Are alienating tendencies essential to visuality? Several other voices from the twentieth century decry vision as inherently alienating — Bergson, Lacan, Debord, Irigaray, and Dewey, to name a few. In response, we need to understand that vision — or, perhaps better, *scopic regimes* — have histories, as Herder, Vico, and Marx made apparent. What is seen, or how it is seen, is not a passive and ideologically neutral affair. Our eyes conceal a past as they reveal our present, and thus what they reveal in our present cannot be taken as a mere registering of what is objectively there. This is not a defect of our human access to reality, but a precondition of its very possi-

---

a project of metamorphosing "its own For-itself into an In-itself-for-itself"; this project he argues is contradictory, so he concludes that "[m]an is a useless passion."

41. Sartre, *Nausea,* trans. Lloyd Alexander (New York: New Directions Publishing, 1964), p. 177.

42. Sartre, *No Exit,* trans. Stuart Gilbert (New York: Alfred A. Knopf, 1948), p. 61.

43. Sartre, *Being and Nothingness,* p. 352.

bility. If the existential and hermeneutical phenomenologists have taught us anything, it is that the biases of our embodiment are what ultimately give us figures standing out *(ek-sisting)* within a background, what open us to a world of otherness and others that matter to us.

Obviously our bodies bring with them an array of limitations and possibilities based on the physiology that underwrites our species's optic capacities. We know that what the fly's eyes see and what the eagle's eyes see are not what our eyes see. And this is a consequence of the differing developmental pasts of our disparate physiologies. The human way of seeing is *not* merely a function of physiology; our sight is not exhausted by its genetic determinants, but is ensconced in a cultural surround which in-forms, that is, re-determines or re-structures, the givens of our genetic endowment.[44] Because we are self-reflexive beings, our vision and visual practices can become objects of our higher-order concerns (e.g., to control others, to distract us from our self-alienation, or to *face* the humanity in the widow, the orphan, and the alien).[45]

Vision is culturally permeable. The normative framework through which I take up a position and configure my attention tacitly comes to co-presence in the field of figures my vision discloses.[46] That is, what we see cannot be finally separated from what we bring to sight. The values that have textured our sensibilities will tacitly in-form our visuality.

44. Norwood Russell Hanson, *Patterns of Discovery* (Cambridge: Cambridge University Press, 1958), p. 19. As Hanson's polemic against sense-data theories of perception never ceases to emphasize, we are not photoplates; seeing is much more than absorbing up optical sensibilia. We must *learn* to see certain things; what we see is seen through our past experiences, assumptions, skills, habits, and language.

45. Paul M. Churchland, *Scientific Realism and the Plasticity of Mind* (Cambridge: Cambridge University Press, 1979), chap. 1. Churchland argues persuasively that perception often involves lots of top-down processing where our higher-order cognitions can significantly in-form what we see. Perception is a compromise between cognition and sensation, or as Arthur C. Danto puts it, "The eye is tainted by the original sin of cognition, and we may as well be conscious of the fact" (from his "Description and Phenomenology of Perception," in *Visual Theory: Painting and Interpretation,* ed. Norman Bryson, Michael Ann Holly, and Keith Moxey [New York: HarperCollins, 1991], p. 207).

46. Here Michael Polanyi's work on the role of subsidiary awareness in the phenomenological transformation of focal objects of attention is relevant; see his "The Logic of Tacit Inference," in *Knowing and Being: Essays by Michael Polanyi,* ed. Marjorie Grene (Chicago: University of Chicago Press, 1969).

With this framework in mind, we contend that vision is *not* inherently objectifying, homogenizing, power-hungry, or oppressive of others. There is an implicit essentialism underlying the ocularcentric critique. Consequently, we are willing to entertain the possibility that vision can be gentle and loving, that it can surmount objectification and be open to difference and hospitable to others. We agree with Foucault that "There are times in life when the question of knowing if one can think differently than one thinks, and *perceive* differently than one sees, is absolutely necessary if one is to go on looking and reflecting at all."[47] Vision, we recognize with Jonas, does have a natural tendency to distance the onlooker from the visual field, giving him or her an enhanced measure of objectivity. This is a crucial dimension of visuality, one that is critical for identifying and critiquing oppressive ideologies. It is also a dimension that Foucault seems to have "overlooked." It is only one dimension of visuality, however. Recognizing this, and not downplaying its proper place in the economy of our visuality, we want to emphasize *counter-visions* and the pursuit of *ocular-eccentricity*.[48] We are seeking a hopeful visuality that can open new and diverse ways of seeing, without forgetting that all disclosure entails concealment, thus ensuring that other visions — or visions of the other — are essential to getting the picture.

Nurturing Counter-Visions

The capacity of vision for intimacy and intersubjectivity must not be overlooked, as it typically has been by post-structuralists, who seem to be obsessed with vision's blind spots and darker dealings with otherness. We will highlight two thinkers whose counter-visions can open our eyes to the possibilities of an optics of hope.

M. M. Bakhtin was renowned for his dialogistic philosophy of meaning and was himself very alive to the enrichments of visuality. In his long essay "Author and Hero in Aesthetic Activity," Bakhtin argues that human meaning is created and experienced through a mutuality

---

47. Michel Foucault, *History of Sexuality*, vol. 2: *Use of Pleasure*, trans. Robert Hurley (New York: Vintage), p. 8 (emphasis ours).

48. Jay, *Downcast Eyes*, p. 591.

of perspectives, or gazes, wherein each vision supplements what is lacking in the other.[49] Here he speaks of an "excess of seeing,"[50] by which he means that in human encounters, each person sees what is inaccessible to the other person. That is, I can see your face, the world behind your back, and a whole series of objects and relations that are not available to you, even as you can see similarly in relation to me. As Susan Felch explains, "Your vision supplements mine, just as mine supplements yours. In order for us to understand ourselves, that is to create meaning, we must each 'fill in' the other's horizon, by offering our 'excess of vision' to the other as a gift."[51] Bakhtin is careful to note that excess of vision allows the seer to "fill-in" the horizon of the other human being "without at the same time forfeiting his [the other's] distinctiveness."[52] This means that I can get a perspective on another person that she cannot get on herself, and this has ethical implications because my perspective might well contain information that is of vital significance to her well-being. It is precisely the *distance* from the other, highlighted by Bakhtin, that is a possible means whereby vision's excess can bring assistance to the other. Again, we need to appreciate that the detachment of sight has a lighter, more positive side than critics of ocularcentrism have been willing to admit, and this, as already noted, has profound import for any ideological critique.

The nonreciprocity of seer and seen is of loathsome importance in Foucault, as a means of implementing the seer's power over the seen. For Bakhtin, however, this nonreciprocity is essential to the communal and redemptive possibilities of sight. It brings an otherness to the seen, which is imbued with power to impoverish, oppress, and normalize, but also to enrich, liberate, and individualize. Bakhtin remarks, "I am conscious of myself and become myself only while revealing myself for another, through another, and with the help of another. . . . I cannot manage without another, I cannot become myself without another."[53]

---

49. In M. M. Bakhtin, *Art and Answerability: Early Philosophical Essays* (Austin: University of Texas Press, 1990), pp. 4-256.

50. Bakhtin, *Art and Answerability*, p. 23.

51. Susan M. Felch, "'In the Chorus of Others': M. M. Bakhtin's Sense of Tradition," unpublished paper (27 October 2000), p. 11.

52. Bakhtin, *Art and Answerability*, p. 25.

53. Bakhtin, "Problems of Dostoevsky's Poetics," quoted in Felch, "Bakhtin's Sense of Tradition," p. 13.

Here the other's gaze descends on me "like a gift, like grace, which is incapable of being understood and founded from within myself."[54] The other's gaze can be healing because the other may well see in me and my circumstances possibilities and potentialities that I cannot see for myself. Your gaze can initiate me into my own possibilities of self-transcendence and development, bringing hope to me, who might be someone who could find no reason to hope for himself.

Martin Heidegger supplements Bakhtin's communal hope for the gaze by highlighting the transcendent and indeterminate otherness that hope feeds on. Much of his discourse about truth and *Dasein's* relation to Being is structured by the metaphorics of vision.[55] Heidegger recognized that vision was a gift that humanity was entrusted with and in which lay great potential for both wholesomeness and impoverishment.[56] He was seeking a new comportment of visuality, one in which otherness is allowed to show itself from itself in its difference from our conception of it. In his writing, two disparate and fundamental kinds of vision emerge, the vision of inauthenticity and the vision of authenticity, or what David Levin refers to as the *assertoric* gaze and the *alethic* gaze.[57]

The *assertoric* gaze is the gaze of inauthenticity, an "ego-logical" vision, a vision nurtured on the necessities of survival that pursues total and shadowless visibility in order that it might master and dominate otherness. This sort of vision is highly reminiscent of Sartre's account of the gaze. It is the vision of the will-to-power, for it allows us to "presence" or "figure-out" beings only as tools to manipulate, or as beings who are objectified substances whose properties and external relations are displayed explicitly before the ego-subject. The operative concern of this vision is correctness, accurately re-presenting objective features (truth as correspondence), and calculative predictability and manipulation (truth as utility). The intentionality of this gaze is ab-

---

54. Bakhtin, *Art and Answerability*, p. 49.

55. For example, he speaks of "presencing" *(Anwesen)*, "the moment of vision" *(Augenblick)*, "the clearing" *(Lichtung)*, "unconcealment" *(Unverborgenheit)*, "circumspective looking" *(Umsicht)*, "horizon," etc.

56. Martin Heidegger, *Parmenides*, trans. André Schuwer and Richard Rojcewicz (Bloomington: Indiana University Press, 1992), pp. 150-51.

57. See David Levin, *The Opening of Vision: Nihilism and the Postmodern Situation* (New York: Routledge, 1988), chap. 4.

stract, anxious, aggressive, rigid, arrogant, one-dimensional, and totalizing, and it is eager either to subsume otherness into the safe confines of concepts or to manipulate otherness into promoting the realization of the ego's desires.

In contrast, the *alethic* gaze, the authentic gaze, is the chastened, non-objectifying gaze of the seer who opens himself or herself in circumspective concern to the "thoughtful maintenance of Being's preserve."[58] The operative concern of this gaze is to allow beings to show themselves from themselves, such that what is undisclosed in their "presencing" is preserved. (Their background, the clearing of their "presencing," is left intact, and not all "figured-out," so to speak.) Unlike the assertoric gaze, which seeks to see what it already knows, the alethic gaze wishes to know what it sees.[59] This gaze is caring, open, relaxed, inclusive, ecstatic, and wholesome, but non-totalizing, and it is eager to let beings be. This is the visuality that gives presence to Being in its playful modulations of disclosure and concealment; and it remains open to Being's way of "presencing" and "absencing" through beings.[60] In contrast to the assertoric gaze of our average everydayness, which "would like to exclude from what is present all absence,"[61] what "presences" before the alethic gaze "presences" together *both* unconcealment and concealment. Because the alethic gaze preserves the interplay of Being's "presencing" and "absencing," it is a humbled vision that is de-centered, whose clearing is a shadow-land and whose closure is never totalized.

Heidegger eschews the visualist essentialism implicit in much of

58. Martin Heidegger, *Early Greek Thinking,* trans. Frank Capuzzi and David Krell (New York: Harper and Row, 1975), p. 36.

59. Abraham Heschel is the source of this distinction between the desire to know what one sees as opposed to seeing what one knows; see *The Prophets,* p. xi.

60. Heidegger believes that the pre-Socratic philosophers got it right — all disclosure brings with it concealment — and suggests that the modern approach to Being deriving from later Western metaphysics cannot reconcile itself to this fundamental modulation of our embodied finitude. The West has forgotten that Being, although disclosed through beings, is not itself a being. Consequently Being has withdrawn. Being is not some *thing* that can be figured out and thus made subject to the will-to-power. Heidegger calls Being the "groundless," and says as long as we seek a ground only in the form of a being, we will surely encounter the "oblivion of being" (Heidegger, *Parmenides,* p. 150).

61. Heidegger, *Early Greek Thinking,* p. 37.

the ocularcentric critique and in Sartre's account of the gaze, suggesting that our vision is malleable over time because its character and tendencies can change. He shows that contrary to Sartre's closet essentialism, which writes conflict into the very nature of human visuality, human beings can embody an alethic gaze, a humbled vision that seeks to be open to and enriched by the transcendence of others and that can provide a clearing where others are freed to disclose and preserve their differences as distinct from our conceptions of them. Heidegger holds out hope that our vision has the potential to yet open us to what Levin calls a "new historical Gestalt formation" in which the disclosive capacities of sight are freed from the disfiguring power of the assertoric gaze.[62]

Similarly, we believe that the prevailing ego-logical, scopic regime of late modernity, with its tendencies toward objectification and commodified otherness, has largely blinded theorists to the perception of the essential humanity of others. We believe, however, that the camera (to take one example) can be a means of re-shaping the intentionality of our vision, such that through its lens we may learn how to feel the world with our eyes and to see the soul of our common humanity in the face of the other.

Facing the Soul

How might a nondualistic anthropology come to bear on the intentionality of our vision, and on our ability to discern the humanity in the other? Unfortunately, we can only touch upon this question here. Descartes, the founder of modern metaphysics, embraced a radical dualism in his attempt to wed the world-machine of science to what he understood to be the Christian perspective of the place, value, and freedom of human existence in the overall picture of things. One consequence of his dualism, and of anthropological dualism in general, is that it undermines our ability to see and to know other persons, to discern the humanity in other human beings. Descartes's dualism brings with it an epistemological and linguistic dualism, where two different

---

62. David Levin, *The Philosopher's Gaze: Modernity in the Shadows of Enlightenment* (Berkeley: University of California Press, 1999), pp. 116ff.

languages with different logics of justification had to be used side by side when the object of inquiry was a human being. The human body itself was considered a point-mass bearing properties of size, shape, location, motion — all features that can be represented objectively on a Cartesian coordinate system. In this framework, science could tell us all there is to know about this object. But the object could not be described as manifesting, bearing, or expressing anything like a feeling, intention, or thought. These properties are hidden in the mind, which itself bears no physical properties. Consequently, then, we cannot *perceive* a human being or features of humanity. Strictly speaking, all we can ever perceive are the objective properties of matter and the space it occupies. That is, we can perceive bodies, but not what it means to exist as a *human* being.[63] The very notion of expressive bodily comportment — for example, a wry smile, a despairing frown, or a loving gaze — is then a category mistake.

For Descartes, the mind becomes a private first-person theater of ideas, and the body a public third-person mechanism of extension. The relation between the two is purely contingent — the state of one warrants no inferences about the state of the other. This obviously leads to the so-called "problem of other minds" that has tantalized modern (analytical) philosophy for centuries. Simply stated, if I can be acquainted only with the content of my own mind, and no one else's, and if I can be acquainted only with the body of other (presumably) human beings, then how do I know — when your body is twisting and moaning — whether *you* are in pain? If you are your mind, and if your mind is only contingently related to the behavior of the body your mind haunts, how can I know what is in your mind?

The rather large ethical question that falls out of this dualism is how are we to discern the humanity in a human. The answer to this question is that we cannot. At best we can inductively infer that that body over there is the site of a human person (mind) because some of its objective properties are similar to my body's properties, and my body is the site of a human person (mind). This is, however, an analogi-

---

63. Only if the human is a form of bodily being could we perceive *human* bodies, but this would entail (given Descartes's commitments to the mathematical physics of the time) that humans were machines — something Descartes could not reconcile with his religious commitments.

cal induction with two rather glaring flaws: it is an induction that has no conditions of falsification or confirmation, and it is an induction based upon a very small sample population — just one, me. But the problem of other minds is not what we want to explore. Our intention is to demonstrate that a dualistic understanding of human Being promotes a kind of blindness to the humanity of the other. If I believe that your soul, your person, is hidden behind the flesh of your bodily being, and only contingently or accidentally related to its gestures and behavior, then what I come to know of your person will be an accomplishment of *my* inferential prowess. Instead of letting you express and disclose yourself out of your bodily difference, in ways that are different from my conception of you, I will be determining your identity through my inferences as to the soul-source of the fleshly manifestations of a body bearing your name. There are big issues here that we must, unfortunately, pass over in silence. The question that we cannot ignore, however, is how a nondualistic anthropology might come to bear on the intentionality of our vision, on our ability to discern the humanity in the other.

There are hints of answers to this question in the writings of Wittgenstein, Merleau-Ponty, and Levinas. If we had the time, it would be illuminating to turn to Merleau-Ponty's discussions of the flesh as expressivity, of bodily gesture as human transcendence, of body as lived meaning, and of the eyes as accomplishing "the prodigious work of opening the soul."[64] We must, however, limit ourselves to the intimations found in Wittgenstein and Levinas on the place of the human body, especially the face, in the quest to discern the humanity in the other.

Wittgenstein, in his *Philosophical Investigations,* responds to Descartes's famous peering out onto the street where men are passing by.[65] Descartes argued that although he is inclined to say, "I see men," he knows that in reality he sees only bodies that might be "pretended men who are moved only by springs."[66] He cannot see men because man-

64. Maurice Merleau-Ponty, *The Primacy of Perception* (Evanston, Ill.: Northwestern University Press, 1964), p. 186.

65. For a helpful discussion of the import of Wittgenstein's thought as it bears on Cartesian dualism, see B. R. Tilghman, *Wittgenstein, Ethics and Aesthetics* (Albany: State University of New York Press, 1991).

66. René Descartes, *Discourse on Method* and *The Meditations* (Harmondsworth: Penguin, 1968), p. 111.

hood (i.e., humanity) is a property of the soul/mind that is hidden beneath the clothes *and flesh* of the bodies he sees. But this is not quite right. Descartes believed that he could "see" humanity, but only with his mind's eye. His mind's eye "saw" (i.e., judged or inferred) that specimen *x* bore sufficient physical properties to his own body for it to be highly probable that *x* also housed a soul.

For the dualist, the process of discerning humanity in the other is an explicit and objective intellectual operation. Having rejected anthropological dualism, however, Wittgenstein can say, "If I see someone writhing in pain with evident cause I do not think: all the same, his feelings are hidden from me."[67] We *see* his pain. Its being is its bodily expression. This is what Wittgenstein means when he claims that when one sees timidity in another's face, timidity is not "merely associated, outwardly connected with the face" — that is, contingently linked — "but fear is there, alive, in the features."[68] Wittgenstein's rejection of Cartesian dualism means that for him "the face is the soul of the body,"[69] and that "the human body is the best picture of the soul."[70] Wittgenstein asks rhetorically, "Can I not say: a cry, a laugh, are full of meaning?"[71] The human physiognomy is not merely inductive evidence for some hidden meaning, say of hope or fear, but quite literally for Wittgenstein, "Meaning is a physiognomy."[72]

Levinas acknowledges that objectification operates in the gaze in a privileged way, but contends that "it is not certain that [objectification's] tendency to inform every experience is inscribed, and unequivocally so, in being."[73] That is, Levinas, like Heidegger, rejects an essentialism of vision's distancing tendencies, and thus refuses to accept that vision intrinsically blinds us to the humanity of the other. Thus, Levinas suggests that vision can be otherwise: "The visible ca-

---

67. Ludwig Wittgenstein, *Philosophical Investigations*, trans. G. E. M. Anscombe (Oxford: Basil Blackwell, 1958), p. 223.

68. Wittgenstein, *Philosophical Investigations*, para. 537.

69. Wittgenstein, *Culture and Value*, trans. Peter Winch (Chicago: University of Chicago Press, 1980), p. 23.

70. Wittgenstein, *Philosophical Investigations*, p. 178.

71. Wittgenstein, *Philosophical Investigations*, para. 543.

72. Wittgenstein, *Philosophical Investigations*, para. 568.

73. Emmanuel Levinas, *Totality and Infinity: An Essay on Exteriority*, trans. Alphonso Lingis (Pittsburgh: Duquesne University Press, 1969), p. 188.

resses the eye. One sees . . . like one touches."[74] The other's face is for Levinas the site where an otherness that is "different in a different way to any other difference"[75] is revealed to those with eyes to see. The other's face is what exceeds "the idea of the other in me,"[76] Bakhtin's "excess of seeing" notwithstanding. Levinas goes so far as to claim,

> The dimension of the divine opens forth from the human face. . . . It is here that the Transcendent, infinitely other, solicits us and appeals to us. The proximity of the Other, the proximity of the neighbor, is in being an ineluctable moment of the revelation of an absolute presence (that is, disengaged from every relation), which expresses itself. His very epiphany consists in soliciting us by his destitution in the face of the Stranger, the widow, and the orphan.[77]

The face, says Levinas, bears a trace of the absolute Other, a trace of the Transcendent, a surplus of irreducible otherness that transgresses the totalizing boundaries of our concepts; it appears without losing its alterity. Levin comments: "The face is like an overwhelming force that erupts into the order of private lives and social history, breaching its defensive causal continuity to command our responsibility and pass the judgment of 'divine' justice on each of us."[78] *The face is where the ought is.* When we encounter the other's face, our world and self-relations are disturbed by a primordial command: "Thou shalt not kill."[79] This command of the face grounds hopes because it can decenter our other-effacing ego-logical (or inauthentic) vision and open us to what is beyond us and our subjectivities' resources. Here we have the putative "object" of sight penetrating the "subject" of the gaze, reversing the vector of violation assumed by the critics of ocularcentrism. The seer who has impoverished vision (i.e., ego-logical vision, which

74. Levinas, "Meaning and Sense," in *Collected Philosophical Papers,* trans. Alphonso Lingis (The Hague: Marinus Nijhoff, 1987), p. 118.

75. To use an expression from Paul Davies's "The Face and the Caress: Levinas's Ethical Alterations of Sensibility," in *Modernity and the Hegemony,* ed. Levin, p. 354.

76. Levinas, *Totality and Infinity,* p. 50.

77. Levinas, *Totality and Infinity,* p. 78.

78. Levin, *Philosopher's Gaze,* p. 275.

79. Levinas, *Totality and Infinity,* p. 262.

can see only what it can re-present) must undergo a certain de-centering before he or she is able to discern the invisible face of human-ity in the visible face of the other.[80] This is not, however, the impossible task that dualism faces (i.e., seeing an invisible thinking substance in the motions of a machine). Rather, it is the infinite task of becoming human ourselves, as being-for-the-other, seeing with human eyes our common humanity in the absolutely unique expressions and manifes-tations of the other, and opening ourselves to the trace of the infinite Other in the face of the finite other.

Divine Vision

Levinas grounds much of his speculation about ethics in the Hebrew Scriptures, particularly in the first section, referred to as the Torah or Pentateuch. It is our assumption that, as Christian thinkers attempt-ing to understand vision and its integral relationship to hope, we must also quarry the rich resources of biblical-theological tradition. Theo-logical grounding for the hopeful gaze developed above may be derived from various biblical texts, but we will restrict our discussion to three Old Testament texts from the Torah, and a few examples from the life of Jesus in the Gospels.

The beginning of the biblical story (Gen. 1:1–2:3) forms an intro-duction not only to the Pentateuchal prologue of Genesis 1-11, and to the Pentateuch at large, but to both the Jewish and Christian Bibles. As an exordium to the central story of Abraham and his descendants in the patriarchal narratives (Gen. 12–50), this introductory prologue also sets up the dialogical contours for how this Israelite deity will relate to the recently introduced human subjects. The most commonly used verb for seeing *(r'h)* first appears in this section in Genesis 1:4, where God validates the goodness of the light: "God *saw* the light, that it was *good;* and God divided the light from the darkness" (ASV). Here we en-counter the beginning of a relatively symmetrical pattern that contrib-utes to the narrative artistry of the book and reinforces its polemical rhetoric. In six occurrences, the material outcome of the divine artist is validated with the designation of goodness — using the Hebrew adjec-

---

80. Levin, *Philosopher's Gaze,* p. 284.

tive *ṭôb* ("good") — subsequent to its seenness.[81] Here *divine vision validates the essential goodness of its spectacle* with the recurring phrase, "And God saw that it was good." Subsequently, after the description of the creation of humans and their terrestrial tasks in verses 26-30, divine vision legitimates the presence of humans on the earth with the phrase, "and it was *very good,*" emphasized with the adverb *mᵉ'od* ("very"). Genesis 1 suggests the beginning of a normative take on divine vision, a vision that recognizes beauty and goodness and celebrates human subjectivity. This divine vision takes the spectacle of the created order and its qualitative/normative dimensions and validates them. The fact that God is said to see these basic human realities suggests that vision itself is not necessarily objectifying or alienating, but can promote the flourishing of human alterity as Levinas and others have suggested.

Another passage on divine vision in the Hebrew Bible can be found in the dialogical encounter that precedes the Israelite exodus out of Egypt. Prefacing the plot's ascent of Exodus 3:1-7:7, the short section of Exodus 2:23-25 introduces the God of the Israelites with intimate language and concern. Contextualized as a response to the incredible suffering and oppression that the Israelites experienced in Egypt (cf. 1:11-14; 2:23), the divine response to this human predicament is described with terms of hearing, remembering, *seeing,* and resolving to take action: "God *saw* [looked upon] the children of Israel, and God took knowledge of them" (2:24-25 ASV).[82] Divine vision translates into committed action — the liberating deliverance of the exodus event. This section portrays divine vision both as *a critical gaze* on oppressive sociocultural structures and practices and as a gaze that ultimately *preserves the subjectivity* of a potentially objectifiable other, thus engendering a community of hope from the fragments of brokenness and violence.

Reading the Hagar story (Gen. 16:1-16) with the exodus story illuminates the liberating character of divine vision.[83] Once again, the

---

81. On day one in 1:4; two times on day three in 1:10, 12; on day four in 1:18; on day five in 1:21, and on day six in 1:25.

82. That is, resolved to do something in response to his concern for them. Contrary to a merely cognitive reading of the verbal root *yd',* the assumption is that God's knowing — like his seeing — will lead to liberating action.

83. Paul Edward Hughes, "Seeing Hagar Seeing God: *Leitwort* and Petite Narrative in Genesis 16:1-16," *Didaskalia* 8, no. 2 (Spring 1997): 43-59.

anthropomorphic verbs used in the Exodus preface appear here, where Hagar says to Yahweh, "You are the God who *sees* me" (v. 13). This gives rise to the toponym *Beer-Lahai-Roi,* "the well of the living one who *sees* me" (v. 14 NRSV). This is a story that deals with divine concern for a marginalized outsider — the *alien* (or sojourner) of the common biblical formula "the alien, the orphan, and the widow" that Levinas adopts.[84] Dealing with the potentially objectified other, this story employs ocular language that alludes to the exodus event and reinforces the biblical-theological notion that God's loving gaze and his liberating action are inseparable. Here, the implications of divine vision emerge: it overlooks prejudicial lines of ethnicity and gender and enlarges the humanity of the other. With divine vision, the divine Other meets other, resulting in hopeful change and transformation. And humans, as bearers of God's image, are therefore capable of a seeing which is alethic, a gaze which has the potential to enlarge human subjectivity and be concerned with the eradication of social oppression.

The New Testament Gospels continue this more positive and humanizing appraisal of vision's possibilities, although they do not neglect mention of vision's darker side. In the Gospel of Mark, the portrayal of Jesus' seeing flows in continuity with the principles of divine vision from the Old Testament that we have outlined above. Instead of objectifying or homogenizing vision's spectacle (as the Pharisees were wont to do),[85] Jesus was deeply concerned about the singularity of the other,[86] and in his vision brought those who were on the margins into the foreground — as is shown in Mark 10:13-16 by the status he ascribed to small children, and, in various places in the Gospels, by the acceptance he offered to those on the lowest rungs of the social ladder. Echoes of the divine vision of the Old Testament can be heard in Mark 6:34 with its description of Jesus' compassion on those he considered

---

84. Levinas, *Totality and Infinity,* passim.

85. For example, in Mark 2:16 where the Pharisees criticize Jesus for eating with tax collectors and "sinners," and also in 7:1-23, where the Pharisees raise concerns about Jesus' disciples who eat with hands that are not ceremonially clean. Both of these examples highlight negatively assessed judgmental implications of the gaze in the Pharisaic attempt to homogenize alterity.

86. Seen in his concern to identify the individual woman in the large crowd who touched his clothing and received healing, unbeknown to him (Mark 5:30-32).

to be like sheep without a shepherd. (Matthew 9:36 adds that he saw they were harassed and helpless.) This is radically different from the distancing, objectifying effects of vision focused on by critics of ocularcentrism; it is, rather, a loving gaze that is anything but ego-logical. And it is exemplified in Jesus' declaration that when his followers embody his vision and see strangers, the poor, the sick, and the imprisoned, they are seeing him (Matt. 25:37-40).

The Gospels also render the darker side of vision and its possibilities. Both the Pharisees and Jesus' followers can have their vision affected by unbelief or spiritual blindness, either by requesting signs (Mark 8:11-12) or having eyes but not using them properly (Mark 8:17-18). More to the point for our purposes, however, is the clear statement that moral transgression can occur in the mere act of looking wrongly (Matt. 5:27-30). As Jesus says, "The eye is the lamp of the body. So, if your eye is healthy, your whole body will be full of light; but if your eye is unhealthy, your whole body will be full of darkness" (Matt. 6:22-23 NRSV).

Photography and the Redemptive Gaze

Although photography institutionalizes ocularity — the gaze — we believe that there are significant examples of photographic practices which demonstrate that photography can be an agent of hope and transformation. Below, we will show a few examples, demonstrating that, despite photography's tendencies toward objectification and de-sensitization, it has, on occasion, surmounted this corrosion of subjectivity and catalyzed hopeful awareness and social change.

Dorothea Lange, one of the most significant female photographers of the twentieth century, produced an image known as *The Migrant Mother* that illustrates how photography can raise public awareness regarding structures of social oppression. The historical context of her work that led to this photograph begins with her involvement with the Farm Security Administration (FSA) in 1935. The FSA was established by the Roosevelt administration as a government agency intent on rebuilding the American economy, and it employed photographers to produce images of agricultural conditions. In this famous portrait of a Californian migrant worker with her three small children,

[t]he face of the young woman is marked by wrinkles, the gaze full of worry directed in the distance. To the right and left the two older children, seeking protection, lean against her shoulders, hiding their faces from the camera, while the small baby has fallen asleep on its mother's lap. This highly concentrated, tightly composed image has made Dorothea Lange an icon of socially committed photography.[87]

Lange's picture highlights paternal absence, the mother's averted gaze, and the dependency of the children who look away, all reinforcing the vulnerability and plight of the poor.[88] The power of this image to focus public attention on the plight of the poor demonstrates Joel Snyder's provocative claim that photographers can educate the public's ocular intentionality.[89]

In what sense, if any, can Dorothea Lange be understood to facilitate the process of vision and photography functioning as means of hope? And hope for whom? Doherty describes how Lange's photographs, depicting labor unrest early in the Depression, caught the attention of Paul Taylor (a professor of economics at the University of California at Berkeley whom Lange later married) when they were exhibited, and Taylor subsequently procured Lange's services for the preparation of reports on the housing problems of migrant agricultural workers.[90] Their work together resulted in the inception of the first federally sponsored housing project in the United States. For many, obviously, this generated hope. But what about the criticism that Lange objectified the woman, a person whose name she did not even know, and erased her individual subjectivity by turning her into a generic icon for the Depression and its perils? What about the testimony of the woman herself — Florence Thompson — who was finally located in 1978 in her trailer home in Modesto, California? She told the United Press that, although she was proud to have been the sub-

---

87. Marianne Bieger-Thielemann, in *20th Century Photography: Museum Ludwig Cologne,* ed. Simone Philippi (Cologne: Taschen, 1996), p. 372.

88. Graham Clarke, *The Photograph* (Oxford: Oxford University Press, 1997), p. 153.

89. Joel Snyder, "Picturing Vision," in *The Language of Images,* ed. W. J. T. Mitchell (Chicago: University of Chicago Press, 1980), p. 230.

90. Robert J. Doherty, "Dorothea Lange," in *Contemporary Photographers,* ed. Colin Naylor, second ed. (Chicago: St. James, 1988), p. 580.

ject of the photograph, she had never made a cent from it and it had done her no good.[91]

It is clear that this photographic encounter and the key image that resulted from it manifest hopeful elements, but also those which are less than hopeful, retaining elements of desensitization and the objectification of the other that tend to confirm the critique of ocularcentrism. Our desire to address the ocular critique and move beyond the predominant ego-logical vision, to one that is more kenotic (i.e., self-emptying) in its orientation, acknowledges that the question of hopeful photography is complex and multidimensional. We recognize that ocularcentrism and photography have the capacity for dehumanization, but we do not believe that this is an inherent characteristic or essential character of ocularity and photography. In fact, we believe that history tends to support ocularity's hopeful possibilities in photography that brings to the public awareness human realities that might be overlooked by more fortunate members of the populace.

In a different context, Nick Ut's Pulitzer Prize-winning photograph of Kim Phuc, the nine-year-old Vietnamese girl whose naked body was scorched by napalm, is credited with bolstering the American anti-war effort and hastening the American withdrawal from South Vietnam. Despite the undoubtedly propagandistic uses this gruesome photograph has been put to, it nonetheless brought these atrocities to light and made it possible for American civilians to actually *see* some of the less popular consequences of their foreign policy. In other words, despite its rather hopeless subject matter, this image inspired hopeful consequences, making such heinous practices subject to public scrutiny. Here, photography serves a prophetic role. Both Walter Brueggemann and Abraham Heschel characterize the beginning of the prophetic task as one of calling attention to the blind spots in the vision of the status quo and criticizing entrenched social injustices.[92] According to Graham Clarke, in his discussion of photography, "the pho-

91. Derrick Price and Liz Wells, "Thinking about Photography: Debates, Historically and Now," in *Photography: A Critical Introduction*, ed. Liz Wells, second ed. (London: Routledge, 2000), p. 39.

92. But this is not the end of the prophetic task. The end of the prophetic task, Brueggemann suggests, is "to present an alternative consciousness that can energize the community to fresh forms of faithfulness and vitality" (Brueggemann, *The Prophetic Imagination*, p. 62). Also see Heschel, *The Prophets*, p. x.

tograph allows us to see what we would otherwise not see. The camera becomes an artificial eye which, through the creative 'lens' of the photographer, probes the world in an act of revelation."[93]

While Ut's image brought to international attention the questionable practices on the battlefields of Vietnam, Jo Spence (1934-1992) — the British photographer and author of *Cultural Sniping: The Art of Transgression*[94] — offered photographic images as reflexive disclosures of the inner warfare of modern consumers and their commodification, and of the male gaze and its dominant definition of femininity. Spence's body of work covered issues such as class, gender, health, and especially the body, from both a strongly political and a critical theoretical perspective. For example, Spence questioned the usual terms of reference for the female body in a series of photographs in which she made her own body, from her diagnosis of breast cancer to her eventual death from leukemia, the subject of representation. Again, as a negative movement, her calling into question the internalized male gaze as defining of feminine identity entails a movement toward liberation, and thus hope.

One final consideration of hope and photography recognizes the possibility for the Levinasian encounter with (and ethical obligation in the face of) the other to take place through the mediated face as represented by a photographic image. Joanna Woodall amplifies this encounter through her art-historical work on the genre of portraiture.[95] Tracing the portrait back to the fifteenth century, she identifies the honorific function of the portrait within aristocratic society and its tie to the nobility. A present-day concern to bring hope to inhabitants of the so-called margins of society can ennoble them through the honorific genre of photographic portraiture. Diane Arbus (1923-1971) was a photographer who demonstrated hopeful elements in this way. A New York fashion-trained photographer, Arbus took to photographing "sub-paradigmatic" humans in order to depict their humanity — even though they were on the margins of society. She photographed people with physical growth abnormalities, those with other socially unac-

93. Clarke, *The Photograph*, p. 20.

94. Jo Spence, *Cultural Sniping: The Art of Transgression* (London: Routledge, 1995).

95. "Introduction: Facing the Subject," in *Portraiture: Facing the Subject* (Manchester: Manchester University Press, 1997), p. 2.

ceptable differences, and even took to photographing residents of a mental institution.[96] Arbus's vision caught something that others had missed. Speaking of her subjects, she stated simply, "They're aristocrats."[97]

The ability of photographers to see the humanity in the face of the marginalized other relies upon an implicit nondualist aesthetic. Why is it important that the photographic aesthetic is nondualist? It is important because, within the confines of a dualistic aesthetic of photography, the person cannot be manifested in the picture of the human body, since the person is only externally related to his or her body, as described above. Levinas's account of the face, when brought to bear on the medium of photography, suggests that through the mediated face, re-presented photographically, the trace of transcendence in the face of the other is the locus of ethical obligation. Therefore, within the normative framework of a theological anthropology guided by assent to the *imago Dei* in human persons, the human body becomes intrinsically sacramental and the depiction of the human body becomes a sacramental act.

Conclusion

As our short discussion of photography and the critique of the ocular sense reveals, we accept the general thrust of the critique of ocularcentrism, especially in relation to the modern scopic regime. We have sought, however, to put forward an ocular eccentricity by showing through Bakhtin, Heidegger, and Levinas that vision, rather than necessarily objectifying the other, can de-center the seer, and provoke the seer to understand with new insight the differences and humanity of the other. For Bakhtin, the gaze is able to supplement what is lacking in the other through the gift of distance; for Heidegger, the alethetic gaze preserves and promotes alterity; and for Levinas, the gaze is open to the epiphany of the Infinite in the face of the other. From a biblical-theological perspective, we argued that normative grounds for divine vision promote the divine gaze as a preserver of human subjectivity.

---

96. See her *Untitled Diane Arbus* (New York: Aperture, 1995) for this collection.
97. *Diane Arbus: An Aperture Monograph* (New York: Aperture, 1972).

The biblical material demonstrates that divine vision celebrates human goodness and assists the marginalized other — the alien, the orphan, and the widow. Photography can embody the divine vision in the prophetic tradition of seeing otherwise, and imagining differently.

Photographers such as Dorothea Lange, Nick Ut, Jo Spence, and Diane Arbus exemplify a photography that uses the very tools that have institutionalized and sustained oppressive social structures but that has the potential to reverse these structures, thereby opening the future to differences, to new possibilities that constitute the essence of hope. Vision and photography are not necessarily objectifying and hostile to alterity. The camera can indeed function as a hermeneutical tool through which we may see our way to a new ethics of vision, a moral vision informed by transcendence, imagination, indeterminacy, and community — essential elements for an ecology of hope.

Determined Hope: A Phenomenology of Christian Expectation

JAMES K. A. SMITH

We have every reason to hope. . . .

Richard Rorty[1]

Introduction: What to Expect When You're Expecting

Whether hearing jeremiads on the Right or hymns of despair on the Left, one is impressed by a seemingly pervasive hopelessness or melan-

---

1. Richard Rorty, "I Hear America Sighing," *New York Times Book Review* (November 7, 1999): 16. See also his discussion of hope in *Truth and Progress* (Cambridge: Cambridge University Press, 1998), pp. 242-43 (where he consistently rejects the notion of radical evil).

Research for this essay was supported by the Pew Foundation and the Calvin College Seminars in Christian Scholarship, whose support is gratefully acknowledged. Special thanks to Miroslav Volf for his assistance and insight. This is in many ways a correlate study to my "Determined Violence: Derrida's Structural Religion," *Journal of Religion* 78 (1998): 197-212, where I critique Derrida's notion of an indeterminate "religion without religion," calling into question the very logic for its production. A similar criticism is articulated in a more Kantian context in my "Re-Kanting Postmodernism? Derrida's Religion within the Limits of Reason Alone," *Faith and Philosophy* 17 (2000): 558-71. That critique is to some extent assumed here; however, while in the earlier pieces the critique of Derrida's "religion without religion" is foregrounded, here my criticism of Derrida's "hope without hope" is taken up within the larger constructive project of thematizing the contours of Christian hoping and eschatological expectation.

choly which characterizes late modernity.[2] Our modern gods have failed us and in this twilight we are left without a sun[3] and with no prospects for new illumination. Having been confidently marching toward the Garden to recapture paradise, we found the gates barred by flaming swords — World Wars, genocide, apartheid . . . (so many swords). And yet the disappointment seems to have caught us by surprise, for as W. H. Auden observed, our confidence had blinded us:

> Til lately we knew of no other, and between us we seemed
> To have what it took — the adrenal courage of the tiger,
> The chameleon's discretion, the modesty of the doe,
> Or the fern's devotion to spatial necessity:
> To practise one's peculiar civic virtue was not
> So impossible after all; to cut our losses
> And bury our dead was really quite easy: That was why
> We were always able to say: "We are children of God,
> And our Father has never forsaken His people."[4]

But "then we were children," he continues, suggesting another loss of innocence. "That was a moment ago/Before an outrageous novelty had been introduced into our lives./Why were we never warned? Perhaps we were."[5] Now everything has changed,[6] our confidence and hope have been shattered, and we late moderns find ourselves slipping under the surface, being pulled down by the eddy of despair.[7] Intellectuals seem

2. For versions of this story and diagnoses from different perspectives, see Andrew Delbanco, *The Real American Dream: A Meditation on Hope* (Cambridge: Harvard University Press, 1999), and Richard Bauckham and Trevor Hart, *Hope against Hope: Christian Eschatology at the Turn of the Millennium* (Grand Rapids: Eerdmans, 1999), pp. 1-43.

3. "What were we doing when we unchained this earth from its sun?" the madman asks in Nietzsche, *The Gay Science*, trans. Walter Kaufmann (New York: Vintage, 1974), p. 181. I was redirected to this by Jeffrey R. Hart, "Resurrection of the Idols: Nietzsche's System of Value" (senior thesis, Loyola Marymount University, 2000).

4. W. H. Auden, "If, On Account of the Political Situation," in *For the Time Being* (New York: Random House, 1945).

5. Auden, "If, On Account of the Political Situation."

6. "It's as if we had left our house for five minutes to mail a letter, and during that time the living room had changed places with the room behind the mirror over the fireplace" (Auden, "If, On Account of the Political Situation").

7. Rorty sees symptoms of this in political philosophy, which no longer con-

especially prone to getting sucked in, Rorty suggests: "Whereas intellectuals of the nineteenth century undertook to replace metaphysical comfort with historical hope, intellectuals at the end of this century, feeling let down by history, are experiencing self-indulgent, pathetic hopelessness."[8] We've lost our faith, and so our hope.[9]

Given this apparent consensus regarding "postmodern hopelessness," we might be surprised to find expressions of hope articulated by two supposedly quintessential "postmoderns": Richard Rorty and Jacques Derrida.[10] With almost evangelistic fervor (but without any desire for "revivals" of old-time hope), both hope against hope, proclaiming hope for a justice to come in the face of the grossest injustices. "In the place of knowledge,"[11] Rorty maintains a pragmatist hope "that full social justice can be attained,"[12] perhaps even in the next hundred

---

structs narratives that engender hope but rather begins from abstract principles. "This seems to me," he concludes, "the result of a loss of hope — or, more specifically — of an inability to construct a plausible narrative of progress. A turn away from narration and utopian dreams toward philosophy seems to me a gesture of despair" (Rorty, *Philosophy and Social Hope* [New York: Penguin, 1999], p. 232).

8. Rorty, *Philosophy and Social Hope*, p. 263.

9. That is to say that hopelessness or despair (or melancholy) is the result or symptom of the failure of a basic trust or commitment. It seems to me that this is thematized in Anthony Giddens's analysis of basic trust, where he argues that it is precisely this trust which produces hope: it is "sentiments of love which, combined with trust, generate hope and courage [faith, hope, and love!]" (*Modernity and Self-Identity: Self and Society in the Late Modern Age* [Stanford: Stanford University Press, 1991], p. 46; see also pp. 38-40). Thus, we can conclude that a loss of hope implies a crisis of trust. This will be confirmed by Rorty, who traces the loss of hope to a failure to *believe* in the stories of progress.

10. On my hesitations with the term "postmodernism," see James K. A. Smith and Shane R. Cudney, "Postmodern Freedom and the Growth of Fundamentalism," *Studies in Religion/Sciences Religieuses* 25 (1996): 25-46. The term perhaps still carries some heuristic value, however; in this essay I have used it interchangeably with "late modernity" as analyzed by Giddens in *Modernity and Self-Identity*. In general, I think we might distinguish between "postmodernity" as a social and cultural phenomenon and "postmodernism" as an intellectual or philosophical "movement" (but if pressed, I would concede that the distinction is a slippery one). In any event, I would resist only analyses which posit some radical discontinuity between modernity and postmodernity, or between the "Enlightenment project" and postmodernism (on the continuities, see my "Re-Kanting Postmodernism").

11. This raises questions about the epistemology of hope, to which we will return below.

12. Rorty, *Philosophy and Social Hope*, p. 203.

years.[13] Derrida's hope — different from Rorty's in important ways (but perhaps not *so* different) — is no less "utopian" in its expectation.[14] His too is a hope for justice which is Marxist "in spirit":[15] a "justice, which I distinguish from law, [which] alone allows the hope, beyond all 'messianisms,' of a universalizable culture of singularities"[16] — which is to say, hope for a "democracy to come."[17] Indeed, as John Caputo comments, "deconstruction comes down to an affirmation, an invocation, a *hope in the future*, and what is that if not a certain *faith*, indeed the passion of an extreme faith in the unbelievable, in *the* impossible."[18] Further developing this Derridean conception of hope, John Caputo concludes: "The name of God is the name of a chance for something

---

13. As envisioned (backward) in his "Looking Backwards from the Year 2096," in *Philosophy and Social Hope*, pp. 243-51, where Rorty suggests a revival of Walter Rauschenbusch's "social gospel" in the latter half of the twenty-first century (p. 249).

14. I use "utopian" here in the sense explicated by Jürgen Moltmann in *Theology of Hope*, trans. James W. Leitch (Minneapolis: Fortress, 1993), and *The Coming of God: Christian Eschatology*, trans. Margaret Kohl (Minneapolis: Fortress, 1996), referring to a mode of thinking that posits a radical discontinuity (or perhaps better, incommensurability) between the present and an absolute future. This is what distinguishes "the spirit of eschatology from that of utopia," and hence permits only Christian eschatology to offer hope (*Theology of Hope*, pp. 17-20). As he summarizes: "Hope and the kind of thinking that goes with it consequently cannot submit to the reproach of being utopian, for they do not strive after things that have 'no place,' but after things that have 'no place *as yet*' but can acquire one" (p. 25). Later, when this distinction is further developed, Moltmann emphasizes that such "regulative ideas" are "utopias," and asks, "[C]an we ever seriously hope for something which we know can never happen?" (*The Coming of God*, p. 34). We will pose just such a question to Derrida below.

15. This is a central claim in Jacques Derrida, *Specters of Marx*, trans. Peggy Kamuf (New York: Routledge, 1994), pp. 92-93. For Rorty's suspicion regarding just which "spirit" deconstruction has asked into its heart, and whether we really need Marx for hope, see *Philosophy and Social Hope*, pp. 210-22.

16. Jacques Derrida, "Foi et savoir: Les deux sources de la 'religion' aux limites de la simple raison," in *La religion*, ed. Thierry Marchaisse (Paris: Éditions du Seuil, 1996), p. 28; trans. Samuel Weber as "Faith and Knowledge: The Two Sources of 'Religion' at the Limits of Reason Alone," in *Religion*, ed. Jacques Derrida and Gianni Vattimo (Stanford: Stanford University Press, 1998), p. 17. On the distinction between "messianisms" (concrete, particular religions) and the "messianic" (as a universal, formal structure of obligation), see my "Determined Violence," pp. 199-207.

17. Derrida, *Specters of Marx*, pp. 59, 64-65.

18. John Caputo, *The Prayers and Tears of Jacques Derrida: Religion without Religion* (Bloomington: Indiana University Press, 1997), p. 133 (first italics added).

absolutely new, for a new birth, for the expectation, the hope, the hope against hope in a transforming future. Without it we are left without hope and are absorbed by rational management techniques."[19]

Both Rorty and Derrida, however, are critical of particularly Christian hopes. Rorty argues that the New Testament, like Greek philosophy, accepts the premise "that the social conditions of human life will never change in any important respect," and it is this conviction which "leads the writers of the New Testament to turn their attention from the possibility of a better human future to the hope of pie in the sky when we die."[20] But while Rorty faults the Christian vision for an "otherwordliness"[21] that is morally and politically debilitating, Derrida criticizes Christian hope for its political violence. Because of its determination of a particular vision of justice, Derrida argues, Christian hope legitimates the worst injustices against those who do not submit to its vision. Alluding to what Derrida describes as a "war of messianic eschatologies"[22] and his concern regarding "the forms of evil perpetrated in the four corners of the world 'in the name of religion,'"[23] Caputo concludes, "The *determinable* messianisms, the specific biblical and philosophical messianic eschatologies, are consummately dangerous. They describe a scene of violence and war, among which is to be included not only the wars that are raged over the holy city of Jerusalem but Marxism itself."[24] So it is precisely the determination of Christian (and Marxist) hope which implicates it in violence, and necessitates Derrida's disclosure of an indeterminate "messianic" religion which is the basis for hope of a justice which is, always, "to come."

While these discourses of hope offer "good news" to a postmodern culture, the task of this essay is to question these hopes in two fundamental ways. First (and here I am primarily engaging Rorty), what, if anything, *grounds* such hopes, thereby distinguishing them from mere "wishful thinking"? What *reason* do these discourses give us to be hopeful?[25] Second (and here I am thinking primarily of Derrida),

19. John Caputo, *On Religion* (New York: Routledge, 2001), p. 10.
20. Rorty, *Philosophy and Social Hope,* p. 208.
21. Rorty, *Philosophy and Social Hope,* p. 207.
22. Derrida, *Specters of Marx,* p. 58.
23. Derrida, "Foi et savoir," p. 22; "Faith and Knowledge," p. 13.
24. Caputo, *Prayers and Tears,* p. 128.
25. Let me here note, to head off initial reactions from post-foundationalists, that

what are they hoping *for*? What is the object or content of their hope? Can hope be hopeful without content? Can we hope for nothing? Here it is not a question of the ground but rather the *determination* of the object hoped for and the *horizons* within which hope is expressed.

I will argue that Rorty's hope is based on questionable and insufficient grounds, and that Derrida's hope lacks determination. As a result, both are disqualified, in a sense, from functioning as genuine hopes. More specifically, my goal is to show (contra Derrida) that determinacy per se cannot disqualify particular hopes; indeed, hope must be determinate and cannot be otherwise. Christian hope thus cannot be excluded simply by virtue of its determinacy. In order to articulate this critique, I will first provide a phenomenological analysis of the formal structure of hoping as a mode of intentional consciousness, in order to discern the features that are common to all hopes and acts of hoping. This will provide the basis for a critique of Rorty and Derrida, which in turn will open the space for a (post-critical) proclamation that a distinctly Christian hope and sense of expectation are viable (and perhaps even our only hope) in late-modern society.

Structures of Hope: A Phenomenology of Expectation

Hoping, like loving and believing (to invoke both a Pauline and a Husserlian relation), is a mode of consciousness and a particular way of "intending" the future. Like other modes of consciousness, such as perceiving and willing, hoping should admit of phenomenological analysis.[26] In order to carry this out, we will need to first briefly outline three

below I will argue that this matter of "reasons" or "ground" is not unjustified even in a post-foundationalist climate, since hoping without reason would be simply *illusion,* of which both Rorty and Derrida are critical. So any knee-jerk reply about the notion of "ground" as (God forbid) "foundationalist," will first have to work through the phenomenology of hope sketched below where I will contend that the very structure of hope demands a ground but that the nature of that grounding is not foundational in the rationalist sense.

26. I cannot here provide a full explication of phenomenology, but rather will be confined to consideration of key aspects as it pertains to hope. For fuller elucidation, see Edmund Husserl, *Cartesian Meditations,* trans. Dorion Cairns (Dordrecht: Kluwer, 1993). To my knowledge, Husserl never undertook a specific analysis of hope as a mode of intentional consciousness.

key elements of phenomenology. First, as Edmund Husserl observes (in contrast to Descartes), consciousness is *intentional;* that is, consciousness is never without an object or a world; rather, I always have before me — whether I am perceiving, judging, feeling, or remembering — an "object" of consciousness. I cannot think without thinking *of* something. Thus, the first fundamental insight of phenomenology, known as the doctrine of *intentionality,*[27] observes that consciousness is always consciousness *of.* . . . Second, the object intended is *constituted* by the ego. This simply means that the ego "makes sense" or, literally, "gives meaning" (*Sinngebung* [*Sinn,* meaning; *-gebung,* given]) to experience by "putting together" or constituting the data of experience into an identifiable "object."[28] The wave of data coming at my senses right now is "put together" and "made sense of" by consciousness so that rather than waves of color and light, I perceive before me a screen, books, a watch, and so on. Anything that would be completely undetermined could not be constituted into an object, and thus could not be "intended" in any way. It would have no "significance" (recalling the connection between something having *meaning* and being *significant*) and could not, in the technical sense, be "experienced." Finally, this process of constitution can happen only within *horizons* of constitution, which provide the context within which I "make sense" of what is before me. In other words, constitution happens within horizons of meaning which enable me to see the object before me *as* a lamp or *as* a cup.[29] Thus these "horizons of expectation," we might say, while functioning

27. Consciousness is described as "intentional" because it always "aims" at objects; the Latin term for this kind of aiming (found in Aquinas's epistemology, for instance) is *intentio.* In Husserl's terminology, to intend an object is also to "mean" an object, to intend it *as* something; this relates to the principles of constitution and horizonality below.

28. This is a largely passive process according to Husserl, and is governed by processes of habituation and the historical formation of the ego (at least as it is described in later works such as *Cartesian Meditations*).

29. This is analogous to the role of *as*-structures in Heidegger's *Sein und Zeit* (Berlin: Akademie Verlag, 2001). It is precisely when these horizons are "out of joint" — as in cross-cultural situations — that I constitute objects differently. I might, for instance, like Ariel the Little Mermaid, find myself in a foreign environment where I have difficulty constituting the objects before me because I lack horizons, or I constitute them differently, as when Ariel spots the fork and constitutes it as an object for combing her hair.

as conditions, are also precisely what enable me to make sense of my experience.

With these three elements of phenomenology in hand — intentionality, constitution, and horizonality — we can now turn to the specific mode of intentional consciousness we find in *hope*. First, as a mode of consciousness, it must be intentional; thus, to hope is to always hope for something.[30] Therefore, hope can never be without an object — *some* intention — even though this object can admit of *degrees* of determination. For instance, I can hope to win my golf game tomorrow, or I can hope to win by five strokes. The former is intentional, but less determinate than the latter. As intentional, however, hope cannot be completely undetermined. This is because, on a phenomenological register, in order for me to "know" or relate to any object, it must be constituted or determined to some degree. The completely indeterminate is also *non*sensical — literally, "has no meaning" *(Unsinnig)*. In addition, the intending of the object of hope and its correlate constitution happens within particular horizons of constitution. Without the horizons, there is no constitution; without constitution, there is no object of hope; and, without an object of hope, there is no hope.

It seems then that a phenomenological description of hope would distinguish five key structural elements of any hope, regardless of its content.[31]

---

30. It seems to me that it is impossible to think of hope as lacking an object, for a couple of reasons: first, if this were possible, it would not be a mode of consciousness, since consciousness is necessarily intentional. And if hope is not an act of consciousness, what else could it be? Who else can hope but subjects? Second, while one might simply *say*, "I hope," the verbal claim seems to necessitate an implicit object of hope on the level of consciousness, even if not verbally articulated. Can I, for instance, simply "love"? If I say, "I love," the first question someone will put to me is: "Love what?" Can I love without some object of my affection? Or consider whether it would be possible to simply say, "I will." Can one will without some determinate end? Perhaps what might help is a distinction between "epistemological" or "linguistic" indeterminacy and, for lack of a better word, "ontological" indeterminacy. One might not verbally be able to articulate the object of one's hope, as when I say, perhaps with tears, "I hope . . ." But that is different than saying that, ontologically or phenomenologically speaking, hope has no object (which, we will see below, is very close to Derrida's claim). This phenomenological analysis would admit the possibility of the former but deny the possibility of the latter.

31. And this would hold even for Josef Pieper's distinction between fundamental,

First, there must be a hope*r,* a subject who hopes; thus, without a person who hopes, there is no hope. While my analysis will not focus on this aspect, one could here focus on the psychological state of the hoper, and perhaps what we might describe as the "virtue" of hope, which disposes an agent to be hopeful.

Second, there must be an object that is hoped *for* (based on our analyses above). As a way of intending the future, hope is expectant and thus is "waiting" for something to come, which is the object hoped for. But we must also note that this expectant intending of the future is hope only if that which is expected is *good* (where "good" is understood in the very broad sense of that which is desired).[32] We can expect other things about the future, including both future *adiaphora* (i.e., things to which we are indifferent, such as the expectation of the phone bill arriving) and future evil — but such an intending of the future would be fear or *Angst,* not hope.

Third, there must be the *act* of hope, which is an act of consciousness. Two things should be noted in this regard: (a) an "act of consciousness," which Husserl describes as a *cogitation,* is not an "act" in the mundane sense of jumping or running; it is an intentional act.[33] Thus, (b) this act of hope or hoping must be distinguished from acts which are done "from" hope, "out of" hope, or "in" hope — for instance, feeding the poor, building low-rent housing, and so forth. The latter are qualitatively different acts which are nevertheless grounded in hope. We might describe them as "hopeful actions," but they are not "acts of hope" or hoping itself in the sense of conscious acts.[34]

Fourth — and here we are trying to "attend to the evidence," as Husserl would say, by simply observing hope in itself — there is the *ground* of hope, which might reside in the subject who hopes, or may lie outside the hoper. I think it important to introduce this concept of

---

genuine, or ultimate "Hope" and penultimate or mundane "hopes." The difference, we will see, would be in the nature of the object-hoped-for. See Pieper, *Hope and History,* trans. Richard and Clara Winston (New York: Herder and Herder, 1969).

32. On this point see Pieper, *Hope and History,* p. 19.

33. I don't mean to say that it is necessarily a "cognitive" or "theoretical" act, however; indeed, I will suggest that hope is a mode of a pre-theoretical being-in-the-world.

34. Perhaps we should note, since someone might protest that this is an overly conscious or intentional model, that even "attitudes" are acts of consciousness insofar as they are "ways of thinking."

ground in order to be able to distinguish hope from illusion and wishful thinking, both of which are modes of intending the future but are unsound because they either lack ground or are flawed in the character of their ground.[35] It is precisely the ground of hope which contributes to the confidence of hope, so that my hope is only "confident" relative to the ground of my hope. Furthermore, an epistemology of hope (which I will sketch below) will need to consider just how one relates to this ground of hope.

And finally, fifth, I think we need to consider *fulfillment* as an integral part of hope. In a sense, this might be an aspect of the object hoped for, or a characteristic of how we intend objects of hope. Nevertheless, it seems important to note that we are not content to simply have objects for our hopes; part of the very way in which we intend objects hoped for means that we want our hopes to be fulfilled. We want our hopes to, one day, no longer be hopes, but realities. And while hope does not guarantee or necessarily entail fulfillment,[36] it certainly seems to imply a *desire* for fulfillment. "Dashed hopes" or "shattered hopes" — hopes that are *not* fulfilled — do not indicate that our hopes were not genuine hopes, but rather remind us of the element of contingency that characterizes any hope. Hope differs from a guarantee, even though it is also characterized by a certain confidence.[37]

We could then diagram the formal structure of hope as in the figure on page 210. This, then, is the *formal* structure of any hope that would qualify as a genuine hope. While I will say more below regarding the concrete embodiment of distinctly *Christian* hope, let me here note a unique characteristic of Christian hope: in Christian hope, the *object* and *ground* are identical, even if they operate in two different modes. That is to say, God is both the *object hoped for* (Titus 2:13) and the *ground* of our hope (Ps. 71:5).

---

35. We will have to return to the question of what would constitute "legitimate" ground below in the context of a critique of Rorty.

36. Indeed, as Pieper observes, that which is guaranteed can*not* be hoped for (*Hope and History*, p. 20).

37. See Pieper, *Hope and History*, pp. 19-22.

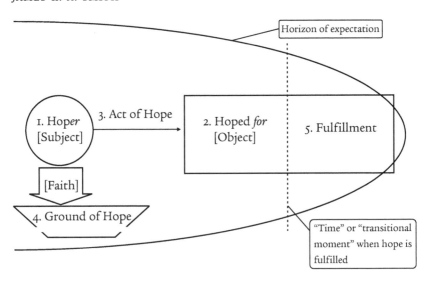

Hope without Hope? A Critique of Postmodern Expectations

If the analysis above is correct, then all hopes — whether ultimate or penultimate, whether regarding eschatological futures or tomorrow's weather — are characterized by this formal structure of a hoper, who intends something in the future, as that which is hoped for, on the basis of a particular ground of hope. If any element is missing, we are without hope.[38]

With this structure in place, I think we are provided with a grid that might help us to both recognize and interpret historical shifts that have taken place with respect to hope. For instance, in modernity — where there is no lack of eschatologies[39] — we still find a structure of

---

38. Though we might still have some mode of intending the future: "wishful thinking," for instance, is a way of intending the future, but without ground; fear and anxiety are also ways of intending the future, but in expectation of something evil or detrimental. Both modes of intending the future, however, are not hopeful in the sense I have specified.

39. In this regard, Karl Löwith offers something of a "secularization" thesis with respect to eschatology in his *Meaning in History* (Chicago: University of Chicago Press, 1949), where he argues that modern philosophy of history is dominated by a secularization of Christian eschatology. As Jürgen Moltmann notes, however, Löwith "meant this in anything but a positive sense" (see Moltmann, *The Coming of God*, p. 133).

hope and expectation about the future. In fact, one might suggest that in important ways, it is not so much the *object* which changes in modernity but rather the *ground* of hope. For instance, both Kant's vision of "perpetual peace" and Marx's vision of justice as embodied in a classless society are very consistent with the Christian hope for a peaceable kingdom and the advent of justice. Even Rorty, commenting on the New Testament and the *Communist Manifesto,* concludes that "both documents are the expressions of the *same* hope: that some day we shall be willing and able to treat the needs of all human beings with the respect and consideration with which we treat the needs of those closest to us, those whom we love."[40] So *what* we're hoping *for* is not so radically different, except in this important respect: in modern narratives of hope, the hoped-for "kingdom" and justice are *immanentized,* so that the object hoped for lacks any transcendence. It is a kingdom which, as a "closed system," is completely continuous with history and the immanent structures of the world. As Rorty indicates, the object hoped for has not really changed, just the locus of its arrival:

> We moderns are superior to the ancients — both pagan and Christian — in our ability to imagine a utopia here on earth. The eighteenth and nineteenth centuries witnessed, in Europe and North America, a massive shift in the locus of human hope: a shift from eternity to future time, from speculation about how to win divine favour to planning for the happiness of future generations. This sense that the human future can be made different from the past, unaided by non-human powers, is magnificently expressed in the Manifesto.[41]

---

40. Rorty, *Philosophy and Social Hope,* pp. 202-3, emphasis added. While he has concerns about the New Testament (see below), he nevertheless recommends that "[p]arents and teachers should encourage young people to read both books. The young will be morally better for having done so" (p. 203).

41. Rorty, *Philosophy and Social Hope,* p. 208. It is not within the scope of my essay here, but I should indicate that I think Rorty's notion of a future advent of justice without any historical discontinuity fails to do justice to the structural depth of injustice which can be eradicated only by revolutionary (though not necessarily "human") change. His hope is, as he confesses, "reformist" (p. 208).

What modernity hopes for carries on the tradition of Christian expectation, but it diverges from that tradition with respect to *where* those hopes will be realized or fulfilled.[42]

Corresponding to this "immanentization" of the locus/*object* of hope to a "this-worldly utopia"[43] is an immanentization of the *ground* of hope, which is the most marked distinction between modern, secular eschatologies and Christian hope. Note, however, that as hope, modern intendings of the future still have a ground, but that ground is no longer transcendent. Thus the confidence of modern expectation does not derive from anything like the providence or faithfulness of God, but rather from the self-sufficiency of humans to realize their own hopes. As Rorty noted above, modernity places its hope in itself, without the need of aid from transcendent powers — indicating a fundamental rejection of *grace*.[44] Thus whether it is confidence in human rationality (Kant), belief in the engine of dialectical materialism (Marx), or faith in the powers of technology and the market (Fukuyama?), the ground of modern "fundamental" hope is always immanent to humanity and history. The problem is, once these foundations crumble beneath us, we lose our ground and so lose our hope.[45] This, we might suggest, is a diagnosis of the postmodern condition.

And yet, in the midst of this late-modern crisis of hope, crying out in this wilderness, we have two prophets: Rorty and his proclamation of hope for a liberal utopia, and Derrida and his hope for a justice "to come." In light of our analysis of the phenomenological structure of hope above, how should we evaluate these postmodern pieces of "good news"? Do they give us reason to hope? And hope for what?

42. It seems to be the burden of Pieper's *Hope and History* to challenge this proposition. Thus he asks, "Is man's hope at all of such nature that it can be satisfied within the area of history?" (p. 28). The answer, for Pieper, is a resounding "Nein!"

43. Rorty, *Philosophy and Social Hope,* pp. 207-8. One sees that it is really only on the basis of a very facile reading of Christian faith as "other-worldly" that Rorty criticizes the New Testament. Somebody should introduce him to liberation theology.

44. A certain tale could be woven here from the starting point of the Thomistic valorization of "natural, unaided reason," through Scotus' radical disjunction between nature and grace, to the modern rejection of grace. But I'll not tell the story here. See John Milbank's weaving of the story in *Theology and Social Theory* (Oxford: Blackwell, 1990), pp. 9-45.

45. For a consideration of this "despair," see Moltmann, *Theology of Hope,* pp. 22-26.

Rorty and Reasons to Hope

Considered against the structure of hope above, Rorty's pragmatic hope is not lacking in the determinacy of its object. Indeed, his vision for a liberal, democratic utopia is stated in the most concrete terms, particularly the features of *equity* and *fraternity*. On the first score, Rorty envisions a world where economic injustices are finally rectified, a world where teachers make as much as lawyers[46] and where the minimum wage is actually a living wage. Thus it is, in light of this hope for equity, that

> [w]e should raise our children to find it intolerable that we who sit behind desks and punch keyboards are paid ten times as much as people who get their hands dirty cleaning our toilets, and a hundred times as much as those who fabricate our keyboards in the Third World. . . . Our children need to learn, early on, to see the inequalities between their own fortunes and those of other children as neither the Will of God nor the necessary price for economic efficiency, but as an inevitable tragedy. They should start thinking, as early as possible, about how the world might be changed so as to ensure that no one goes hungry while others have a surfeit.[47]

Such concrete hope for economic and material equity is made possible by the expectation of a coming, fundamental "fraternity" which overcomes current selfishness, prioritizes "love of neighbor," and encourages the virtue of self-sacrifice.[48] Imaginatively writing from the utopian viewpoint of 2096, Rorty envisions the greatest transformation to be from a selfish, rights-based political discourse to a sacrificial, fraternal understanding of responsibility; from a focus on "I" to a sense of "we"; from considering myself first to first considering my neighbor. "Perhaps no difference between present-day [2096] American political discourse and that of 100 years ago is greater than our assumption that the first duty of the state is to prevent gross economic and social inequality," he imagines.[49] One might say, then, that it is precisely frater-

---

46. Rorty, *Philosophy and Social Hope*, p. 121.

47. Rorty, *Philosophy and Social Hope*, pp. 203-4.

48. Rorty, *Philosophy and Social Hope*, pp. 206-7.

49. Rorty, *Philosophy and Social Hope*, p. 246 and passim. This article, when originally published, was entitled "Fraternity Reigns."

nity which is the condition of possibility for equity. In any case, this is the future Rorty confidently expects and for which he hopes.

Indeed, now looking from the present to the future, Rorty declares: "We have every reason to hope that once today's economic bubble bursts, once we start reinventing the interventionist state, Americans will relearn what Delbanco calls 'the lesson of Lincoln's life' . . . that the quest for prosperity is no remedy for melancholy, but that a passion to secure justice by erasing the line that divides those with hope from those without hope can be."[50] That is, we have every reason — we do not lack reasons — to hope for the realization of justice in America. But, unfortunately, Rorty fails to give an account of the reason for his hope that lies within.[51] It is here that his hope, in light of our phenomenological analysis, must be called into question. In order for hope to be hope, as opposed to mere illusion or wishful thinking, there must be (a) *some* ground or basis for that hope, and (b) some *proportionality* between the ground of hope and the object hoped for. For instance, to choose a mundane example, if I hope to slam dunk a basketball (despite the fact that I am 5'6") on the basis of my mother's assurance that I can do anything I put my mind to, then it seems to me that I am being deluded. There is some basis or ground for my hope, but that ground is not proportionate or relevant to my hope.[52] It does not constitute a "good reason" to hope for such a telos. Such expectations of the future we often describe as "wishful thinking" or as "*false* hopes."[53] They must be distin-

---

50. Rorty, "I Hear America Sighing," p. 16, referring to Delbanco, *Real American Dream*, p. 74.

51. I am alluding, of course, to 1 Peter 3:15 and will return to consider this more carefully below.

52. And to assert this is not to require that there be a one-to-one correspondence between the ground and my hope, since hope is precisely that which is not guaranteed (Pieper, *Hope and History*, p. 20). In other words, the ground of my hope does not need to yield "certainty" in order to qualify my expectation of the future as *hope*; in fact, such certainty or guarantee would disqualify it from being hope, since I don't hope for that which is inevitable (Pieper, *Hope and History*, p. 20). Nevertheless, in order to distinguish hope from false hopes or wishful thinking, there must be what I am calling here a *proportionality* of the ground to the hope. (What needs to be worked out, then [if possible], would be the criteria that would determine whether a ground is proportional or not.)

53. One can see this very concretely in medicine, where promises are sometimes made under the name of "hope," when in fact one is trafficking in *illusion* (this becomes particularly complicated in some traditions that believe in divine healing). For a discus-

guished from (genuine) hope. And this distinction is not a merely theoretical one: when people operate on the basis of false hopes, the most disastrous consequences can often follow.[54]

What is the ground of Rorty's hope for a liberal, democratic utopia? Is there a ground for this expectation? Or is it merely a false hope, perhaps a delusion? Rorty is not entirely forthcoming in this regard — he offers no *apologia*. But if we look carefully, it seems that he thinks the narrative of history itself is the reason for such hope. Criticizing contemporary political philosophy for abandoning historical narration (in particular, a narrative of progress),[55] he argues that "it is the kind of historical narrative which segues into a utopian scenario about how we can get from the present to a better future. Social and political philosophy usually has been, and always ought to be, parasitic on such narratives."[56] Thus elsewhere he emphasizes that reflecting on this historical narrative of progress will keep buoyant our hopes for a liberal utopia:

> If human hope can survive the anthrax-laden warheads, the suitcase-sized nuclear devices, the overpopulation, the globalized labour market, and the environmental disasters of the coming century [can it?], if we have descendants who, a century from now, *still have a historical record to consult and are still able to seek inspiration from the past,* perhaps they will think of Saint Agnes and Rosa Luxemburg, Saint Francis and Eugene Debs, Father Damien and Jean Jaurès, as members of a single movement.[57]

---

sion, see J. R. Petrie, "The Cruelty of False Hope," *British Medical Journal* 308 (June 1994): 1723; J. Penson, "A Hope Is Not a Promise: Fostering Hope Within Palliative Care," *International Journal of Palliative Nursing* 6 (February 2000): 94-98.

54. See, for instance, Daniel Callahan, *False Hopes: Why America's Quest for Perfect Health Is a Recipe for Failure* (New York: Simon and Schuster, 1998); J. A. Roberts et al., "Factors Influencing Views of Patients with Gynecologic Cancer about End-of-Life Decisions," *American Journal of Obstetrics and Gynecology* 176 (1997): 166-72; A. Jirillo et al., "Survey on the Use of Questionable Methods of Cancer Treatment," *Tumori* 82 (May-June 1996): 215-17; and William B. Schwartz, *Life without Disease: The Pursuit of Medical Utopia* (Berkeley: University of California Press, 1998).

55. Rorty, *Philosophy and Social Hope,* p. 232.

56. Rorty, *Philosophy and Social Hope,* p. 231.

57. Rorty, *Philosophy and Social Hope,* p. 203. Rorty is here making the connection between Christian and Marxist hope in the pairing of these figures.

But can history really function as the ground for Rorty's hope? Will our consulting of the historical record give us good reason to believe that his vision for justice will be realized? Could not a look at the history of the past century — of much regress alongside some progress, of increased violence rather than perpetual peace — equally lead to despair and hopelessness? The problem here, it seems to me, is a *dis*proportionality between Rorty's hope and that which seems to ground it. The ground simply cannot yield the hope he has described; in fact, this history would seem to lead us to expect just the opposite and intend the future in the mode of fear and anxiety rather than hopeful expectation.

Thus, at times, Rorty himself seems to suggest that this hope is *without ground.* Considering some of the "reasons why it seems absurdly improbable that we shall ever have a global liberal utopia,"[58] he basically concedes these as valid reasons for "historical pessimism." As he admits, "[t]his shift leaves us nothing with which to boost our social hopes." With nothing to boost our hopes, we would seem to be without ground — without good reason to hope. *"But,"* Rorty continues, "that does not mean there is anything wrong with these hopes. The utopian social hope which sprang up in nineteenth-century Europe is still the noblest imaginative creation of which we have record."[59] Though we have no reason to do so, we should continue to hope. But without ground, can this really be hope? Given our analysis above, an expectation for good in the future which lacks ground is not hope. If Rorty counters that we have fallen prey to a "foundationalist" understanding of hope — that we just need to "get over" this need for grounding — then he seems also to concede that we cannot make any distinction between hope and false hope, illusion, or mere wishful thinking. I don't think this is a concession that he would want to make, since it would undercut his own criticisms regarding alternative expectations for the

---

58. Rorty, *Philosophy and Social Hope,* p. 273. The reasons for lack of hope are (a) global democracy would require a global standard of living equivalent to that in European nations, but there are too few natural resources to sustain this globally; (b) "greedy and selfish kleptocrats" and military leadership always find new ways to subvert democracy and adapt well to changes; and (c) "achieving a liberal utopia on a global scale would require the establishment of a world federation," which seems increasingly impossible to achieve (pp. 273-74).

59. Rorty, *Philosophy and Social Hope,* p. 277, emphasis added.

future (e.g., expecting the consummation of history on the grounds of a belief in Providence, which he would describe as deluded, would not be qualitatively different than Rorty's expectation for a liberal utopia). Further, as mentioned above, to undercut the distinction between hope and wishful thinking or false hope would have important negative consequences in the practical and political spheres. Thus, in order to maintain the distinction, we need to understand hope as grounded in some sense; and, accordingly, Rorty's hope for a liberal utopia — which lacks ground — is disqualified, so to speak. When we have no "good reasons" to do so, we ought not hope.

Derrida and the (In)Determination of Hope

While we might also question the ground of Derrida's hope, here I want to focus on problems concerning the object hoped for and the act of hoping. What does Derrida expect when he is expecting? For what does Derrida hope and pray? Or, to put it otherwise, does deconstruction have an eschatology?[60]

While deconstruction is concerned to call into question any notion of a programmable future[61] (there are no dispensational charts in *Specters of Marx*), Derrida does nevertheless sketch what he describes as

60. Derrida, unlike Caputo (*Prayers and Tears,* p. 96), is not spooked by the notion of an "eschatology." In fact, Derrida says that his project is in contrast to French Marxists such as Althusser who attempt to "dissociate Marxism from any teleology or from any messianic eschatology" (*Specters of Marx,* p. 90), whereas his concern "is precisely to distinguish the latter from the former," that is, to distill a "messianic eschatology" dissociated from the determinate content of Marxism (which is, on Derrida's accounting, a messia*nism*).

61. Derrida reminds us that one of the first jobs of deconstruction was to call into question "the onto-theo- but also archeo-teleological concept of history — in Hegel, Marx, or even in the epochal thinking of Heidegger" (*Specters of Marx,* p. 74). This was to "open up access to an affirmative thinking of the messianic and emancipatory promise as promise: as *promise* and not as onto-theological or teleo-eschatological program or design" (p. 75). While I cannot do so here, I would argue that Christian eschatology — when it retains its integrity and resists the lures of modernity — is *not* onto-theological but rather closer to the structure of "promise" Derrida describes. Perhaps this is the flipside of my argument that Christian faith is not grounded in a meta-narrative in the technical sense. (For this argument, see my essay "A Little Story about Metanarratives: Lyotard, Religion, and Postmodernism Revisited," *Faith and Philosophy* 18 [2001]: 261-76).

a "messianic eschatology."[62] As such, it is a structure of radical expectation, of waiting for the future; but as "messianic" it is divorced from any particular, determinate messian*ism* (i.e., any determinate religion or tradition)[63] and thus is without any determinate expectation for what is "to come." Consequently, he explains,

> We will not claim that this messianic eschatology common both to the religions it criticizes and to the Marxist critique must be simply deconstructed. While it is common to both of them, with the exception of content,[64] it is also the case that its formal structure of promise exceeds them or precedes them. Well, what remains irreducible to any deconstruction, what remains as undeconstructible as the possibility itself of deconstruction is, perhaps, a certain experience of the emancipatory promise; it is perhaps even the formality of a structural messianism, a messianism without religion, even a messianic without messianism, an idea of justice . . . and an idea of democracy.[65]

This messianic — which elsewhere he argues is a "general structure of experience"[66] — would be "the opening to the future or to the coming of the other as the advent of justice, but without horizon of expectation and without prophetic prefiguration."[67] So this messianic eschatology awaits and expects justice "to come" *(à venir)* as a democracy "to come."[68] But, at the same time, this messianic hope must remain completely indeterminate; otherwise we might begin to confuse democracy "here and now" (which is fraught with injustice) with the democracy which is (always) "to come." Thus Derrida asserts that this "idea"[69] of justice and democracy signals

---

62. Derrida, *Specters of Marx,* pp. 59, 90.

63. Again, for a fuller discussion (and critique) of this distinction and the *epochē* by which it is produced, see my "Determined Violence: Derrida's Structural Religion," pp. 197-212.

64. It is interesting to note that Derrida sees a disjunction between Christian hope and Marxist hope, whereas Rorty emphasizes their continuity and similarity.

65. Derrida, *Specters of Marx,* p. 59.

66. Derrida, "Foi et savoir," p. 28; "Faith and Knowledge," p. 18.

67. Derrida, "Foi et savoir," p. 27; "Faith and Knowledge," p. 17.

68. Derrida, *Specters of Marx,* pp. 64-65.

69. Because of his employment of this Kantian language of the "idea" of justice,

the opening of this gap between an infinite promise . . . and the determined, necessary, but also necessarily inadequate forms of what has to be measured against this promise. To this extent, the effectivity or actuality of the democratic promise, like that of the communist promise, will always keep within it, and it must do so, this *absolutely undetermined messianic hope* at its heart, this eschatological relation to the to-come of an event *and* of a singularity, of an alterity that cannot be anticipated.[70]

To wait for the messianic is to be expectant for — *who knows what?* Literally. "For it belongs to the very essence of *venir* and *à venir*," Caputo comments, "that what is coming be unknown, not merely factually unknown but structurally unknowable. . . . Otherwise nothing is really coming, nothing *tout autre*."[71] As such, "[t]he messianic exposes itself to absolute surprise and, even if it always takes the phenomenal form of peace or of justice, it ought, exposing itself so abstractly, be prepared (waiting without awaiting *itself*) for the best as for the worst, the one never coming without opening the possibility of the other."[72] It is the "absolutely undetermined" character of this "messianic hope" which exposes us to this danger, all the while expecting the advent of justice.

Given this "object" of Derrida's hope, we must also consider *how* one can hope for such, or what we might describe as the correlate mode of expectation. Recalling the structure of hope above, we here consider the *act* of hope: How can one hope for the indeterminate? How does one wait for who-knows-what? As Derrida recognizes, the (conscious, inten-

---

one finds him constantly protesting that his notion of justice is *not* a regulative ideal (e.g., *Specters of Marx*, pp. 64-65; see also Caputo, *Prayers and Tears*, p. 129). While methinks he doth protest too much (and unsuccessfully), Derrida's claim is that this cannot be a regulative ideal because it is indeterminate, and therefore there is no way to gauge our "progress" toward it. But if the claim to absolute indeterminacy is impossible (see below), then Derrida is left with no way to distinguish his democracy "to come" from a simple regulative ideal.

70. Derrida, *Specters of Marx*, p. 65, emphasis added.

71. Caputo, *Prayers and Tears*, pp. 101-2. Aside from a curious resurrection of "essences," I would question by which logic this is necessary (see below).

72. Derrida, "Foi et savoir," p. 28; "Faith and Knowledge," p. 18. On the dangers of this openness, see Richard Kearney, "Desire of God," in *God, the Gift, and Postmodernism*, ed. John D. Caputo and Michael J. Scanlon (Bloomington: Indiana University Press, 1999), pp. 112-45, esp. 122-28.

tional) act of hope must be a waiting "without horizon of expectation" (*sans horizon d'attente*).[73] Why? Because any horizon of expectation would predetermine — which is to say, *determine* — what is expected and that for which we hope. Since Derrida has contended that we must be open to the absolutely indeterminate, our expectation must be without horizon, without predetermination, because any predelineated anticipation would undo the "universality" of such justice, and represent an *in*justice.

This brings us to one final, and perhaps most important, component of Derrida's messianic hope. He has argued that our hope for the future, though a hope for justice, must be "absolutely undetermined"; and in order to await such an indeterminate "object," we must be waiting without horizons of expectation, since these horizons would always already condition the wholly other of the future, would cram the democracy "to come" into our current understandings, converting it into some kind of "law." But why must we be so vigilant about preventing the determination of justice? Because determination itself is unjust insofar as it *limits* possibilities and necessarily entails *exclusion*. Every decision is an incision,[74] and every determinate erection of justice is attended by injustice. And not only does determination itself constitute a kind of violence, the determination of justice by particular religions or regimes often leads to real violence and injustice, all "in the name" of religion or communism or — if you can believe it — democracy. Thus Caputo suggests that "[i]f the *tout autre* ever won the revolution, if the Messiah ever actually showed up, if you ever thought that justice has come — that would ruin everything."[75] Thus Derrida emphasizes the indeterminacy — the *absolute* indeterminacy — of justice "to come" in order to safeguard against the inevitable *hubris* which would want to identify a particular political system or policy with the very advent of justice. The way to avoid wars of determinate messianistic eschatologies is to adopt an absolutely indeterminate messianic eschatology.[76] Unfortunately, this means that hope is always deferred, that justice is

73. Derrida, "Foi et savoir," p. 27; "Faith and Knowledge," p. 17; *Specters of Marx*, p. 168.

74. Derrida, "Force of Law," in *Deconstruction and the Possibility of Justice*, ed. D. Cornell et al. (New York: Routledge, 1992), pp. 24-26; this is also alluded to as the "law of finitude, law of decision and responsibility for infinite existences" in *Specters of Marx*, p. 87.

75. Caputo, *Prayers and Tears*, p. 74.

76. Derrida, *Specters of Marx*, pp. 58-59.

always (i.e., structurally) "to come" — which is why we are always "waiting." Justice, we must remember, is impossible.

Before undertaking a critique of Derrida's "messianic hope," let me first note what is salutary about this account, notably, Derrida's critical concern with and reminder of the injustices that can take place when we identify our particular regime with "Justice Itself." That, it seems to me, is an important point that triumphalist Christians (but not only Christians) can often forget and which we do well to recall. I think, however, that we can maintain this critical posture without adopting Derrida's fundamental logic regarding determination and violence, which, to summarize, goes as follows: determination itself is violent and leads to violence; therefore, in order to avoid violence we must have a hope which is *in*determinate; and insofar as our hope — the way in which we intend the future — is *in*determinate, our mode of expecting must be "without horizon." Let me unpack my criticism by working back through these three components.

First, as I have argued elsewhere[77] (and so will only summarize here), Derrida's premise, which equates determination with violence, can and must be called into question. The determinate and finite would be construed as violent and exclusionary only if one assumes that finitude is somehow a "failure," implying that we are somehow called to be infinite.[78] Further, Derrida conflates what I have called "the historical production of violence" with the "necessary production of violence" in its relation to religion. Not all finite decisions produce injustice, unless one operates with a notion of "infinite" responsibility which "faults" humanity for being finite, and this would be a Neoplatonic move. In short, I think that in order to accept Derrida's premise that all determination or finitude constitutes violence one would have to adopt some version of a Neoplatonic ontology, or at least be

77. This concern regarding the conflation of finitude and violence has been central to my critique of Derrida. For development within general understandings of language and interpretation, see my *The Fall of Interpretation: Philosophical Foundations for a Creational Hermeneutic* (Downers Grove, Ill.: InterVarsity, 2000), pp. 115-29; in the context of religion as central to this essay, see my "Determined Violence"; and with respect to "violence" and God-talk, see my "Between Predication and Silence: Augustine on How (Not) to Speak of God," *Heythrop Journal* 41 (2000): 66-86, esp. 78-84.

78. I have suggested that Wolfhart Pannenberg's theology is guilty of the same in *The Fall of Interpretation,* chap. 2.

haunted by its ghost.[79] And if one does not adopt this premise, the logic which motivates the evacuation of all content from this messianic hope is averted. In other words, one would not need an absolutely indeterminate, messianic hope in order to avoid violence; rather, a determinate, "messianistic" hope could be adopted without implicating oneself in necessary or inevitable violence.

Second, turning to the question of the indeterminacy of the object hoped for: (a) I would now note, given the rejection of the logic which equates determination and violence, that there is no need to maintain the absolute indeterminacy of hope. But two further points must also be made: (b) On the basis of our phenomenological analysis of hope earlier in this essay, hope cannot be "absolutely indeterminate," since then it would have no object (and since hope is an intentional mode of consciousness, if there is no object, there is no hope). One can intend only that which is constituted to some degree; therefore, hope can be hope only insofar as it has an object which allows for some degree of determinacy. Hope does not require absolute determinacy; rather, as in Christian eschatological expectation, there are a degree of determinacy and a degree of indeterminacy, or what we might more properly describe as "mystery."[80] Even from the perspective of Christian hope, *over*-determination is problematic. And (c) there is an important sense in which Derrida's messianic is *not* indeterminate but rather "does have *certain* determinable features."[81] For one, we know that it is a *democracy* to come; and we know enough about that to know that it is *not*, for instance, a *theo*cracy to come. Further, it is very heavily indebted to the biblical prophetic tradition of justice, not only in its rhythms and nomenclature but in its very structure and concern (mediated by Levinas). But once one admits this "content," the gig is up: absolute indeterminacy has been compromised[82] (not that it was ever possible) and one either admits that deconstruction's messianic hope is also violent or concede my point above, that determination should not be equated with violence. This means that the door is also opened for other determinate hopes, since they can no longer

79. This is what I have argued in *The Fall of Interpretation,* pp. 127-29.

80. See Kevin Hughes's essay in this volume on the indeterminacy of Christian eschatological expectation.

81. Caputo, *Prayers and Tears,* p. 142.

82. I have developed this point more fully in "Determined Violence" and "Re-Kanting Postmodernism?"

be disqualified simply by virtue of their determinacy — and that has important implications for the viability of Christian hope.

Finally, hope, as a conscious mode of intending the future, cannot be without horizon. Again recalling the phenomenology of hope above, and our conclusions regarding the necessary determination of the object of hope, it follows that such constitution of the object of hope must take place within determinate horizons of expectation. As Caputo comments, Derrida resists "the very idea of 'horizon,' for any horizon, be it that of a regulative idea or of a 'messianic event,' sets limits and defines expectations in advance."[83] Thus Derrida speaks of messianic hope as "[a]waiting without horizon of the wait, awaiting what one does not expect yet or any longer."[84] Phenomenologically speaking, this is impossible, simply *Unsinnig*, Husserl would say, since any mode of intentional consciousness, such as hope, cannot escape the conditions of horizonality.[85] And in this respect, I follow Derrida's own affirmation, in "Violence and Metaphysics,"[86] that the "wholly other" must appear within the horizons of our experience, otherwise it would never appear for us at all. This is due simply to the structure of intentional consciousness described above, which Derrida would not want to deny. Indeed, we might say that he has been more scrupulous about nothing else than the conditions which attend the constitution and appearance of the other. One cannot wait for (literally) nothing.

83. Caputo, *Prayers and Tears*, p. 117; cf. 73.

84. Derrida, *Specters of Marx*, p. 65; cf. 168.

85. In this respect, Derrida begins to sound remarkably like Levinas and Jean-Luc Marion, of whom he has been critical on just this point. For my own critique of Levinas and Marion, Derridean "in spirit," see my "Respect and Donation: A Critique of Marion's Critique of Husserl," *American Catholic Philosophical Quarterly* 67 (1997): 112-31; and more fully, my *Speech and Theology: Language and the Logic of Incarnation* (London: Routledge, 2002), chaps. 2 and 5.

86. Derrida, "Violence and Metaphysics: An Essay on the Thought of Emmanuel Levinas," in *Writing and Difference*, trans. Alan Bass (Chicago: University of Chicago Press, 1978), pp. 79-153.

Waiting in Hope: Christian Expectation

On the basis of a phenomenology of hope, I have critiqued Rorty's hope for a liberal utopia as, at best, wishful thinking, and Derrida's messianic hope as either impossible (in the straightforward sense) or in fact more indebted to the biblical prophetic and messianic tradition than he acknowledges. In both cases, the critique of these "postmodern hopes" has opened the space, I think, for a reconsideration of a robust, determinate Christian hope as not only viable in postmodernity but perhaps its only hope. So in this brief conclusion, I will consider the elements of Christian expectation in light of our phenomenology of hope above.

First, if we consider the subject as hoper, and the subject's *act* of hoping, we see that the Christian community expectantly, even if somewhat impatiently (James 5:7) and anxiously (Jude 21), awaits in *eagerness* (Rom. 8:19, 23, 25; 1 Cor. 1:7; Heb. 9:28). But this hope is one that is produced by and sustained in suffering, which produces perseverance, character, and ultimately hope (Rom. 5:3-4). Thus it seems that the Christian has a certain *disposition* to hope — that hope is a certain "virtue."[87] The waiting and awaiting of the Christian community is therefore anticipatory and confident, since "hope does not disappoint" (Rom. 5:5). And given our expectation, the advent of our hope is not something that will take us by surprise, even though we cannot determinately know when it will be fulfilled (1 Thess. 5:1-10).

But the sanctified impatience of Christian hope — which exclaims so loudly, "Come! *Viens!*" (1 Cor. 16:22; Rev. 22:20) — is markedly different from the perpetual waiting that characterizes Derrida's "messianic hope." Derrida's hope delights in waiting. On Caputo's accounting, "[t]he very idea of the Messiah is that he is *to* come, *à venir,* someone coming, not that he could actually arrive."[88] In that respect, the best we can do and hope for is to wait. But this, of course, is Maurice Blanchot's "idea" of the Messiah, not the biblical prophetic understanding, for which the "essence" of the Messiah is his *anointing* for justice for the poor and oppressed who have known

---

87. On this notion of a virtue of hope, see the work of Scott Daniels. Caputo suggests the same in *On Religion,* chap. 1.

88. Caputo, *Prayers and Tears,* p. 78.

nothing but injustice (Isa. 61:1-2; Luke 4:14-21). There is, then, no virtue in waiting; rather, the biblical awaiting for the Messiah is characterized by just this impatience, out of which the cries of "Come, Lord Jesus!" resonate with the prophetic laments, "How long, O Lord?" (Rev. 6:10-11). Hope deferred makes the heart sick (Prov. 13:12), and there is a certain *dis*-ease which attends Christian waiting for the eschaton and the advent of justice.[89]

Second, with respect to the object hoped for, this space is hardly adequate for working out a comprehensive vision and analysis of the telos of Christian hope.[90] But it is important to recall that given our analyses above, we know that our hope must have some object, that that object must be determined to a certain extent, and that such an object of hope is constituted or determined within particular horizons of expectation; in other words, ours is (as must be any hope) a waiting *with* horizon and a messianic hope *with* a Messiah. The horizons of expectation are those provided by the tradition and community (Scripture and Church). Further, a phenomenology of Christian expectation will note that, contra Derrida's "messianic hope," there is an important degree of determinacy; but also an important, and perhaps helpful, *lack* of specification and *in*determinacy.[91] In other words, we know what to expect, but do not have a comprehensive knowledge of such; thus with Derrida and Caputo, we could agree that this degree of indeterminacy functions as something of a safeguard with respect to attempts to institute the kingdom on earth, retaining the important distinction between the eschatological kingdom and our attempts to establish justice in the here-and-now. Further, Christian eschatology expects a future advent of justice which is both *continuous* with the present order, as a redeeming of creation, but also *dis*continuous, insofar as it represents a revolutionizing of fallen structures. In this way, it is not a sheer "otherworldly" utopia

---

89. On this tension between imminence and delay, see Richard Bauckham, *The Theology of the Book of Revelation* (Cambridge: Cambridge University Press, 1993), pp. 157-59.

90. For this kind of comprehensive vision and exposition, see Moltmann, *The Coming of God*.

91. This indetermination might also be due to a certain "excess" and "fullness" which exceeds description and determination. On this point, see Pieper, *Hope and History*, pp. 78-79. On this tension, and the apophatic strategies adopted in the book of Revelation, see Bauckham, *Theology of the Book of Revelation*, pp. 44-45.

(as Rorty charged), but neither is it an "immanentized" eschatology which finds the resolution of injustice within the mechanisms of history itself. Thus, Christian hope is characterized by a fundamental *transcendence* which is not opposed to immanence but is opposed to the "immanentization" characteristic of modern eschatologies; further, Christian expectation is "open" in the sense that Derrida advocates, but open precisely to the necessary *grace* which alone can revolutionize a fallen world. Thus we markedly disagree with Rorty, and other defenders of modernity, when they claim that humanity, in itself, has the resources necessary for its own redemption. In short, we reject the myth of progress in favor of a narrative of grace.

And if Christian eschatological hope counters the immanentization of the object of hope, so also does it resist any attempt to immanentize the *ground* of hope. Perhaps the most important discussions of Christian hope in postmodernity will concern this question of ground. What is the ground of Christian expectation? And how can such a hope be viable in postmodernity? Christian hope, I would argue, is grounded in the revelation of God's faithfulness and the promise of his continued faithfulness, particularly as grounded in God's revelation in the cross and resurrection of Jesus Christ. Most elemental to this account is that this ground is ultimately grounded in *revelation* (not "propositions," let alone detailed "plans," but the revelation of God in Christ) and that this revelation reveals God's faithfulness to his creation, his identification with the struggles of creation, and his power and providence to bring about its restoration. Without what Pieper describes as "prophecy,"[92] we are left in a position not unlike Rorty: speculating and positing a hope for the future without a genuine ground. Thus, I think Christian hope can properly be *hope* only insofar as one accepts and believes this revelation. But with respect to the epistemology of hope, this is not unlike any other kind of hope: the hoper must relate to the ground of hope via a fundamental trust and commitment; it is because hope is grounded in faith that hope does not yield apodictic guarantees.[93] On this score, even the hopes of mo-

92. Though there is a tendency for Pieper to reduce this to prophetic "statements" and "divinely authenticated information" (*Hope and History,* pp. 44, 78).

93. Space does not permit me to develop this any further here, but I would argue that hope is not "known" in a cognitive or rational sense, but rather "believed" and

dernity rest on faith: whether in the myth of progress, dialectical materialism, technology and the market, or the rationality of humanity. In any case, these hopes rest on a faith in a particular ground; so unless one wants to undo the idea of hope altogether, we cannot exclude Christian hope simply by virtue of its grounding by faith commitments in a particular revelation. This is not to say, of course, that one could therefore "demonstrate" the superiority of this ground (that would be to confuse faith and knowledge);[94] but one can certainly proclaim such a hope and demonstrate the integrity and coherence of its ground. Finally, because of the Christian's commitments to God's revelation in Christ and God's faithfulness to creation, a Christian eschatology must argue that, ultimately, God is our only hope. In that regard, the question of the viability of Christian hope in late modernity differs little from the context of Augustine's *De civitate dei:* it represents both a scandal and good news. My hope is that the demise of modern eschatologies, and the critique of postmodern hopes above, indicate an open space for Christians to unapologetically proclaim a hope that does not disappoint.

"known" "affectively" — known otherwise. As such, hope should be communicated or proclaimed via affective modes, particularly the aesthetic, and perhaps even more particularly via images that activate the imagination. On this point, see Paul Hughes and Robert Doede, "Wounded Vision and the Optics of Hope" (in this volume), as well as the discussion in Bauckham and Hart, *Hope against Hope,* pp. 172-73.

94. As Pieper notes, "those reasons can convince only one who accepts the truth of Christian doctrine" (p. 87).

Contributors

David Billings
Assistant Professor of Philosophy
Calvin College

Robert Paul Doede
Associate Professor of Religious Studies
Trinity Western University

Kevin L. Hughes
Assistant Professor of Theology and Religious Studies
Villanova University

Paul Edward Hughes
Associate Professor of Religious Studies
Trinity Western University

Daniel Johnson
Associate Professor of Sociology
Gordon College

William Katerberg
Associate Professor of History
Calvin College

John Milbank
Francis Ball Professor of Philosophical Theology
University of Virginia

Jürgen Moltmann
Emeritus Professor of Systematic Theology
University of Tübingen

James K. A. Smith
Associate Professor of Philosophy
Calvin College

Miroslav Volf
Henry B. Wright Professor of Systematic Theology
Yale University Divinity School

Nicholas Wolterstorff
Noah Porter Professor of Philosophical Theology
Yale University

Index of Names and Subjects

Index of Scripture References

Lightning Source UK Ltd.
Milton Keynes UK
UKHW010144090219
336979UK00005B/560/P